A Greatness of Spirit

Dave Van Cleve

A Greatness of Spirit

Tales of Extraordinary Rangers at the
Heart of California's State Park System

By David Van Cleve

Copyright © 2018 by David Van Cleve

All rights reserved.

Book design by Beth Edwards.

This book is dedicated to the thousands of park rangers,
worldwide, who protect our parks,
as well as the natural and cultural resources these parks were established to conserve.
They also serve as park ambassadors – welcoming and serving the visiting public.
Rangers operate at all levels of government – cities, counties, states, and countries –
to defend parks, threatened species, natural processes, and irreplaceable
cultural sites and artifacts.
A tip of the Stetson to the men and women, current and past, who form this
"thin green line." All the while, they also remain mindful
of the philosophy that, above all,

Parks Are For People!

"Inspiration is not the exclusive privilege of poets or artists generally. There is, has been, and will always be a certain group of people whom inspiration visits. It's made up of all those who've consciously chosen their calling and do their job with love and imagination. It may include doctors, teachers, gardeners – and I could list a hundred more professions. Their work becomes one continuous adventure as long as they manage to keep discovering new challenges in it. Difficulties and setbacks never quell their curiosity. A swarm of new questions emerges from every problem they solve. Whatever inspiration is, it's born from a continuous 'I don't know.'"

— *Polish Poet and Nobel Laureate Wislawa Szymborska*

TABLE OF CONTENTS

A Greatness of Spirit 1

MARK JORGENSEN	Iconoclastic Icon of the Desert	17
JERRY HENDERSON	The Comet That Lit Up the Sky of Mt. San Jacinto State Park	40
DAVID AND JANET CARLE	Save Mono Lake	62
CARLOS PORRATA	El Guardabosques	81
MIKE TOPE	A Benevolence of Tenacity	95
GARY STRACHAN	Bird Nerd, Surfer, Hero	117
MIKE LYNCH	Sultan of Swag – One Very Busy Chap!	134
PAULA PETERSON	Reluctant Groundbreaker	153
BILL DEITCHMAN	The Rafting Ranger	177
JON MUENCH	Renaissance Ranger and Ace Pilot	199
DAN WINKELMAN	Win With Winkelman	222
MARK FAULL	Poet, Guardian, Scientist	238
GREG HAYES	Writer and Poet, Loved by Everyone He Touched	259

Afterword	286
Bibliography	288
Acknowledgements	290
About the Author	292

INTRODUCTION

A Greatness of Spirit

We park rangers never get tired of people telling us, "I wish I could live my life over and be a park ranger," or "My daughter wants to become a park ranger. How does she do that?" It makes us feel good – park visitors think that we are doing good things in the world, and it remains a profession that is admired.

We get to live in special landscapes. National and state parks are typically found in places where people like to visit on vacation or in their free time. Parks are popular sites where one can enjoy the scenery, observe nature, watch wildlife, hike and backpack, enjoy water sports like surfing, scuba diving, boating, and fishing, camp and picnic, photograph and paint, have family outings, or just relax.

Almost invariably, when we get hired, the position of field park ranger seems to us the best possible job in the world. We get to work outside, often in a beautiful natural setting or an important historical site, and our goals are to protect the park and its resources while helping the park visitor have a good experience. Initially, we want to stay in the field. It is the rare ranger who immediately wants to "move up the career ladder." Why do more paperwork and become a supervisor when you can patrol California's beautiful state parks and greet our visitors?

Often, however, the allure of promoting to higher levels in the Parks Department becomes stronger. The attraction

Ranger skiing at Calaveras Big Trees State Park in 1948.
Copyright ©1948, California State Parks (Image 090-S20767).

varies from one ranger to another. It could be a pay increase, a better fit for one's skill set, a desire for more responsibility and more influence, or any number of factors. And clearly, the Parks Department benefits greatly from having bright, talented, and motivated individuals promote to positions of greater responsibility. Eventually, the career ladder may lead to roles of influence in Sacramento. We need these great leaders in headquarters.

On the other hand, many rangers decide to spend almost their entire career at one park in the field. Again, there are many different reasons for this – a desire not to move their kids around every few years, the reality of having a working spouse who makes a lot more money than the field ranger, the inability to buy a house or rent in communities where parks are located, or simply finding a park they fall in love with – a park where they believe they can really make a difference.

This book is about rangers who fall into that last category. These individuals, at some point in their careers, either chose to work at a park that sounded interesting and attractive, or they were assigned to a park by the personnel section. Whatever the reason for this transfer, they discovered they were really at home there. They decided that this was where they were going to spend their time and effort – improving the park, becoming involved in the local community, and changing the world through their incredible dedication, character, park values, and will.

These rangers are storytellers, guardians, and scientists. As scientists, they explored the literature of "their" park, and also spent a lot of time in the field discovering for themselves the park's natural and cultural features. For example, Mark Jorgensen, through his field research, became one of the leading experts on the desert bighorn sheep. After he retired from State Parks, he co-authored a beautiful book on the history and behavior of this iconic desert mammal.

Gary Strachan is now recognized as an expert on the northern elephant seal and the birds of the coastal region between Santa Cruz and San Francisco.

Mark Faull taught himself the science of archeology. He spent thousands of hours poking around the washes and canyons of Red Rock Canyon State Park, looking for prehistoric sites and artifacts, paleontological remnants, and natural features. Mark ultimately became so knowledgeable in archeology that he was asked to co-teach, for over a dozen years, a class on that topic at the Parks Department's Mott Training Center at Asilomar in Pacific Grove.

Rangers play an extremely important role as guardians for parks. The common phrase used to describe one part of their job is "to protect the park from the people, protect the people from the park, and protect the people from other people." These are the roles of law enforcement and public safety, but also included are search and rescue and first responder duties. Understanding the science of the park is very helpful in this assignment, since visitors are often unaware of the impact their actions might have on a park's sensitive resources. Rangers can use the "interpretive" approach, based on their knowledge of the local resources, to help change visitors' behaviors and attitudes.

INTRODUCTION

Jon Muench spent years as the ranger/pilot for Anza–Borrego Desert State Park. He spent so much time in the plane that it almost became his "partner," much as a canine or patrol horse would. He wrote manuals for the pilots who would follow him in order to make their jobs easier and safer, and he performed search and rescue operations that were as remarkable as they were dangerous.

Jerry Henderson developed the entire wilderness management program at Mt. San Jacinto State Park. This program has lasted over 40 years in pretty much the same condition in which he created it. The wilderness protocols Jerry implemented have effectively provided visitor safety – protection from the extreme conditions that often exist at the park – and have restored the local wilderness ethic that was eroding quickly in the early '70s.

Bill Deitchman was the whitewater river ranger at Auburn State Recreation Area. In addition to rafting the American River regularly, he managed the entire river program at the park. In these roles, he ensured that private boaters, as well as those visitors traveling with a commercial guide, were able to have a fun, yet safe, experience.

One of the best attributes of good park rangers is their ability to tell stories. And these are stories with a point – not just some rambling tale. One of the mistakes made in "interpreting" parks to the visitors is to confuse the tendency to recite facts with the ability to relate the park's story to the visitor's experiences. Talented rangers have the ability to hold their audiences spellbound, whether by their personality or their skill at making a story resonate with the lives of visitors.

Greg Hayes, stationed at Jack London State Historic Park, went back to college and wrote his master's thesis on author Jack London. One park employee joked that not only did Greg know more about the park than the author did, he knew more about Jack London than did the park's eponym. Rather than list a bunch of dates when London did this or that, Greg would tell the author's story in as exciting a style as that in which London wrote his tales.

Janet and Dave Carle developed the knack of telling the story of Mono Lake, and they did not just tell this story to park visitors. As a result of a major legal action, the park was often host to scientists, lawyers, agency managers, volunteers, lobbyists, and the media. Janet and Dave do not take credit for "saving" Mono Lake. Instead, they acknowledge that, based on their extensive scientific understanding of the lake and its concomitant management and legal issues, they were able to translate the legal and scientific arguments into layman's terms. They could break down the complex issues into building blocks that a judge could understand and that the media could provide to their readers and listeners in straightforward copy. In retrospect, this storytelling was, without doubt, key to saving the lake.

Carlos Porrata was a storyteller of the highest order. He delivered environmental living programs to over 17,000 fifth-graders during his stay at Tomales Bay State Park! He taught the students how the Coast Miwok Indians made tools, prepared food, and set up their tribal governance. To this day, it is common for former students to approach Carlos in his hometown of Inverness and thank him – not only for telling them stories of the native peoples, but for inspiring them to be better land stewards.

Mike Lynch not only was adept at telling stories, but his historical research also provided him with the tools to discover some heretofore hidden stories, and to correct other, oft mistold tales. He became convinced that certain parts of the State Parks legacy were missing, so he set forth to fill those gaps. For instance, he believed we should all celebrate the accomplishments of the Department. Celebrations of the anniversaries of the appointment of the first park ranger, the creation of the first state park, and of a variety of Departmental programs came to fruition under Mike's guidance. He collected important historical memorabilia, such as patches, badges, insignia, hats, and state park postcards. And when he found gaps in the postcards record, he used his own time and funds to produce the missing cards. Most importantly, he was able to articulate the plight of the state park rangers during collective bargaining, and the rising tide that he insisted upon eventually "lifted all ships."

Dan Winkelman may be the only park ranger in history to make a run for president – not president of the local natural history association or Kiwanis chapter, but of the United States! This whimsical and quixotic campaign was a product of the imagination of famed cartoonist Phil Frank of the San Francisco Chronicle. Phil's brilliant concept gave Dan the opportunity to market the park, give campaign speeches to varied audiences, and even pass out "Win With Winkelman" bumper stickers.

Why is this work of being a scientist, guardian, and storyteller so important to park rangers? The worth of parks and open space reserves has been demonstrated on many levels – physical and mental health, economic contribution to local businesses and citizens, better understanding of our local environment, and civic pride. Parks provide hope – hope that the very best parts of our natural and cultural heritage are being protected in perpetuity by park rangers and other staff, and hope that we are leaving our grandchildren and their grandchildren a healthy and sustainable planet.

Some of the key points in the history of the "park movement" demonstrate this hope. The first official "state park" was the 20,000 acres of land at Yosemite Valley and the nearby Mariposa Grove of giant redwoods. On June 30, 1864, President Abraham Lincoln signed federal legislation that ceded this property to the State of California. The bill required that the premises "be held for public use, resort, and recreation, and shall be inalienable for all time."

It is hard for us to imagine the mood in Congress in 1864, during one of the very darkest periods in our country's history. Perhaps it was this ray of hope, provided by the creation of a permanently protected park, that allowed lawmakers to think long-term and to embrace a vision of an action that would outlive not only themselves, but last at least seven generations into the future of our country.[1]

Another example occurred during our country's economic depression. In 1928, the first state park bond act was enacted by the California legislature and approved by the state's voters. This enabled the state to sell bonds in order to seek and buy lands to create the State Park System. Although this voter ratification preceded the stock market crash of 1929 and the great depression that soon followed, the real work of

---

[1] The Seventh Generation Principle, from the Great Law of the Iroquois Confederacy

A ranger at Humboldt Redwoods State Park in 1936. *Courtesy of California State Parks (Image 090-11037).*

acquiring parklands, through purchase and donation, really took place from 1930 through 1934 – during the heart of the very worst of economic conditions in the history of our nation.

Again, hope was at work at the time. People had trouble finding work, feeding their families, and living productive lives. However, they found the ability to peer into the future and recognize the opportunity to leave a legacy – a legacy of some of the state's most beautiful and important landscapes. These were places that they could afford to take their families to and enjoy life, if only for a few hours or days. Even in those dark times, they knew that these beautiful parks would be available for their children's children and well beyond.

Think of some of the iconic state parks that were added to the California State Park System during those difficult years – Del Norte Redwoods, Mt. Tamalpais, D.L. Bliss, Mt. San Jacinto, Santa Monica State Beach, Calaveras Big Trees, Palomar Mountain, Jedediah Smith Redwoods, Cuyamaca Rancho, Pt. Lobos, Anza–Borrego Desert, Pfeiffer Big Sur, Castle Crags, San Juan Bautista State Historic Park, La Purísima Mission, and Silver Strand State Beach. Had they not become state park units during that period, it is not difficult to speculate that some of them would have been purchased for other, non-park purposes – that is, they would have been developed for commercial applications.

Looking back, it is clear these were good decisions, based on the amount of use these state parks received. In 1928, the State Park System was composed of 12 parks, five historic monuments, and 13,700 acres of land. Six years later, in 1934, there were 49 parks, 11 historic monuments, and 300,000 acres of park property. Incredibly, usage went from 60,000 park visitors per year in 1928 to almost six million in 1934 – a nearly 10,000% increase! These new parks were definitely filling a need.[2]

Another tale is told by Terry Tempest Williams in her excellent book, *The Hour of Land*. Although Grand Teton National Park had been established in 1929, thousands of acres that made up the spectacular Snake River Valley remained outside the park boundary. John D. Rockefeller Jr. quietly began buying up these lands, and offered them as a gift to the United States – but only if they would be added to the National Park Service's holdings. President Franklin Roosevelt was reluctant to accept this gift, due to local opposition to increasing the size of the national park.

Finally, in March of 1943 – a mere 15 months after the bombing of Pearl Harbor – Roosevelt issued an executive order. This proclamation established the Jackson Hole National Monument, which was composed of over 220,000 acres of public and private land. Again, this incredible act took place during the planet's worst war ever, and represented optimism during what was a famously hopeless time in world history.[3]

These were incredible leaps of faith for another reason – none of these actions included operating funds for these lands. The enabling acts did not attach appropriations for staff, maintenance, or operating funds. In

---

2 Engbeck, Joseph H. Jr. *State Parks of California, from 1984 to the Present.* Charles H. Belding, Publisher. 1980

3 Williams, Terry Tempest. *The Hour of Land.* Sarah Crichton Books. 2016

these instances cited above, and in countless others, the Congress, two U.S. presidents, and the California legislature all provided these amazing gifts to their constituents – without really knowing how these parks would be operated.

After World War II ended, more new parks were added, visitation went up dramatically again, and military veterans returned to the work force. These veterans filled many of the state park ranger jobs – jobs that at that time included all field work necessary to keeps parks running and safe.

When Ronald Reagan became governor of California in 1967, he appointed a man who was one of the most creative and influential directors in the history of the Parks Department – William Penn Mott, Jr. Mott was one of two state park directors (the latter being Donald Murphy) who, 24 years apart, took disjunct actions that created the perfect environment in the Parks Department – ideal for a generation of rangers who were bright, educated, mission-driven self-starters.

These rangers believed they could change the world, and were not afraid to take risks to effect this change. They did, without question, change the parks they came to love, and changed them for the better – the much better.

Perhaps not surprisingly, William Penn Mott, Jr. and Don Murphy were two of the small handful of State Parks directors in the past 50 years who actually had park experience. After their stints in California State Parks, both were appointed to high-level positions in the National Park Service.

Governor Reagan appointed Bill Mott after Mott had served as director of the East Bay Regional Parks Department – one of the most highly regarded regional parks agencies in the United States. One of his highest priorities was to "professionalize" the California state park ranger profession.

During his term as director, Mott separated the civil service classifications of the rangers and the maintenance workers. This meant that rangers would focus on visitor services to the exclusion of doing routine maintenance work. Naturally, this split led to some hard feelings; some of the maintenance staff believed the rangers were now the favored class – "Mott's Babies," according to some. But this change did have the effect of allowing rangers to focus more on visitor services – direct contact with the park's visitors. The director also increased the minimum qualifications for rangers – a four-year college degree became the new standard.

Mott then decided to increase the training for all staff. And in order to handle the tremendous new emphasis on training, he established a training center at the Asilomar Conference Grounds, near Monterey. The Asilomar Training Center was staffed up, dormitories and classrooms were constructed, and it soon became the gold standard for state park training in the nation.

One of the first classes the ranger trainees had at Asilomar was "Park Philosophy," taught by a veteran regional director named Jim Whitehead. Jim had a very distinguished career, and remains the only State Parks employee to be named to the California Park and Recreation Commission after he retired.

Jim was the perfect instructor to teach this class. Well-respected by staff, he in turn had tremendous regard for the profession of park ranger. He insisted that rangers in his region (Southern California) wear their Stetsons, have a clean and pressed uniform, protect the heck out of the parks, and be friendly ambassadors. At Whitehead's direction, on the back of each park vehicle in Southern California was a sign with these words – **"PARKS ARE FOR PEOPLE!"**

He recognized that the mission of State Parks could not be fulfilled without the support of the people of the state of California. It was these citizens who clamored for more parks to be established and who voted for the state park bond acts that helped provide the funds necessary to create those very parks.

A key element of Whitehead's philosophy class was his recounting the story "From Little Acorns." A short and powerful fictional tale, it tells of Elzeard Bouffier, a simple shepherd in the mountains of southern Europe. Bouffier lived by himself, over a day's walk from town, with his flock of sheep, in a very barren region. Every evening, he would sort through bags of acorns, looking for the best 100. He would discard most until he had his "good" acorns ready for the following day.

The next morning, he would soak his acorns in water, then set out to walk the treeless hills and ridges nearby. Every so often, he would thrust into the ground the iron staff he carried. He would drop an acorn into the hole, and then cover it with earth. He continued this for hours, and he later recalled that he had planted over 100,000 acorns over a span of three years. About 20,000 of those sprang to life, and half of those saplings survived as oak trees.

He did not know whose land he was planting trees on, nor did he really care. He did not have permission to plant trees, because he had never asked for approval. Bouffier had not prepared environmental documentation, nor did he have a timber management plan. He simply planted oak forests where no trees had previously existed.

Ten years later, the oaks were taller than Bouffier, and birch and beech trees that he had planted also sprouted among the oaks. The streambeds that had been dry before now were flowing with water. Wildlife was now abundant in the young forest, and the harsh dry winds were now gentler and more refreshing.

To paraphrase the narrator of this story, "When I reflect that one man, armed only with his own physical and moral resources, was able to cause this land of Canaan to spring from the wasteland, I am convinced that in spite of everything, humanity is admirable. In order to achieve this remarkable result, an unfailing greatness of spirit and tenacity of benevolence were required."

Here are these bright, impressionable, young ranger trainees whom Mott hired because he believed they could change the world. Now add in Jim Whitehead, a high-level park manager who is telling them that not only CAN they change the world, but they MUST change their world – for the better.

The result was a highly trained, motivated, well-educated cadre of park rangers. Classes in resource management, interpretation, management, administration, maintenance programs, and law enforcement were mandatory. Then, after a ranger had a couple of years experience, he or she would be invited back to Asilomar for refresher classes and higher level training classes. The expectation was that these trained

Jeff Jones, Alex Weiss, and Carol Nelson playing music at Angel Island State Park, much to the delight of park visitors.
Courtesy of California State Parks (Image 090-S18114).

employees would be the best and brightest and would serve the public well their entire careers. One metric for this generation is the fact that at least 50 of these rangers have written books.

Retired park superintendent Mike Wells calls this group of rangers "the pig in the python." As these graduates advanced in experience and longevity, they exerted greater influence on the Department. They wanted better working conditions, modern and functional equipment, even more and improved training, clearer policies, and better supervisors and managers. In the late '70s, these desires got even more traction as collective bargaining for state employees became law. A public employees' union was now able to speak for and negotiate for the park rangers.

At that time, it was a common belief and practice that rangers, particularly those who wanted to promote to higher levels, should relocate every two years or so. The theory was that a supervisor or manager should possess experience at a wide variety of park units – a redwood park, a reservoir, a beach, a resource park, a recreation area, a historic unit, or an off-highway vehicle park. While there is some validity to that theory, the people featured in this book chose another path. They were not as interested in promoting to the highest levels in the Department as they were in protecting the park that they had chosen – or, perhaps, the park that had chosen them.

Of course, some of these rangers became those better supervisors and managers. Others decided that their skills and desires, and sometimes their personal situations, led them to stay in one park for a number of years. And some of those who became associated with one park focused on improving this park as much as possible. They defended it from outside threats, managed its natural and cultural resources, interpreted it to the public, helped visitors have excellent experiences, educated schoolchildren about its wonders, and inspired volunteers and visitors to become ambassadors and stewards of "their" park. These were "persons of place."

Then California Governor Pete Wilson appointed Donald Murphy as director in the early '90s. Murphy had a background in parks – actually, he was one of the rangers in the Department who was part of the "Mott" generation. Well-educated, highly trained, and very motivated, Director Murphy had been moving up through the ranks of State Parks supervisory and management positions when he was selected as director.

Now, management philosophy and management theory ebb and flow in state government, just as they do in the private and non-profit sectors. During Murphy's tenure as director, a lot of companies and organizations were moving towards an approach called "total quality management." He decided he was going to implement this TQM at State Parks (Some eventually called it PQM, or Parks Quality Management). Although this theory was more geared to private industry, Murphy was able to single out the parts that were germane to, and would work in, a state agency. These included a laser focus on mission, excellent customer service, reliance on teams, data-driven decision-making, and continuous improvement.

Another extremely valuable component of TQM was the practice of empowerment. To Director Murphy, empowerment meant placing decision-making authority at the appropriate place in the organization. Sometimes the appropriate person to make a decision is the director, and sometimes it is the seasonal park aide in the park's entrance station who sees an opportunity to provide outstanding customer service directly to the customer. Usually, of course, it is someone in between these two people. This took tremendous courage on the part of the director. He would be held responsible for the decisions of the district superintendents and other field staff, yet he still empowered his people to represent the Department in dealings with the public, universities, other agencies, local government, the media, and elected officials.

By some fortune – there is disagreement whether it was good or bad fortune – the Department was required to severely cut its budget at that time. The director recognized that this budget cut, rather than a disaster, presented a remarkable opportunity.

To implement TQM and empowerment into the Department's organizational structure that existed then (1993) would have been very, very difficult. There would have been tremendous resistance from all quarters. Well, there was resistance anyway, but it was more manageable while the Department was being turned upside-down financially and organizationally.

Murphy appointed a crosscutting team of well-respected supervisors and managers to design a new State Parks Department. This was the most comprehensive and significant reorganization the Department had ever sustained. The result was a much "flatter" organization – that is, there were fewer layers of supervision. The regional offices were eliminated, and the size and scope of field district offices were increased. A key outcome was that staff experts, such as resource ecologists, archeologists, historians, interpretive specialists, engineers, landscape architects, and even paleontologists, were assigned to the districts. Higher level and technically sophisticated administrative and maintenance managers were also relocated to these field offices.

One of the most important results of this reorganization was the appointment of district superintendents who had progressed and matured under the Mott program. These trained and educated rangers, now roughly 20 years into their careers, were promoting into management positions.

Through empowerment, they had also now been given the authority, responsibility, and accountability to manage their district and to make a lot of decisions that heretofore needed to be approved by a legion of reviewers in the regional offices and in Sacramento headquarters (many of whom had zero field experience). Wisely, district superintendents delegated a lot of these decisions to their staff – the real experts in running parks and protecting park resources.

The district superintendent now had a team of subject matter experts and high-level managers working for them who could provide reasoned advice on any number of issues. Another vital change in the Department's culture was that, should the district superintendent or one of their staff make a mistake of consequence, it was treated as a learning opportunity. The prevailing theory was that everyone could learn and improve when mistakes are made. The goal was to ensure that the district superintendent had the information, data, and feedback necessary to consider the next time in order to make a better decision.

A subsequent director, Rusty Areias, encouraged staff to adopt the management style embraced by President John F. Kennedy. Director Areias said that President Kennedy would be addressing members of his cabinet or his Joint Chiefs of Staff at high-level meetings, and would tell attendees that the behavior he abhorred the most at these meetings was to have everyone sitting around the table and silently nodding while he was talking. The president would say something along the lines of, "If I am talking and everyone else is nodding, that means I am the only one in the room doing any critical thinking. I encourage all of you to voice your opinions, no matter how much they deviate from mine. Your job is to provide me with your best thinking. My job is to make decisions once I have all the best ideas available for consideration. You all have experience that far outweighs mine in your field of expertise. If you are not courageous enough to present me with your thoughts, I am not sure why you are in this room."

Director Mott set in motion the creation of a generation of truly exceptional rangers. Regional Director Whitehead told them they had a mandate to achieve remarkable results through their spirit and tenacity. Director Murphy then told them to go forth and carry out the mission of the Department to the best of their ability, and to do it while using their best judgment. Director Areias told them they needed to be courageous.

The district superintendents no longer needed to ask permission to take actions that were mission-based, reasonable, and well-justified through supportive data. Again, the district superintendents were expected to empower their staffs similarly. These leaders created a perfect storm – a beneficial storm that turned loose remarkable rangers who achieved spectacular results.

However, as with all good things, they must, at some point, come to an end. The principle of empowerment was eventually eliminated, while decision-making was largely brought back to Sacramento. This reversal was not the result of egregious errors that were made in the field. Director Murphy was cut from the same cloth, woven at the same time, as the majority of field superintendents – he knew and trusted them. When he left the Department, subsequent directors did not possess the same field experience that he had. Further, the Department's training center (now the William Penn Mott Jr. Training Center) is severely under-utilized, and instead of rangers employing a broadly based skill set, there is a much greater emphasis on law enforcement.

Having a well-trained and competent cadre of law enforcement rangers to provide protection in and for our state parks is absolutely necessary. One of the key questions facing the Department today is whether there should be a law enforcement team that is separate from the rangers who present day hikes and campfire programs, and staff the interpretive centers.

The people featured in this book were fortunate in that they were of the generation who were convinced they could change the world. They had no reason to be disabused of that notion.

What made them such fierce defenders of parks? Those who love nature see parks as places where natural features and natural processes can be protected and sustained. Those who love the cultural aspects of our parks honor the role that state parks play in preserving the stories of our historical and prehistoric periods. We have little control over what happens outside the park boundary – the habitat fragmentation, urbanization, wind farms, strip mining, and infrastructure projects – so we tend to defend like crazy those lands we are sent in to protect.

So, the persons of place, in this book, are those individuals who fell in love with a particular geography. When I think of Anza–Borrego, Mono Lake, Mt. San Jacinto, Tomales Bay, Red Rock Canyon, Año Nuevo, Auburn, Crystal Cove, Angel Island, or Jack London, my first thought is of the ranger who was so closely associated with that place.

For some of these rangers, their "place" was a park they were assigned to by chance, and the park became their passion. For others, it was a park they had known as a child and where they had always wanted to work. Or there may have been a situation where a ranger viewed a somewhat undesirable park as a career stepping-stone and was shocked when it became their life's passion. Then some of our subjects had the goal of a really fun and adventurous job – whether it was hiking and skiing the wilderness, flying an airplane, scuba diving, patrolling on horseback, or rafting whitewater rivers.

Whatever their motivation, these "parkies" inspired the rest of us to be bold, creative, fierce, courageous, humble, and wise. Although these women and men are park heroes, they all downplay their role, and they are quick to credit other individuals or teams as sharing the responsibility for successful outcomes. None of them sought recognition for their accomplishments – they were, and remain, true and humble public servants.

When I set out to write this book, I identified five goals:

- I wanted to honor several of the incredible individuals who were so committed to making "their park" or their profession so much better. These rangers were dedicated to improving their geography – they were persons of place. They accomplished miracles, and these successes were, in several instances, enacted at great risk to their professional career in State Parks.

- There are several iconic jobs in the California Department of Parks and Recreation, and I wanted to describe those jobs and the people who take them on. These include wilderness patrol ranger, airplane pilot, and river rafter.

- I wanted to call out the courage of "groundbreakers." Paula Peterson faced incredible resistance when she became the first full-time, permanent, female state park ranger. Janet and Dave Carle had to invent the protocols for a married couple sharing a job – a job at a remote park in the midst of a political cauldron. Greg Hayes, upon retirement, eventually became the president of the cooperating association for Jack London State Historic Park. When that park was threatened with closure, Greg had to lead the effort that ultimately handed the reins for running "his" park over to a nonprofit corporation. Mike Tope had to face down unruly crowds at public meetings, work to terminate a signed multi-million dollar contract, evict hundreds of residents, and create a new model for an operating agreement, all in order to create an extraordinary and unique state park at Crystal Cove.

- While honoring these individuals, I hope to inspire current employees to accomplish more than they might feel possible in today's State Park System. I want people to look outside their real and perceived boundaries and aspire to do more. If rangers in today's Department do not believe they have the capability or authority to effect necessary changes and accomplish miracles, we need to ask why not.

- It is highly desirable to recruit a new generation of exceptional rangers and lifeguards who are excited about entering this line of work and who will excel at it.

I started interviewing subjects for this book in the fall of 2014, and I reckoned I would have this in print in about a year. Well, a few things got in the way. A close relative received a cancer diagnosis, I had a pacemaker implanted, and then my mother had a bad fall and broke several bones. At the age of 90, her prognosis was not good. She lived in four different levels of care facilities within a three-month period. I was traveling to her home in Northern California two to three times a month to help her out.

Then the big one hit. Anza–Borrego park ranger Steve Bier (Esteban Cerveza, in his words), widely regarded as the "ranger's ranger," committed suicide. I, and many others, had trouble reconciling this act with the Steve we thought we knew – an upbeat, funny, extremely bright and knowledgeable, do-it-all kind of ranger. Obviously, few of us knew the demons Steve was dealing with.

It was so maddening – Steve was a "throwback" ranger. He was a creative storyteller and interpreter, a knowledgeable and inspired resource protector, and an excellent enforcer of the law. I never saw him on duty without his Stetson on, and it was rare that he was not wearing a huge grin.

Ranger Steve Bier at an overlook of the Borrego Badlands. *Courtesy of Mark Jorgensen.*

I was driving up Fish Creek in Anza–Borrego Desert State Park one hot day, came around an outcropping of rock, and there was Steve – digging a hole to install a sign. He was wearing his Kevlar vest, his Stetson, and his omnipresent smile.

Finally, it struck me what I should do. I could not explain Steve's death – perhaps no one can – but I can honor him by telling the stories of rangers and others who shared his commitment to excellence.

When I started to write these stories of extraordinary men and women, I wanted to discover what the conditions were that enabled them to succeed. I found the following traits to be the most common:

- Humility

- Courage

- Tenacity

- A genuine desire to share credit with their colleagues

- Almost all acknowledged that they were shy growing up.

- They are all very nice people, but don't let that fool you. They also have spines of steel, especially when it comes to protecting parks.

- A sense that they had been lucky, or "blessed," to have had a wonderful job and splendid career during a magical time. That is not to say there were not challenging times and experiences that frustrated them in significant ways. But the same challenges, at the end of the day, were overcome, and those successes led to a feeling of pride and self-worth.

- A fierce allegiance to the mission of the Department – not necessarily allegiance to the Department, which can sway to and fro in the political winds, but to its mission –

To provide for the health, inspiration and education of the people of California by helping to preserve the state's extraordinary biological diversity, protecting its most valued natural and cultural resources, and creating opportunities for high-quality outdoor recreation.

They were certainly not always loyal to the Department's directors – in some cases they actively and publicly opposed the director, especially when the leader of the Department was taking actions that were not in line with the mission.

Several of these featured men and women won director's awards for excellence. One of the rangers featured in this book earned the State's Medal of Valor. But that medal is awarded for a singular act of courage. This book seeks to honor these rangers, and their many worthy colleagues, for their commitment and service over several decades to the people of California and the state's magnificent parks.

NOMENCLATURE

Although all the individuals portrayed in these chapters wore the khaki and green uniform of California's State Park Rangers at some point, that was not everyone's job title their entire career. Seasonal Park Aide, Seasonal Lifeguard, State Park Ranger, State Park Ranger Trainee, State Park Technician, Supervising Ranger, Lifeguard, Lifeguard Supervisor, Aquatics Specialist, Park Naturalist, Resource Ecologist, Park Superintendent, and District Superintendent were among the job titles held, at least for some period of time, by these extraordinary men and women. For the sake of brevity and simplicity, I used "ranger" throughout the book. I personally held several of these jobs in my 31-year State Parks career, and I worked another nine years for a nonprofit organization after leaving state service. But when people ask me today what I did for a living, I am proud to say, "I was a park ranger."

Every few years, the Parks Department decides that job titles and job responsibilities should change. I used these terms as follows:

Park Supervisor or Park Superintendent – The administrator of a single park unit.

Sector Supervisor or Sector Superintendent – The administrator of a small number of park units.

District Superintendent – The administrator of a cluster of park units.

Regional Director – The administrator of several park districts.

Division Chief – The administrator of a program at State Parks Headquarters.

Stetson – the broad-brimmed "campaign" hat that is closely associated with park rangers. Sometimes called the "Smokey Bear" hat.

MARK JORGENSEN

Iconoclastic Icon of the Desert

It was almost like a scene out of an artsy Western movie. As the park ranger drove up to a group of 20 Boy Scouts and their two adult leaders in the spring of 1963, he kept the desert sun at his back. When he climbed out of his yellow CJ-5 Jeep in the Fish Creek Mountains area of Anza–Borrego Desert State Park, George Leetch was the archetype of the desert ranger. He was tall, fit, and lean, with the look of the desert about him – leathery skin and a deep dark tan. He belonged in the desert. The sun was in the eyes of the scouts, and this silhouetted ranger added to the mystique of the moment.

The legendary Ranger Leetch was wearing his crisp khaki and green ranger uniform, polished badge, and flat, faded Stetson – the fading due to years of exposure to the desert's savage and holy light. George walked to the back of the Jeep and pulled out a large skull of a bighorn ram with a full curl of horns and laid it in the sand next to his patrol vehicle.

Eleven-year old Mark Jorgensen, one of the Boy Scouts, recalls that the scouts were a "bunch of mouthy squirrels" most of the time, but the image and demeanor of Ranger George Leetch commanded total silence.

Little did Mark realize at the time that this one encounter with a ranger would spark a 50-plus year love affair with Anza–Borrego Desert State Park in general, and more specifically, with research and management of the magnificent desert bighorn.

When Ranger Leetch picked up the ram skull and passed it around, he was utilizing a powerful interpretive technique known as the "hand-held object." When he described how the age and gender of a sheep could be determined by its skull and horns, the scouts were engrossed – looking at it close up and trying to determine its age.

George Leetch kept talking to the scouts about other aspects of the desert. He described the dynamics of the desert experience for them – flash floods, earthquakes, rescues, the desert heat, and rattlesnakes. Five years later, in 1968, immediately after an extremely powerful earthquake, Ranger Leetch drove up through Split Mountain, dodging falling boulders and rock slides to rescue a number of people. This rescue effort won George the state's highest honor – The Medal of Valor.

Desert bighorn sheep

George also described the rigors of being a ranger in Anza–Borrego to the scouts. In those days, rangers "air-conditioned" their Jeeps in the blazing hot summers by taking off the doors and windows.

At the time, the park was so large that the State Parks Department created a series of "outpost" ranger stations. These outposts were composed of a water tank, generator, underground gasoline tank, a travel trailer, and a storage building. This was where the ranger was expected to live with his wife and, in George's case, a pet monkey. Rangers lived many miles from their neighbors, and the main form of entertainment (well, maybe in the top two) was getting together with nearby rangers for a potluck dinner and a fair amount of alcohol.

Although this was interesting information, Mark was intrigued during the entire ranger talk with the bighorn sheep. A self-described "shy kid" (Yeah, right!), Mark kept asking Ranger Leetch question after question. Today, Mark recalls that he never raised his hand in school to ask questions, but that experience in Fish Creek with the bighorn skull sparked an extraordinary lifelong passion in him that has never waned.

Finally Mark asked, "How many sheep are there, what do they eat, how do they find enough water, where do they live?" George admitted that there was a lot of science still needed on the bighorn. Although George was the local park expert on sheep, he did not have enough answers to satisfy young Mark Jorgensen. George had hiked around Fish Creek (Mark likes to add that this area is blessed with neither fish nor creek), as well as Rattlesnake Spring, to observe the bighorn, but freely acknowledged big voids in data on the sheep.

Finally, to the last of Mark's many questions, George said that in order to get all these answers, someone needed to hike out into the desert wilderness and spend a lot of time studying sheep behavior and analyzing their findings. This was music to Mark's ears – it inspired him to follow a course that spanned the next five-plus decades and has not diminished since.

Ten years later, Mark was hired by Park Superintendent Bud Getty to conduct studies on the bighorn. George Leetch had left his Fish Creek Ranger Station in 1969, but returned to work in Anza–Borrego in 1975. When they met again as fellow rangers, Mark approached George and told him that one talk of George's had really inspired Mark's life work. George smiled and responded that he had probably given that same talk to 5,000 kids in his career, and he was delighted to learn that it had had a positive impact.

After that experience in Fish Creek in 1963, Mark was determined to further the research on the desert bighorn. He was only 11 at the time, so he bugged his older brothers to drive him out to Anza–Borrego for exploratory trips. They would take a little telescope for stargazing and walk up canyon after canyon looking for sheep. Mark recalls that it took him over five years to see his first live bighorn, and that was not even in the park. Mark frequented known bighorn habitat in the park, climbed Rabbit Peak, and searched the Colorado River banks near Picacho State Recreation Area, but he just kept "getting skunked."

At Picacho, he talked to a guy who told him he had just seen a bighorn around the next bend, but when Mark got there – nothing. On the Rabbit Peak hike, one of the hikers in the party was lagging behind the rest of the group, and, of course, he got to see three rams that the rest of the group missed. Many people probably would have thought that there must be a more rewarding research pursuit – one where you actually SEE your target species every once in a while.

Finally, Mark and long-time friend Don Sterner were in Chino Canyon, near Palm Springs, looking for lizards, when Mark ran out of water. He hiked back to their vehicle to refill his canteen, and when he tilted his head back to drink, he espied a ram on a boulder some 300 feet away. That sealed the deal as far as Mark's career path right there.

Besides the iconic bighorn, Anza–Borrego Desert State Park is remarkable for many reasons. One of the greatest compliments it receives is from visiting National Parks staff. They invariably ask, "Why is this not a national park?"

In addition to its size (at 1,000 square miles, it comprises over 40% of the California State Park System and is one of the largest state parks in the country), it is also incredibly diverse biologically. It is home to several endemic and endangered species.

Anza–Borrego has a rich historical and archeological record. The park is home to stagecoach routes, old stage stations, the Juan Bautista de Anza National Historic Trail, ancient rock art, fish traps, pottery, geoglyphs, solar sites, and rock circles – the list goes on and on.

Unique and perhaps most remarkable, though, is its paleontological record. In the past, ancient seas, rivers, lakes, and savannahs were present in what is now the park, and this abundance of water supported an incredible array of marine, fresh-water, and terrestrial flora and fauna.

It is a landscape that invites people like Mark to a life of intimacy with the park. It has so much to offer, and Mark, more than most, dedicated his life to getting to know every aspect of the park and sharing that knowledge and passion with others.

Mark just fell in love with Anza–Borrego Desert State Park, and was determined to know it inside and out, hot and cold, high and low. Without question, Mark knows more about the park than anyone ever has. However, at about 640,000 rugged acres, the park does not make it easy to become intimate with its every nook and mountain peak. Mark reckons that he knows about 10% of the park pretty well.

In order to get to know Anza–Borrego at its most challenging time, he and Don Sterner cooked up this scheme to backpack the length of the park, over 100 miles, south to north, in the middle of summer.

This was an "unsupported" hike – that is, no one met them occasionally with supplies or water or drove them to an air-conditioned motel once in a while. However, the two young men did stash water jugs along the way in order to, well, just stay alive.

They began their 22-day journey in the lovely town of Jacumba, in the southwest corner of the park and headed to the northeast corner, near the town of Mecca, California, from August 10 through August 31, 1971. They hiked through Carrizo Gorge, across the Carrizo Badlands, up Fish Creek to Hapaha Flat, north through Harper Flat and Harper Canyon, over to Buttes Pass, then across the Borrego Badlands to Calcite Mine. They turned north and east once they reached the foot of the Santa Rosa Mountains, trekking cross-country from Calcite into Travertine Palms Wash.

By the time they reached Travertine, they had run out of water, but gained comfort in the knowledge that one of their water caches was nearby. They found the site where they had buried their water jugs, but the first bottle they dug up had broken and was empty. They looked at each other, knowing that if the second jug was empty, their lives were over. Fortunately, the second jug was intact, so they rehydrated and continued hiking on north to Mecca.

Despite spending time in jail for having spent a night on the linoleum floor of an air-conditioned school classroom (Ah, luxury!), Mark recalls that the trek that he and Don survived was a life-changing hike. They learned a lot about the desert and its summer ecology, mostly because they took time to sit and contemplate life and the desert. Don Sterner went on to a career in conservation of endangered species at the San Diego Zoo and Safari Park.

Mark was still a student at Sacramento State when he submitted a proposal to study bighorn sheep. Park Superintendent Bud Getty found out about the proposal and thought it was a great idea. Bud hired Mark at $2.51/hour with funds that had to be spent by the end of the fiscal year, which terminates June 30. Bud took a risk and spent some of the following year's money in July and August, so the young biologist could conduct the majority of his field research in the heart of the summer. Of course, this is the season when it is common to have temperatures over 110 degrees during the day. It is also the time of year when bighorn are most evident to scientists and other observers.

Anza–Borrego badlands

When Mark did get hired by Getty in 1972 as a seasonal researcher, he was told that the park did not want to send researchers into the desert alone, so Mark would be paired up with another young student – Bob Turner. Bob and Mark became great friends and colleagues, and both young men went on to become state park rangers. After a few years as a ranger, Bob switched over to State Fish and Game as a warden.

Bob and Mark did this for the next three summers as well, and worked on answering questions that Mark had posed to George Leetch some 10 years earlier – how many sheep were there, where are their watering holes, where do they cross highways, and what is their habitat and range. They recorded every sheep sighting and every possible source of water, and mapped this information.

The young researchers would talk to the park staff and ask them how many sheep were in the park, how important the water and forage in Carrizo Gorge were, or what were the sheep's movement patterns in the Rattlesnake Spring area. They were surprised that no one really had good answers for them. They slowly realized that they – these two young college students – were quickly becoming the experts on bighorn in the park.

They met frequently with Park Superintendent Getty and gained his confidence vis-à-vis their growing expertise on bighorn. They raised concerns about the management of the sheep, or lack thereof. Intuitively, they knew that sustainability of the sheep population was precarious. Although much of their study preceded the enactment of the Federal Endangered Species Act (passed in December, 1973), their work in the field informed them that human activities had put this population at risk.

Mark and Bob were concerned about the lack of scientific data on the sheep. They realized that, as visitation in the park increased, new forms of recreation developed, and infrastructure projects were proposed to cross the massive park, it would be necessary to assess the impacts of those trends and projects on this species. In order to make decisions that protected sheep and their habitat, good science was needed.

One of the first issues that arose after a few summers of field surveys for bighorn was in Coyote Canyon – a beautiful riparian corridor in the northwest corner of the park. Water in the desert is, of course, very important to plants, animals, and humans. The presence of a stream with summer surface water was particularly crucial. At that time, motorized vehicles were allowed in the stream, and that caused problems.

It seems odd now that motor vehicles would be allowed to drive up a riparian corridor. However, one can imagine that in the early days, only a few cars or Jeeps would meander up the creek. Then usage continued to increase to the point where there were organized caravans. Also, the development of off-road motorcycles made this canyon more and more of a playground than a peaceful riverine zone.

Mark recalls the time he and Bob were watching ewes and lambs come down the mountainsides towards standing water in Coyote Creek one summer day. In the summer, water is very scarce in the desert's mountains, and the sheep were descending cautiously and very slowly. In the summer, it is critical that sheep drink water at least every third day.

As the ewe band neared the creek, a motorcycle came flying up the creek and scared the sheep back up the mountainside. Given the sheep's need for regular water, this disruption could have had serious consequences. When they presented this concern to Bud Getty, the superintendent told the young researchers that he could not close the area to motor vehicles or close it during the hot months without more data and scientific justification.

Mark's older brother Paul, an esteemed biologist in his own right, was hired by Getty in the summer of 1973 to study this interaction between vehicles and bighorn. The basic question Paul was trying to answer was whether the activity of motor vehicles in Coyote Canyon in the summer affected the bighorn's success at accessing water. After a very hot period of research, Paul concluded that the sheep spent less than a third as much time near water on weekends, when there was regular vehicular traffic, as on weekdays, when there was virtually no traffic in Coyote Canyon.

Based on these data, Bud Getty was able to justify the summer seasonal closure of Coyote Canyon to humans. This was the first time in the park that scientific surveys had been used to make a controversial land-use decision. This episode was to set a standard for the park for decades. As numbers of people in the park increased and as threats to the park and its resources mounted, the use of science-based information was crucial to good park management and decision-making.

Mark went on to earn his degree in environmental resources at Sacramento State in 1973, and he credits this seasonal work on sheep as an inspiration for his career with California State Parks.

State Parks was hiring a lot of ranger trainees in those years, and Mark was hired to work at the coastal state parks of San Diego County. Trainees would split their first nine months between on-the-job training in the field and formal training – law enforcement, interpretation, resource management, and administration – at the Mott Training Center at Asilomar in Pacific Grove, California.

His first "permanent" assignment was at the coastal state parks of Ventura County. Typical for Mark, his best remembrance of his two years at the Channel Coast District was when he observed a couple of least terns nesting on the beach at McGrath State Beach. Again, Mark was aware of the threats to this bird species and its recent steep drop in population numbers. Mark called upon brother Paul, who had a lot of experience with tern nesting.

On Paul's recommendation, Mark gathered fencing and posts, borrowed a few closure signs for least tern nesting from State Fish and Game, and created a protected area for the terns to nest successfully. Soon, Mark and others noted another sensitive species, Belding's savannah sparrow, in the vicinity. The presence of these two resident species led to the State Park and Recreation Commission eventually establishing a natural preserve at the mouth of the Santa Clara River.

During his assignment at Ventura, Mark was constantly itching to return to Anza–Borrego Desert State Park. In 1978, he transferred to Ocotillo Wells State Vehicular Recreation Area, immediately adjacent to his beloved Anza–Borrego. "OW" was created as part of the solution to the rapidly increasing popularity of off-roading – visitors used dune buggies, rails, Jeeps, quads, and motorcycles for riding dirt roads and cross-country travel. At that time, OW and Anza–Borrego were lumped together administratively, so Mark also did some field time as a ranger at Anza–Borrego when called upon.

Mark was at Ocotillo Wells from 1978-1980. In those days, a few parks, like Anza–Borrego and Torrey Pines State Reserve, had a position called "park naturalist," whose primary job was to work on interpretation and education.

In the fall of 1980, the former park naturalist left state service, and Mark was hired to fill that position. Incredibly, the immense Anza–Borrego Desert State Park had no staff dedicated to resource management – natural, cultural, or paleontological. So Mark took on those roles in addition to the more traditional naturalist tasks of writing brochures, leading nature hikes and campfire programs, giving talks at schools, training local staff, and creating bird and mammal lists.

During his 13 years as the park naturalist, Mark undertook what he considers his two greatest achievements during his State Parks career. Given the plethora of successes Mark had, these two accomplishments were really something special.

The first was the designation of "state wilderness" in the park. Now, in 1974, the state legislature had passed the California Wilderness Act, which established the "designated wilderness" program in the state. At the same time, the legislature approved two wilderness areas in state park units – the Santa Rosa Mountains

Anza–Borrego's beautiful Wilderness..

Wilderness in Anza–Borrego, and the Mount San Jacinto Wilderness in Mount San Jacinto State Park. Mark and Bud Getty had written the proposal for the Santa Rosa Mountains State Wilderness while Mark was still a seasonal employee.

The act also established the criteria for designating additional state wildernesses, as well as the process for such designation. Further wilderness designation in units of the State Parks System would be subject to public hearings and approval by the California State Park and Recreation Commission.

Basically, potential wilderness had to be on lands owned by the state, have the characteristics of wilderness, and be at least 5,000 contiguous acres in size. The legislatively created wildernesses at the Santa Rosa and San Jacinto mountains met these criteria, but the state was slow to legally establish new state wildernesses.

Anza–Borrego Park Superintendent Bud Getty, looking over the political landscape in the early '80s, recognized a window of opportunity. The secretary for resources (one level above State Parks director in the state hierarchy) in the Edmund G. Brown Jr. administration was a fellow named Huey Johnson. Johnson had a reputation for being an advocate for wilderness, and Bud was aware that Johnson would leave that position in January of 1983 at the latest, since that is when a new governor would take office and appoint his or her own management team. Bud realized that they had better get any proposed wilderness before the park commission for consideration and approval while Johnson was still in office.

Mark was tasked with developing the proposals for state wilderness for the park. He recognized right away that there would have to be several separate wilderness areas. Because the park has a large number of dirt roads in its backcountry, and since motor vehicular travel is not allowed in wilderness, a single wilderness area would not be feasible.

Mark spent many months drawing maps, putting together resource summaries for each proposed study area, and surveying the backcountry to ensure that his proposals made sense. In 1981, the park commission held public hearings to take testimony about the proposed wilderness. Surprisingly, there was almost zero opposition to any of the wilderness proposals in the park. At the time, 12 separate wildernesses were established, and slight expansions were approved the following year.

In 2005, that same commission approved the general plan for the entire park, following more than a decade of preparation. The general plan added acreage to three of the original wildernesses, and it created one new state wilderness.

There exists now more than 460,000 acres of official wilderness in the park. This dwarfs the amount of state wilderness owned and managed by all other state agencies, and it comprises 95% of the wilderness in California's State Park System. This wilderness designation affords exceptional protection for the park and its incredible resources. New roads, power lines, and new facilities – including park structures – are now prohibited, and the land will remain wild and free for visitors to enjoy in perpetuity.

Mark's other top achievement was participating in the team effort in 1987 that led to the removal of green-sticker and unlicensed motorized vehicles from the park. This was a great example of a grass-roots effort of staff in the field on a major policy issue – not only was there little leadership from the director's office on this issue, there was direct and forceful opposition.

In the early '70s, the "green sticker" program had been authorized by the legislature, which allowed non-street legal motorized vehicles a means to be registered for legal operation. The program also authorized the creation of legal areas for off-roaders to ride in. A part of Anza–Borrego Desert State Park was sliced off to become part of the new Ocotillo Wells State Vehicular Recreation Area (SVRA). Additional lands were soon acquired to expand this boundary. In a short period of time, Ocotillo Wells became the largest SVRA in the state and served users from all over the Southland.

The park staff of Anza–Borrego at first thought this was a good arrangement. There were a lot of families using the SVRA, and staff supported the notion of families spending time together in the outdoors. Due to the tremendous and rapid increase in this recreational activity, it was recognized that it made sense to establish legal riding areas throughout the state. After all, it was reasonable to have off-roading in a site that was patrolled and staffed with rangers that had first responder training.

Soon, however, off-road use began to spill over, illegally, into Anza–Borrego Desert State Park. And the California Public Resources Code, which spelled out regulations for the Parks Department, clearly stated that all vehicles operated in state parks had to be licensed for the highway and operated by a licensed driver.

For several years, no effort had been made on the part of the park staff to enforce existing laws. Like a lot of

After only one vehicle goes off the approved road, many others often follow. In short order, it looks like a regular road, and the damage becomes permanent.
Courtesy of Jimmy Smith

activities, usage of the park by off-roaders did not seem to be that much of a problem. After all, there were over 500 miles of dirt roads in the park. As long as the green-sticker vehicles stayed to the legal, established dirt roads, it did not seem as though significant damage to park resources was occurring.

Gradually, though, things kept getting worse. The volume of green-sticker vehicles in the park kept increasing significantly. And, instead of vehicles staying in the washes on designated park roads, there was an increasing number of incursions off the designated routes, as well as hill climbs and cross-country riding. It was as if the state park had become a testing ground for high-performance machinery rather than a peaceful respite for park visitors and wildlife.

In 1985, the local staff finally decided that they could no longer permit this illegal activity. Even the green-sticker vehicles that stayed on the roads were breaking the law. The damage to resources from off-roaders was becoming a major issue. Additionally, the peaceful nature of the park had disappeared – it was now a noisy, busy place.

Staff recognized that the notion of removing an entire recreational activity – especially one with a powerful political lobby – would necessarily require a huge, whole team effort. The entire park staff, from the chief ranger to the park auto mechanic, got together to discuss the issue at Mark's house.

It became clear to all that the damage had become too severe, and disregard for laws and the reasons for those laws too widespread, for benign neglect to persist. So the staff wrote up the justification for beginning to enforce the provisions of the law that restricted the dirt roads in the park to street legal vehicles.

One of the main proponents of this grassroots action was Ranger Joe von Herrmann. Joe possessed a razor wit, a strong belief in the rule of law, a sharp tongue, and a spine of steel. These attributes made him a formidable foe and a strong ally. Fortunately for the park and its resources, Joe was a motivated co-conspirator in the movement to rectify this intolerable and illegal situation. An issue of this magnitude needed a "public face" or two to talk with the media, appear in print or on camera, and provide legal and scientific input at public meetings. Joe was more than willing, along with Mark, to risk his job and career in order to do the right thing and become a public figure on this controversy.

Mark and a park aide started collecting photographic evidence of damaging activity. They would go in Mark's private vehicle, out of uniform, and park near sensitive areas. Then they would record the number of vehicles that would approach the area and drive right by the sign that said "No Motor Vehicles." They took thousands of photographs of the illegal activities and the damage caused by off-road drivers. Vehicles with no green sticker or license and unlicensed drivers were commonplace. This helped build their case and, when presented to decision-makers, gave those managers confidence in the staff's concerns.

Once the staff recommendation that proposed the removal of all illegal off-road activities from the park was released, a major public firestorm erupted. There was support from local management and from the regional director in San Diego, but Mark and the other rangers knew they were in for a major battle in the media, legislature, and courts.

A major disappointment arose almost immediately – one of the major hurdles was the opposition to their plan from the new State Parks director, Henry Agonia. Based on its funding sources and its lobbying efforts, the Off-Highway Vehicle (OHV) community was very powerful. Organized OHV support groups donated to political campaigns, and therefore had many allies in the legislature. They could fund legal actions and public relations campaigns. Every public meeting on this topic was advertised among that community, so there was always a large contingent of OHV supporters at those meetings.

The director was unwilling to take on the OHV community and kept trying to find a compromise solution. None of his proposals addressed the issues of unsustainable resource degradation and lawlessness, so park staff held fast to their goal of the removal of OHVs from the park.

At staff meetings in those days, Mark, the rangers, and the maintenance staff recognized that they were putting their jobs and their careers at risk. To directly oppose the director of your department, and to do it publicly, is usually not seen as a wise career move. Unanimously, however, they agreed that they had to do the right thing by the park, and that they were willing to take the consequences.

Mark was personally threatened with disciplinary action if he did not back off on this controversial issue. However, he found it difficult to reconcile the notion of defending the park and Department from damage with the idea of being punished for that effort, so he and the rest of the team persevered in their battle.

Needless to say, there was a lot of political and legal maneuvering, many field trips with managers and media pointing out resource damage, vandalism, threats, and tales of woe from the local businesses that serviced off-roaders. In the end, however, Mark and the local staff prevailed.

Ron McCullough, the State Parks regional director for Southern California, organized one of the key meetings during this decision process. Now, although the director of the Department, Henry Agonia, was opposed to the staff proposal to eliminate green-sticker use in the park, many middle and high-level managers in the Department, such as Ron, supported the staff proposal. As career park professionals, they nearly unanimously recognized that strong action was needed to adequately protect one of California's premier state parks. Part of their task was to find a way to convince the director of the wisdom of the staff proposal without appearing to defy him openly.

Ron had the idea for a field trip to the park that would include all the high-level managers in the Department. He believed that if managers, including those unfamiliar with the park, could be shown the magnificence of the park and the damage off-road activity was inflicting on those resources, he would be able to build a large and strong coalition of support. McCullough also reasoned that the director could not ignore or dismiss a coalition of unified top-level managers as easily as he could a gang of renegade rangers and one mouthy naturalist.

So all the field regional directors and all the division chiefs in Sacramento took a field trip to the park. Mark was assigned the job of leading the field trip, discussing the issues, and pointing out areas of damage.

Serendipitously, (Mark maintains), the managers came across a ranger in the Borrego Badlands who was repairing damage caused by illegal OHV activity. The ranger demonstrated to the group where an off-road motorcyclist had torn up a natural area of the desert. The ranger had a hard rake and explained that, while the motorcyclist had probably been there for only 10 or 15 minutes tearing up the desert, it would take him (the ranger) three or four hours to "rake out" all the tracks and try to restore its more natural appearance.

One of the managers on the field trip was Les McCargo, chief deputy director of the Parks Department – second in command to the director. Obviously, it was important to try to get Les on board to support the staff proposal. As Mark and the ranger were explaining the reason for raking out the vehicle tracks, Les interrupted, "Well, Mark, if you were smart, you would have brought 30 rakes and given each of us one. Together we could have raked out all these tracks in about 10 minutes and let this poor ranger get on with his job." Mark fired back, "Well, Les, I know you would be good at that, because you have been raking out your tracks your whole career!"

There was stunned silence for about five seconds, and many were probably thinking that the staff proposal just got torpedoed, when Les started laughing heartily at Mark's jab. Unbeknownst to most there, Mark and Les had recently taken a lengthy work trip together to advise the kingdom of Saudi Arabia on establishing protected desert areas and had become friends on that trip. That story probably was retold many, many times when those attendees got back to their offices. McCargo was on board with the staff's recommendation, and McCullough's strategy of building a broad internal coalition had succeeded. Director Agonia was ultimately persuaded to stand down.

In 1987, the Department agreed to eliminate green-sticker off-highway vehicles from Anza–Borrego Desert State Park. Shortly thereafter, the State Parks and Recreation Commission voted unanimously to support the elimination of OHVs from Anza–Borrego. The local staff had won! No disciplinary actions resulted from the actions of the staff members who defended the resources and integrity of the park.

Mark felt fortunate to have been part of this grass-roots team that exhibited bravery, resolve, and a passion for protecting and upholding park values and resources. As Mark can say about his compadres now, looking back at those tumultuous times, "I can think of no better example of park staff doing the right thing, even in the face of tremendous pressure, adversity, and potential risks to their careers."

That was also a good year for the park in other ways. A few years earlier, the Department began distributing small amounts of funding for resource management projects. Typical projects that received funding included removal of non-native species, restoring native plant habitat, and performing prescribed burns on forest understory. Mark was not afraid to think a little bigger.

He proposed that all the feral cattle be removed from the park. These were thought to be animals that had escaped from neighboring cattle ranches or, in most cases, descendants of those escapees. Research showed that the cattle were passing diseases on to desert bighorn sheep through the common use of waterholes. While these diseases were benign in the cattle, they were fatal to the bighorn sheep. A local park scientist estimated that there were about 80 cattle in the park, and Mark became determined to eliminate this very

Mark Jorgensen transferring a net-captured bull into a cargo net for helicopter transfer.

real threat to the local population of these endangered wild sheep.

Cattle ranchers also have a very strong and powerful lobbying group and a lot of support in the legislature. Again, Mark knew he would have to develop a proposal that was legal – the specter of legal action is always in the air during the planning and execution of bodacious projects – and guaranteed to accomplish its stated goal of zero cows at the end of the project. The project would also have to be accomplished humanely in order to maximize its public acceptance.

Mark talked to a number of experts and settled on a plan that met all these criteria. The plan was to have the cattle live-captured in a net shot out of a helicopter, which had never been accomplished with cattle before. Once the cow was ensnarled in the net, "cowboys" would jump out of the helicopter, hobble and blindfold the cow to decrease its stress, and transfer it to a net that would then be attached to the bottom of the helicopter. The chopper would fly it back to a holding pen, where it would be tended to by a veterinarian, released, and eventually trucked to Brawley. One of the cowboys who transported the cattle to Brawley joked, "I have been working with cattle for 70 years, and this is the first time I have ever seen a cow fly – much less fly upside down!"

Mark now laughs, "Out of the estimated 80 cattle in the park, we only caught 142!" Needless to say, the project went way over budget. But Mark, through the force of his conviction and passion, was able to go out and raise additional private funds to keep the operation functioning until every cow had been removed from the park.

It sounds like a dangerous project – helicopters flying very low, people jumping out of them and running through the desert to get to the cow, wrestling a scared and angry 1,000-pound animal into a net and attaching the net to the helo, and then releasing the cow at the holding pen from its hobbles, blindfold, and net. There was not one reported injury during the entire project, and no cattle have been sighted in the park since 1987.

During this very eventful decade of the '80s, Mark also met and married the tall and beautiful Kelley Blackledge. He laughs now and recalls that he and Kelley had crossed paths in the '70s, but did not meet in person until 1985.

Mark was a park aide at Anza–Borrego from 1973-75, helping rangers patrol the Split Mountain and Buttes sectors. One of his favorite places to patrol was Borrego Mountain Wash, where he would often stop by a sandstone pillar that stood in the middle of the wash. It was shaped like an Easter Island statue, complete with hollows for eyes and a mouth.

He became frustrated because park visitors could not resist placing stones in these three hollows, and Mark saw his job as keeping the pillar more natural. So he would stop and pick the stones out of the statue and discard them.

It turns out that Kelley's grandparents lived in Borrego Springs at that time, and she would visit them on summer vacations from her home in Nebraska. Grandpa Dick used to take the grandkids on tours of the desert in his Jeep, and one of their favorite routes included a deep canyon in the Buttes, where "The Old Man in the Mountain" resided. Every time they would drive by this sandstone pillar, Kelley would have her grandpa stop so she could fill up the eyes and mouth of the "Old Man" with rocks. Mark chuckles that he must have emptied out the statue's hollows a dozen times, but it was not until 10 years later that he learned that his bride-to-be was the culprit!

They finally met in person in 1985 when Mark was the park's naturalist, living in state housing in Borrego Palm Canyon, and Kelley had returned to Borrego Springs on a more permanent basis. She had been hired as a park aide to work in the Palm Canyon entrance station, a few hundred yards from Mark's house. Mark had to drive through the entrance station to get home, and the first time he saw her in the kiosk, he got out of his car and introduced himself to this lovely six-foot tall brunette.

They started dating soon thereafter, and they were able to laugh when they realized that they had been frustrated by each other, in absentia, over philosophically different efforts to "improve" the sandstone statue 10 years earlier. They moved in together and were in no hurry to get married.

In October of 1987, Mark was helping to conduct, via helicopter, a survey of bighorn sheep with two other biologists over the Santa Rosa Mountains, when the engine failed. The helicopter plummeted from the sky

Mark and Kelley visit the "The Old Man in the Mountain." *Courtesy of Carly Jorgensen*

into a deep desert ravine, and Mark said he had about 15 seconds to consider his life and how it was going to end very soon. When they crash-landed, the helicopter was demolished, yet the pilot and all three passengers miraculously survived. They slowly and painfully hiked out of the mountains and finally reached an occupied farmhouse in the Coachella Valley, where Mark called Kelley. He got home about 3:30 in the morning, and Kelley met him on the front porch crying, "Now can we get married?" Mark hugged her and responded, "Of course we can!"

The following January they did get married beneath the beautiful cliffs of Split Mountain in the park. Mark recalls, "The full moon was rising, we could see and hear the bats flying around the cliffs, and a great horned owl called from above. It was magical, and we have lived happily ever after!"

In 1992 and '93, the philosophy of how to staff state park units drastically changed. As a result of severe budget reductions, a team of State Parks employees regarded as creative thinkers was challenged to design a "new Parks Department" – one that focused on customer service and core missions. Importantly, the department also became de-centralized. One key philosophical change was the idea of putting "specialists" in the field, rather than all at headquarters or at one of the four regional offices. The regional offices were actually eliminated, while park ecologists, interpretive specialists, archeologists, engineers, planners, and historians were then assigned to field units. Along with this change, field managers were "empowered" to be more pro-active in managing their park units.

The civil service position of park naturalist was eliminated, while the position of resource ecologist was made more ubiquitous. For Anza–Borrego Desert State Park, the result was that scientists and interpreters were now stationed in Borrego Springs, and they took over the duties previously fulfilled by the park naturalist.

Mark's science background and education qualified him for this position of ecologist, and between 1993 and 2002, Mark filled this rewarding and exciting role. He officially gave up responsibility for interpretive and educational work, but willingly provided the benefit of his experience and wisdom to the new staff responsible for managing that program.

In 2002, Mark applied for the position of park superintendent of Anza–Borrego Desert State Park. After being selected, he had to go back to the ranger academy for six months to get his status back as a sworn officer. He was in this position until his retirement from state service in 2009.

Mark continues to help the park and its local nonprofit partner, the Anza–Borrego Foundation, as an active volunteer. So, over the past nearly 50 years, Mark has served Anza–Borrego as a seasonal park aide, a ranger, a naturalist, a resource ecologist, a park superintendent, and finally, as a park volunteer.

In addition to his two favorite accomplishments, Mark has effected significant change at the park and elsewhere. He led the effort to rescue 29 wild horses (which were later released at approved wild horse sanctuaries in South Dakota and Nevada), made a heroic effort with others to save historic structures during the catastrophic Cedar Fire, helped create a "Sister Park" in Mongolia, advised the Saudi Kingdom and Abu Dhabi in the United Arab Emirates on establishing and managing desert parks, assisted in leading the opposition effort to a totally inappropriate 500 kV power line in the park, did a ton of research to help craft the park's first ever general plan, helped justify the addition of an airplane and pilot to the park's asset base, and became an expert on desert bighorn sheep and the flat-tailed horned lizard. (A local park scientist likes to joke that, prior to the advent of off-highway recreation in the desert, this local species was called the "round-tailed" horned lizard.)

One of Mark's recent accomplishments was writing a splendid book on these native ungulates, entitled *Desert Bighorn Sheep – Wilderness Icon*. Along with photographer Jeff Young's remarkable images, Mark conveys his high regard for this species and the wilderness it inhabits – in a truly beautiful edition.

Mark is probably best known for his efforts to conserve the park's population of desert sheep, along with their habitat. "DO NOT call them longhorn goats," he chuckles. An example of this dedication is the annual summer bighorn census, which Mark has helped organize almost since its inception. This count, which relies on about 80 volunteers each year, began in 1971, and has continued ever since. In early July, these volunteers set up observation posts throughout the park, at documented water sources, in an attempt to monitor the status and size of the population of the park's sheep – a species that wildlife biologists call "mega-charismatic macro-fauna." This is a wry reference to the belief that large mammals, such as grizzlies, bison, whales, dolphins, and bighorn sheep, receive more public support, media attention, and funding than do, say, San Diego fairy shrimp, California gnatcatchers, and least Bell's vireos.

Although it is blazing hot in Anza–Borrego Desert State Park in July, mid-summer is the most effective and reliable time of the year to count bighorn. Research has shown that these wild sheep need water, at a

In the summer, water is most often found in known, reliable sources.

Ranger Steve Bier "assists" sheep counters during annual summer census. *Courtesy of Mark Jorgensen*

minimum, every three days when temperatures are high. In the summer, it is crucial that sheep are able to have access to surface water – streams, springs, tenajas (natural depressions or cisterns in rock that retain water), and even artificial sources, such as man-made wildlife guzzlers and ponds.

The park is located in the Colorado Desert – a region that normally receives most of its rain during the winter months. Summer rains, which occur during the desert's monsoon season, most often arrive from mid-July through the end of August. Therefore, early July is regarded as the time when surface water is at a premium. When water is more widely available, the sheep are more dispersed. In early July, the sheep have to find water in well-known locations. The park staff bases the locations of observation posts for the volunteers in spots where they are most likely to see the sheep come to water.

Volunteers for the annual census spend roughly three days looking for sheep – this coincides, of course, with the needs of sheep for access to drinking water. Although it can be almost unbearably hot to sit in the desert looking for bighorn, there are several ways to mitigate this discomfort. Shade tarps, an abundance of drinking water, water spray bottles, and appropriate clothing are necessities.

There are also several different strategies that volunteers can use for the census. The first of these is the most challenging. Sheep-counters (usually a group of two to four people) backpack all their supplies into a count site – they have to carry food, water, sleeping gear, binoculars, safety equipment, perhaps a beach chair, and a shade tarp to their observation post. This is often several miles from the trailhead, and the hike in – usually uphill – is best undertaken at a time other than mid-day. It is impossible to carry enough water to last 72 hours, so they typically bring a water filter with them that they can use at the water hole when the sheep are not present. Some counters even hike extra water into their site days or weeks ahead of time to ensure a supply of drinking water.

At these backpacking sites, the group erects their shade structure and establishes a protocol for observation. All four sheep-counters do not need to scan the hillsides for sheep all day – it is more effective to have one or two people "on duty," while the others rest their eyes for a while. Each person has a turn on binocular patrol – looking up, down, and across the hillsides, scanning for sheep. Although the sheep blend in well with their surroundings, they are more obvious when they are moving. Usually, by the end of the third day, the observers are very ready to come down out of the hills – their drinking water stays at "room" temperature by this time.

The second option for sheep counters is to drive to a staging area, where they make their campsite. They have to hike a short ways to their observation post, where they set up their shade tarp and wildlife blind. These "base camp" sheep counters also spend three days in the backcountry, but they can carry a lot more gear, since they are in a vehicle. These volunteers camp out for two or three nights and hike into their count site every day.

The third option, while still difficult, offers a little more comfort. These counters drive up and back to their count site every day. At the end of the day, they come back to an air-conditioned home or motel – preferably one with a swimming pool and a large supply of iced beverages. Sitting around the pool each night with a cold beer, they are happy to toast the efforts of the sheep counters in categories one and two. Most of their conversations focus on the wisdom of choosing option number three.

All volunteers make detailed notes of the sheep they observe – number of animals, time of day, location, gender, age, color, markings of the sheep, and the presence or absence of a radio collar. On occasion, the same sheep visit more than one count site during the three-day period, so staff compares the notes of the counters to ensure that sheep are tallied accurately. While every observer buys into the concept of an accurate count, it is discouraging to have your tally reduced due to double counting a sheep with your neighboring counters. It can be a grueling three days, and the payoff for that effort is observing sheep in their native habitat.

After nearly 50 years of involvement with the sheep count, Mark retired from being the census coordinator, and went back to being a volunteer in the field. For decades, he trained the volunteers, helped with the logistics of recruiting and directing them to their count sites, and allayed the concerns of new volunteers. He now continues to serve as the subject matter expert for this iconic desert mammal – a vivid symbol of desert wilderness. Mark still spends a fair amount of time worrying about the well-being of the sheep counters – three days in the desert heat can cause some serious problems.

The count numbers are tallied and compared to previous years. The count provides a reliable trend of population size, in addition to anecdotal information on the population. One of the highlights of the three-day weekend is arriving back at the sheep count's staging area and drinking about a gallon of really cold water. Surrounded by other exhausted, shower-deprived folks, it is a delight to meet with Mark while he

Mark has played a key role in the recovery of the desert bighorn sheep.

smokes an enormous cigar and discusses census results and population trends. Even more delightful are the electric fans and air-conditioning.

As a sheep counter, you want to see sheep. Occasionally, though, bighorn do not utilize a regular count site during the entire three-day census. Sheep bands move around for forage, water may not be present, predators may be active, or sometimes it is just bad luck. You almost feel as though you have failed if you have to report a lack of sheep at your count site. Then the counters from a nearby count site report in, and, of course, they invariably relate that they saw so many sheep, it was hard to keep track of them all.

Mark always had a good response if you got "skunked." He always kept a straight face when he said, "You know, from a biological perspective, it is important to know what sites the sheep are avoiding. Wildlife biologists can really utilize those data for making informed management decisions." Logically, you can agree with this reasoning, but you still feel compelled to demand a more productive site next year.

Conservationists tend to think long-term. Mark, with the assistance, advice, and counsel of thousands of others – park staff, agency biologists and veterinarians, university professors and students, citizen scientists, volunteers, private citizens who fund recovery efforts, legislators, and the media – has worked tirelessly toward the recovery of the desert bighorn sheep.

The following actions that Mark has led, or at least been deeply involved with, have been, at least in some measure, directed towards the recovery and sustainability of the park's bighorn sheep population: removal of 142 cattle from the park, construction and maintenance of wildlife guzzlers, emplacement of radio collars on hundreds of sheep, outfitting the park airplane with a wildlife antenna, writing up the justification for the designation of over 460,000 acres of wilderness, creating a bypass road for the Lower Willows section of Coyote Canyon, eliminating motor vehicle traffic from the Middle Willows section, removing the use of illegal off-highway vehicles from the entire park, dozens of aerial or ground surveys for sheep, almost 50 years of organizing the summer sheep census, restoring scores of acres of tamarisk-infested wetlands to a natural condition (which recreates vital water sources for desert wildlife), hundreds of presentations to park visitors, service clubs, conservation groups, and schools at all levels, live capture of sheep to study the presence of fatal diseases, and authoring an award-winning book.

In the early '70s, when the young Mark Jorgensen and Bob Turner began to conduct field studies of the bighorn, the population of the sheep in the vicinity of the park was approximately 390. Since then, diseases have been identified that are fatal to the bighorn, and agency and university biologists strive to protect the sheep from them.

Fires in the nearby Cuyamaca and Laguna mountains have killed scores of mule deer – the favorite prey of the legally protected mountain lion. At least for a while, that, along with other factors, drove these predators to lower elevations in search of food. There, the lions were delighted to find the desert bighorn sheep. Biologists and agency managers have had to deal with this uncomfortable situation – one protected species just happens to be eating another one.

Meanwhile, habitat fragmentation, infrastructure projects, and other human activities have continued to put pressure on this species.

Because of the incredible dedication of Mark towards the conservation of the desert bighorn sheep, great strides have been made. Now, almost 50 years later, the bighorn population within the state park is estimated to stand at between 550 and 600 – an increase of roughly 50%.

Mike Wells, former Anza–Borrego park ranger and retired superintendent of the Colorado Desert District, has a funny, yet complimentary, observation about Mark: "If you work here long enough, you begin to talk like Mark Jorgensen without realizing it. Gradually you develop this gravelly Southern accent, which is sort of crazy since Mark was born and raised in nearby El Cajon, California."

More remarkable is the impact Mark has had on others in more serious and sustaining ways. He credits writers like Aldo Leopold, Edward Abbey, and Wallace Stegner with stimulating his thinking and helping him develop his environmental ethic. And, like those writers, Mark dearly wants to pass that ethic on to others.

In addition to his positive influence on young rangers, local and visiting scientists, and even his bosses, his role in shaping visitor attitudes and behaviors has been legendary. This legacy will be passed on through generations to come.

The biodiversity of Anza–Borrego Desert State Park is as beautiful as it is phenomenal.

It is impossible to capture all of Mark's accomplishments in one chapter. Rather than go over what he has done, perhaps it is better for him to relate why he is still on fire for Anza–Borrego, more than 55 years after seeing Ranger George Leetch display a bighorn skull in Fish Creek.

"I think a large part of it is the sense of discovery," Mark says.

"In a big national park like Yosemite or Yellowstone, you have the feeling that there are a lot of researchers looking into the array of resources and visitor impacts there. But at Anza–Borrego, there are still new discoveries all the time. When I started working here, we did not know about the sandstone night lizards, we did not know that there were elephant trees in the Santa Rosas, we did not know about this little hidden grove of palm trees in Palm Wash, and we did not know about the fossil trackways of prehistoric animals in Fish Creek. I still feel thrilled when I look into a small cave and find a clay pot the Kumeyaay people left there hundreds of years ago. My appreciation for and awe about the park has continued to grow over the years.

"Over the decades, I have thought about the philosophical drive about working for parks – I, along with thousands of other parks employees, have inherited a long heritage of protecting parks and their natural and cultural resources. I learned from incredible park stewards ahead of me the importance of accepting the responsibility of maintaining this park – 'my little slice of the world' – and leaving it better than I found it. When I look back on the legacy our team has put together at Anza–Borrego and, biased as I am, I have to say we left that place a lot better than we found it.

"However, in addition to the discoveries that continued to add to the body of knowledge about this splendid park, we also improved local policies and management practices. We mitigated the impacts of the OHVs – dust, illegal trails, and noise. When I started at Anza–Borrego there were cattle in Grapevine Canyon, Peña Spring, Big Spring, Hellhole Canyon, and especially Coyote Canyon. The first time I ever went to Coyote Canyon, there were cattle crapping in the lower creek, and there were real old-time cowboys running cattle – part of it was private land back then.

"I always thought it took a team of amazing people to bring about these achievements. It took people with fire in their belly. It took administrators who acknowledged that they did not know a lot about the details of our projects, but were willing to support us. We earned their trust by doing complete staff work, providing solid justifications, and achieving often spectacular results. At the end of the day, we measured our work against the Department's mission statement. As long as we were in line with the mission, we were willing to take calculated risks. I would ask myself, 'If this project does not succeed, what are they going to do? Send me to the desert for punishment?'

"I have a great wife, home, and family, and I wake up every morning and am thankful, appreciative, and grateful for the good things in my life – every single day. I am able to recognize that and can appreciate it. It is a gift to be able to share our knowledge and environmental ethic. Unfortunately, sometimes it takes setbacks – like the loss of friends or family members, or a near-fatal helicopter crash – to teach us important lessons. We need to acknowledge and appreciate the grace and humility in our friends and family. One of the best lessons I have learned in my life is how to accept the gifts and love of other people."

For more information —

Jorgensen, Mark C., and Jeff Young
Desert Bighorn Sheep – Wilderness Icon
Sunbelt Publications, Inc. 2015.

Huell Howser – 2009. Anza–Borrego Desert State Park.
Huell talks to Mark Jorgensen about the state park.
https://blogs.chapman.edu/huell-howser-archives/?s=Anza+borrego.

JERRY HENDERSON

The Comet that Lit Up the Sky of Mount San Jacinto State Park

During his six-year assignment to Mount San Jacinto State Park, beginning in 1972, Ranger Jerry Henderson turned the management of the park and its incredible wilderness resources completely upside down. The result was a modern and effective wilderness program that rivaled that of federal agencies, such as the National Park Service and the United States Forest Service, that managed wilderness lands on a much larger scale.

Since the State Parks Department at that time was not actively managing any other state wilderness, Jerry had to create and implement the modern tools of wilderness management – permits, carrying capacities, trail and campsite locations, campfires, and safety programs. It is possible that, in those six years, Jerry had more effect on improving any particular state park than any other field ranger, past or present. He also created more positive changes at the park than it sustained in its other 80 years. Incredibly, during many of those changes, he was a State Park Ranger I (field ranger), although he did promote to Supervising Ranger (Ranger II) in 1974.

Jerry was not only an excellent ranger, he enjoyed immensely the opportunities that Mt. San Jacinto State Park provided.

Mount San Jacinto is one of the most amazing parks in the State Park System. Rising to 10,831 feet in elevation, it towers over the surrounding desert landscape. Its eastern face is said to be one of the steepest escarpments in the country.

When park visitors see its forests of pine and fir trees and deep winter snowpack, many find it hard to believe they are actually in Southern California. Although the name of the park since its inception was Mount San Jacinto Wilderness State Park, the term "wilderness" really had no legal meaning for state-owned lands in California until 1974. Because of the wild and rugged character of the nearly 14,000-acre park, the state legislature created a state wilderness there in 1974, more than four decades after it had been first established as a unit of the state park system.

In addition to defining an official state wilderness of about 10,000 acres, the legislature laid out some broad provisions for management of state wilderness areas. This means that for the majority of the changes that Jerry effected to protect and manage state wilderness, he really had to be creative and innovative – there was no road map to follow in state government. Once these changes were put into practice and accepted by the visiting public, they were codified in the California Public Resources Code. It is important to note that, typically, the law is changed before management practices can be put into place – this was not the case where Jerry Henderson was involved.

Jerry on winter wilderness patrol.

The conditions in the wilderness can change quickly and present challenges for those who are not prepared. *Courtesy of Jerry Henderson.*

Its wilderness status gave the park additional legal protection – the influence of humans was supposed to be minimal, if not absent altogether. More importantly, this status inspired its staff to manage it in a manner that not only protected the park and its resources, but provided a "wilderness experience" for its visitors. "Wilderness" became a management philosophy in the mindset of the park staff, as much as it was a legal construct.

Jerry – with his effusive personality, park and wilderness ethic, physical conditioning, "wilderness defender" mindset, and people skills – was the perfect park ranger to implement these changes, lead a team of young rangers and seasonal aides, and inspire hundreds of others to support the Department's most famous and iconic wilderness area.

Along with Departmental luminaries such as Ken Jones and Denzil Verardo, Jerry was hired in the very first class of state park ranger trainees. Director William Penn Mott Jr.'s plan to professionalize the Department's ranger corps was underway, and hiring rangers with college degrees and idealism was the first step to transforming the culture of California State Parks. A well-educated and idealistic cadre of rangers began to permeate the organization, in a good way. These rangers would soon begin to move into supervisory and, ultimately, management positions.

Many of these new rangers had very little direct park experience when they joined the Department. All were college graduates, and many had been in the military, but few had held seasonal state park jobs or had worked for other park organizations.

Ranger Trainee Jerry Henderson was sent to Big Basin Redwoods State Park in Santa Cruz County in 1970, the inaugural year of the ranger trainee program. Jerry was married, was soon to have four children, and also had been a captain in the U.S. Marine Corps, serving in Vietnam. So, although he lacked park experience, he was not a wide-eyed kid right out of college. From day one as a ranger trainee, Jerry maintained strong personal convictions about how things should be done, and what things should not occur in a state park. He was not shy about sharing those views – sometimes very publicly.

For example, during his first year in the Department, at Big Basin, one of his jobs was to patrol the campgrounds. If he found someone collecting down wood for use in their campfire, he would contact them and give them the "interpretive" talk. That is, rangers were not expected to be hard-core about minor infractions. Instead, they took the opportunity to educate the public about the role the down wood played in the ecosystem, while providing a legal alternative for the camper to have a fire in their campsite.

Jerry learned that the park had just entered into a concessions agreement with a contractor who would get visitors to pay to ride his horses and take wagon rides in the park. So that the contractor could keep his horses and wagons in the park, the Department approved his request to clear an acre of trees and brush of state park property. Jerry thought it incongruous that, while he was hassling a camper for picking up a stick or two, the park was permitting this contractor to build corrals and the infrastructure required for a horse-and-wagon outfit.

One of the rangers' other tasks was to contact noisy campers, since the philosophy of the park was to provide a quiet, calm camping experience. The fact that the same contractor was allowed to set up loudspeakers and broadcast through the campground, "All aboard for the wagon ride!" further irked Jerry.

Park managers made little effort to address Jerry's concerns or calm him down. After all, he was a rookie and on probation. So Jerry started writing articles for publication in the newsletter of the association of park rangers. The California State Park Rangers Association was a professional organization – this was in the days before state employee unions – and it was composed, in part, of Departmental supervisors and managers. When Jerry publicly challenged management practices, it stands to reason that those managers responsible for raising his ire were not happy about reading an article about their ineptitude – especially an article written by a newbie ranger.

Although Jerry did it the right way – certainly writing an article for publication in the newsletter of a professional association did not meet the standard for insubordination – he certainly grabbed the attention of managers in Sacramento who could, and would, influence his career.

Towards the end of his first year at Big Basin, he received, as did all fellow ranger trainees, a letter from the personnel department asking for his priorities for his first permanent ranger assignment. As Jerry recalls, "I was thinking – what a great outfit. Last year they asked me where I want to work as a trainee, and I say Big Basin Redwoods State Park, and boom! I am working at Big Basin. Now they ask me where I want to go next, and there are vacancies at lots of great parks. My wife Pat and I spent a lot of time figuring out which assignment will meet our needs best, and I submit my list of terrific parks. Then I get my assignment, and it is Huntington State Beach, which was not anywhere on my list – in fact, it was hundreds of miles from any of my priorities."

Jerry knew that he was being punished with this assignment to Huntington State Beach. Upon arriving there, he quickly became friends with the administrative officer for the district, Louise Short, and she confirmed Jerry's suspicions. She told him to be very careful, because he had a reputation as a troublemaker, and management was "keeping a file on him."

For a lot of people, of course, Huntington State Beach is a great assignment. After all, being a ranger on a beach in Southern California does not seem so bad. But for someone whose goal is to hike mountains and forests, it is not such a great fit. Jerry reckoned he would spend his time at Huntington and see if he eventually could arrange a transfer to a park more in line with his goals and desires.

At the time, it was the policy of the Parks Department that rangers would have to stay in each assignment at least two years. For a "troublemaker" like Jerry, it could have been a lot longer.

In March of 1972, Jerry was working in the park office when a man walked in to chat. He said that he was a ranger at Mount San Jacinto State Park. He had just gone through a divorce and he wanted to move back to Huntington Beach to be closer to his family. Jerry realized that this was a great opportunity for him (while he could not believe that a ranger would want to transfer from Mount San Jacinto to Huntington Beach).

View from the Tramway.

In today's department, there are strict rules governing how vacant ranger positions are advertised and filled. In 1972, however, the regional director for Southern California had great authority and autonomy over moving people around. In large part, this old system, perceived as an unfair "old boy" network, is responsible for the strictly regulated transfer system of today.

Anyway, Jerry arranged to meet with the park superintendent of Mount San Jacinto. He drove to Idyllwild to meet with Bill Stahlberg, and the two of them went for a hike, where they really hit it off. Bill called the regional director, Jim Whitehead, and told him that he really wanted Jerry to transfer to the mountain to be the wilderness ranger for the park. Whitehead agreed, and it was a done deal! The position was never advertised, and Jerry and wife Pat soon moved to Banning to begin the next phase of their life.

Now, Mount San Jacinto State Park is, unofficially, really made up of three sub-units. The park headquarters and traditional campground for tents and recreational vehicles are in the charming mountain village of Idyllwild, on the west slope of the mountain. Then there is the state wilderness, which includes the mountain peaks and the vast majority of the park's nearly 14,000 acres. The park staff jokingly calls the third sub-unit "Tramwayland."

For years, following the end of World War II, the city leaders of Palm Springs proposed that an aerial tramway be constructed to carry visitors up the steep eastern side of Mt. San Jacinto. Finally, in the early

The tramway ascending the steep and rugged Chino Canyon.

1960s, the concept was approved and the tramway was built. It carries tourists from the valley station, in the city of Palm Springs – from an elevation of 2,643 feet – nearly 6,000 feet vertically, up through the state park's rugged Chino Canyon.

The authority for the tramway was approved by the legislature, which created a "quasi-state agency" to manage the tram, and the legislature established a governing board to oversee its operation. When Jerry was asked to define a "quasi-state agency," he laughed and said, "Well, when it is to their advantage to be a state agency, they are a state agency. When it is to their advantage to be a private corporation, they act as a private corporation."

The tramway authority is not constrained by civil service or state purchasing regulations. However, it is exempt from some of the rules that private corporations are bound by. The tramway starts on city property and terminates on state property, which further complicates matters. And although it operates just as a concession would for any other state park, there exists an operating agreement between the State Parks Department and the Tramway Authority, rather than a formal concession contract.

Although the vast majority of the park is state wilderness, the tramway hauls thousands of tourists a year and dumps them on the threshold of the wilderness area. At the upper terminus of the tramway, visitors exit the tramcar into a large lodge, known as the mountain station. Many visitors never venture out of the building. There are gift shops, restaurants, restrooms, a bar, and spectacular views of the mountains and the desert.

They may spend an hour or so looking around and get on the next tramcar for the descent back to Palm Springs.

One of the goals of the tramway authority is to remain financially solvent. They do not receive state tax revenues, so their operating funds come principally from fees paid by tramway riders. Understandably, they want to see as many people as possible ride the tramway, and they want to provide an experience at the mountain that not only attracts tourists, but makes them want to return frequently and bring friends and family back with them.

It is this issue that probably causes the most tension between the tramway authority and the state park staff. State park rangers and managers think that Long Valley is a fine place for walks, wildlife viewing, and picnics. The tramway staff thinks there should be more man-made attractions, like sleigh rides in the winter, an ice-skating rink, toboggan runs, and horse rentals.

As with many issues in State Parks, a balance is usually struck that both sides can accept. After all, the Parks Department wants people to enjoy the park and return often, as well. Figuring how many facilities are needed, how oversight is provided, and mitigating their impacts – those are the tricky parts. It is also this idea of providing lots of rides and a variety of man-made experiences that led to the moniker of Tramwayland.

The only realistic and cost-effective means of getting supplies and employees to the mountain station is on the tramcars themselves. Food for the restaurants, gift for the gift shops, people to cook and clean, toilet paper, and towels all must come up on a tramcar. It is how the rangers and seasonal employees get to work. Similarly, trash, bank deposits, and other materials must go down the mountain via that same tramcar. In many ways, the mountain station and the state park are like an island – you must rely on public transportation to get to and leave the mountain station. There are no roads. It is possible to hike out to Idyllwild on the west side of the park, but it is an 11-mile hike that takes all day in good weather and trail conditions.

One problem that most do not consider is how to get rid of human waste. That cannot be put on the tramcars to go down the mountain, so leach fields have been constructed in Long Valley to handle the sewage. The leach lines have not always held up well, shall we say, to the extreme changes in temperature at that altitude.

There is a contingent of tramway riders that comes well prepared for the wilderness, while others do not. In general, there were five types of visitors that Jerry and his staff had the opportunity to deal with.

The first type was the vast majority of tramway riders – they never left the mountain station. They came for the tramway ride, the view, and maybe a meal or a gift. They would stay a short while and head back on the tram to Palm Springs. Some would manage to visit the park store or see the movie about the park and the tramway. But otherwise, these thousands of park visitors often had no idea that they were even in a state park.

Next were the visitors who wanted a short experience in the park. They would venture down the steep trail into Long Valley for a short hike, have a picnic, or just enjoy the local mountain wildlife, such as jays and squirrels. They might stop in at the ranger station to ask questions, or "just to see a real ranger," as one visitor commented. Unless they got rowdy or left trash, there were usually no issues with these visitors either.

Rarely, there are more serious problems. On one occasion, there was a sexual assault, but that was in the early '70s. Sometimes, people scramble down the big boulders on the steep eastern escarpment of the mountain and get stuck. Jerry ensured that the park staff was trained in first aid and cliff rescue.

The park staff does not typically spend a lot of time with these first two categories of park visitors. For people who do not leave the mountain station, the only contact with staff is usually on the tramcar itself, as the staff is getting to work, or to buy a book or map at the park store.

Visitors who spend a short time in Long Valley enjoying the natural features of the park rarely have contact with park staff, unless a child wanders away from its parents, someone gets stuck climbing a boulder, or there is an issue with noise, trash, injury, or illness.

The third category is those people who venture into Long Valley and decide spontaneously to hike into the wilderness. Long Valley contains a forest of pine and fir trees, and has a beautiful mountain meadow with a small running stream. When people get to the tramway's mountain station, they can get an incredibly attractive and inviting view of the park's magnificent wilderness area.

To appreciate the problems this scenario can present, it is necessary to understand the geography, climate, and tourism patterns in the region. Palm Springs, and the rest of the Coachella Valley, are in the Sonoran Desert – a region of temperate winters and very hot summers. Most tourists to the desert, as well as the "snow bird" residents, come to Palm Springs in the winter, late fall, and early spring. Since there are more tourists in town during the months of October through April, it follows that those seven months are the peak rider months for the tramway.

Now consider the climate and the weather. The elevation of the Palm Springs airport is 477 feet. The elevation of the tramway's mountain station is 8,516 feet, and the peak of Mount San Jacinto rises to 10,831 feet. A park visitor who starts their trip at 1 p.m. in Palm Springs for a visit to the state park might be enjoying a nice December day of 80 degrees. Accordingly, they wear a T-shirt, shorts, and sandals. They decide to go up the tramway, and they arrive at the mountain station while it is still a comfortable

Day-use visitors hiking to Long Valley.

60 degrees. Although they did not really plan to take a long hike, it is great weather in the forest, and the sun is still shining. They may have read on the internet that there is a beautiful mountain lake only about a mile away. Without water, food, warm clothes, or any gear whatsoever, they decide to hike to Hidden Lake.

It is not difficult to see where this venture could go wrong. Even if these visitors stay on the trails, on the way back from the lake (Hidden Underground Lake, the rangers call it), the sun dips below the elevated horizon of the mountain. The temperature drops quickly. Any unexpected occurrence – a sprained ankle, mountain sickness, or a wrong turn – could quickly lead to a serious predicament.

The fourth type of visitor rides up the tramway, and is prepared for a wilderness experience. These visitors are great fans of the tramway, for it does about 6,000 feet of hard climbing for them. These hikers and cross-country skiers have the right gear, are usually in decent shape, carry maps and a compass, and have an idea of what challenges face them in entering the wilderness. However, they still may have to deal with heavy snowpack, winter and summer storms, mountain sickness, and lack of drinking water.

Cross-country skier on a trek to the peak of Mt. San Jacinto. *Courtesy of California State Parks [Image 090-S10238].*

The last type of visitors that the park staff interacted with was day-hikers, backpackers, and horseback riders who entered the park wilderness from the west side of the park. Eschewing the tramway, they arrived via the much steeper, longer, and challenging trails of the "Idyllwild side" of the mountain. Of course, they had to be prepared physically and possess the right equipment for the wilderness, too.

In the late '60s and early '70s, wilderness activity throughout the United States exploded in popularity. Hiking, backpacking, cross-country skiing, snowshoeing, and river rafting started to put a real strain on the resources of the nation's wilderness areas – this increase in usage led to a sense that the wilderness experience was being compromised, as well.

Mount San Jacinto State Park is very popular with outdoor enthusiasts. There are many reasons for this popularity: 1) the tramway does 6,000 vertical feet of work for hikers and backpackers, 2) it is a very beautiful montane park, 3) it is close to the population centers of Southern California, 4) it has potable water at Round Valley, which is the most popular wilderness campground – only two miles from the mountain station, 5) visitors who want to enjoy the snow for play or cross-country skiing can use the tramway and thereby avoid the need for tire chains and slick roads, and 6) bears, mosquitoes, and rattlesnakes are not major nuisances or dangers in the park.

Jerry, Pat and family enjoy the igloo they built in Long Valley. *Courtesy of Jerry Henderson.*

Since the park is easy to get to, and since the hike to the first wilderness campground in Round Valley is only two easy miles from the tramway's mountain station, many groups use the park for a "shake-down" backpacking trip. Boy Scouts and private groups often plan a one- to two-week backpacking trip to the Sierra Nevada mountains late in the summer. In order to ensure that all individuals for that longer trip have the right equipment, know how to use their gear, and actually enjoy the experience of backpacking, they will go to Round Valley for one or two nights of camping. This also means that a lot of the backpackers are not very experienced that first weekend.

When Jerry arrived to work at Mount San Jacinto State Park in 1972, he quickly realized that some changes in the way the park, and particularly the wilderness area, were being managed would greatly increase visitor safety, resource protection, and wilderness appreciation. Jerry is quick to acknowledge that the previous wilderness ranger, Phil Claude, came up with some of these ideas. It was Jerry and his staff of rangers and park aides, however, who implemented these policies and effectively explained the need for them to the public and the tramway staff. Jerry laughs again, "Some guys are good at thinking up ideas, some are good at putting others' good ideas into practice, and some are good at both. Phil was REALLY good at coming up with ideas."

The first new procedure was to implement a system for wilderness permits. This certainly was not unique to Mount San Jacinto State Park – many federal wildernesses were facing skyrocketing visitation numbers in the '70s. Managers of these wildlands had to come up with solutions – and quickly – in order to deal effectively with this dramatic increase in usage.

It may seem counter-intuitive that, in order to protect the wilderness from people and the wilderness experience for people, more complex, bureaucratic policies were being initiated. Park visitors would have to fill out more paperwork, plan further ahead, stand in more lines, and would be subject to being turned away on busy weekends under a permit system. Indeed, at the beginning, there was a lot of chafing at this change. That is why Jerry trained his staff to explain well – and passionately – the need for limitations on usage. Eventually this change was widely accepted.

The procedure Jerry designed was for both day-users (hikers, skiers, snowshoers, and horseback riders) and overnight campers (backpackers). Everyone entering the official state wilderness needed a wilderness permit with basic information – name, contact info, number in party, how long was the stay, and time and date of their planned exit.

Day-hikers and backpackers alike would have to possess a wilderness permit if they were in the state wilderness. In order to minimize disappointment at being turned away, backpackers could also apply for overnight permits by mail.

There was no limit on the number of day-users allowed into the wilderness at any given time – the day permit was required for day-users more for safety reasons than it was to limit the number of people. The permit requirement meant that all those people who showed up and suddenly decided to take a hike would have to visit the ranger station first to get a permit. The ranger or park aide on duty would be able to warn unprepared visitors about the weather conditions, trail conditions, and other factors. The park staff, after assessing the equipment, attitude, and knowledge of the visitor, would be able to provide them with the appropriate level of safety information.

Jerry had a creative idea for how to maximize compliance with this new regulation. Prior to the implementation of the wilderness permit system, there were myriad trails that led from Long Valley into the wilderness, and many of these did not pass by the ranger station. Jerry had his staff reroute all these wilderness access trails so that they funneled into one main trail. Not only did that one trail go directly by the ranger station, it also began with a significant climb in elevation. This was not done to discourage prepared hikers – rather, it was created to give all hikers the realization that hiking the wilderness was not, well, a "walk in the park." This also made it more difficult for people without a permit to claim they were unaware of the need for a wilderness permit, since signage at the ranger station was very clear.

For backpackers – those staying overnight – the permit system was more complex, as was the re-design of the wilderness campgrounds. Jerry decided that, in the wilderness area of Mount San Jacinto State Park, backpackers would be required to camp at established campgrounds. The adjacent U.S. Forest Service wilderness did allow more dispersed overnight camping. However, due to the popularity of the park and the damage to resources that was being caused by indiscriminate use, allowing visitors to camp anywhere in the state park was no longer feasible.

Jerry and the staff spent considerable time and thought on this issue. Where would campers be allowed, and how many backpackers would be allowed at each campground on any given night? They did a remarkable job of coming up with campgrounds that provided a variety of experiences and attributes. Available drinking water, distance from the tramway, solitude, and resource impacts all were considered. Eventually five campgrounds – Round Valley, Tamarack Grove, Strawberry Junction, the peak of Mount San Jacinto, and Little Round Valley – were all established. The peak has since been eliminated as a legal campground, due to safety issues.

The park and recreation industry refers to this limit on the number of people in any given area as its "carrying capacity." The carrying capacity for any given area, say Round Valley wilderness campground, in theory is the number of people who could use that area at any time and not cause unacceptable damage or impacts. Carrying capacity is supposed to be designed with both physical (soil compaction, erosion rate, number of plant species impacted) and social (excessive noise, a perceived feeling of crowdedness, fear) factors included.

When this concept originated in the cattle industry, carrying capacity was used to determine how many cattle could be grazed on a certain number of acres with a certain amount of ground cover or feed for a given number of months without overgrazing that site. Now if you know these factors, and you know the age, size, and number of cattle in your grazing herd, you can come up with a pretty reliable and predictable estimate for how much impact that herd will have on that particular field over a given period of time. These data allow the site administrator to move the herd around to meet management goals.

With humans, it is not nearly so easy to determine a reliable carrying capacity. Let's say there is a nature trail loop in a redwood park. On Monday, one thousand tourists walk the nature trail. All the visitors are quiet and well-behaved, and leave almost no trace. On Tuesday, however, only one person walks that trail. Unfortunately, they have a handsaw and stepladder with them, and they cut 100 burls off the redwood trees. After Monday, the ranger can hardly tell the trail has been used at all. After Tuesday, she is irate at the damage – one person left 100 permanent scars.

So it is difficult to say with total confidence what the human carrying capacity of any site is. Jerry believed that they developed the best estimate possible, and knew that a feedback loop would be necessary. That is, every year, the carrying capacity numbers would be reviewed and, if necessary, revised upward or downward. In addition, the locations and efficacy of campgrounds and campsites required review.

Further, Jerry was able to think outside the box. There exists a stone shelter a few hundred meters from the peak of Mount San Jacinto. It was built as an emergency shelter in the 1930s by the Civilian Conservation Corps, under the direction of a stonemason from Idyllwild, shortly after the park was established. Due to the extreme weather conditions that can occur at the peak in the winter, the reason for building it was that people who got caught in a winter storm could seek refuge there. Although cold and extremely drafty, the theory was that being inside this stone icebox was better than being outside! However, experience would soon disabuse staff of that notion.

During Jerry's stay at the park, the staff decided to establish the peak as an approved campground. Although there are several beautiful outdoor campsites tucked among the boulders at the peak, many campers felt more comfortable staying inside and sleeping on the wooden bunk beds.

Several fatalities occurred near the peak shelter, usually when backpackers were trying to reach the cabin during extreme weather. Interviews with survivors revealed that the members of the party kept thinking, "If we can just get to the shelter, we will be alright." It was clear that, had the party set up an emergency campsite when the storm first rolled in and not attempted to reach the peak shelter, they probably would have survived. This was one of the reasons the peak was eventually eliminated as a campground.

Another consideration was exactly where campers would be permitted to set up their campsite at each designated campground. Again, this was a tremendously popular wilderness area with relatively easy access, and it was used a lot by beginning backpackers.

Before Jerry's arrival, people were allowed to camp at the edge of the meadows in the campgrounds. Although these campsites were very picturesque, the meadow soils and flora were impacted by this heavy use. And while campers had a great view of the meadow and the mountains surrounding the valley, they also saw a plethora of other brightly colored tents.

Again, Jerry came up with a solution. Staff developed a plan for establishing individual campsites, with little pathways to each one, so that campers could find them. Campsites were placed in locations that made sense – they were flat, had good views, but were separated visually from other campsites. In short, they were campsites that campers really enjoyed, but might not have found on their own had staff not put a little wooden post at each site. A map of their locations was printed on the back of every wilderness permit.

Next was the issue of campfires in the wilderness. Again, many federal wildernesses were dealing with this management issue, especially in light of the increase of wilderness visitation. At Mount San Jacinto State Park, the decision was made to eliminate wood fires in the wilderness, although camp stoves that used liquid gas or propane remained acceptable. At that time, tremendous improvements in camping gear were being achieved, and advancements in camp stoves were part of that progress in technology.

In very short order, Jerry had established the wilderness permit system, designed approved campgrounds, established a recreational carrying capacity for each campground, designated individual campsites, stopped the use of wood campfires, and re-routed several trails.

Again, Jerry is quick to share credit with others. In the mid-'70s, there were incredibly bright, dedicated, and creative park aides working at the park. They were also capable with their hands, whether it was installing plumbing, rigging an emergency phone line, or routing and building new trails. It was a terrific and innovative time for the park and for those who worked there.

Jerry was also famous for having, let us say, absolutely no sense of rhythm. The staff would put on campfire

Jerry giving a campfire program at Round Valley to wilderness campers. *Courtesy of Jerry Henderson.*

programs in the summer on weekend evenings, and Jerry was very enthusiastic about leading songs. If only that enthusiasm had been matched by the ability to carry a tune or keep a beat! Campers had no idea whether to clap when Jerry clapped during a song, or actually keep the real beat. It was a chaotic and immensely joyful experience.

After campfires, if there were a decent moon, the park aides would lead a night hike to the peak. They created experiences that backpackers would never have had otherwise. Through their enthusiasm, they created a whole generation of park supporters. Now, night hikes are thought of as having too much liability, both for campers and staff.

Another unusual feature of the state wilderness at Mount San Jacinto State Park is the fact that it is contiguous with the federal wilderness at the San Jacinto unit of the San Bernardino National Forest. The U.S. Forest Service operates its wilderness with several different rules than does the State Parks Department. The feds allow dogs on their trails, permit wood fires in campsites, and do not require campers to stay in established campgrounds. In addition, the federal wilderness is much farther from the tramway.

When Jerry was effecting these amazing changes at Mount San Jacinto State Park, he talked to the Forest

Jerry removing the old emergency phone line from the wilderness.

Service staff about trying to align these policies. At first, it seemed fairer to the public to have both agencies use the same rules and regulations.

Over time, however, both agencies realized that the public was actually happy to have different rules. Some hikers wanted a place to take their dogs, while others believed that dogs detract from the wilderness experience and negatively affect native wildlife. Some backpackers wanted to camp wherever they felt like it, while others felt unaccustomed to the wilderness, and preferred having designated campgrounds and campsites. The state's experience was that campers would frequently set up their tent as close as possible to other backpackers, and managing that camping experience actually provided a better wilderness experience for all.

While working as the supervising ranger for the wilderness and helping to raise four little kids, Jerry took night classes and fulfilled the requirements for a master's degree in environmental administration at UC Riverside. For one class, he told his advisor he was going to write a paper on creating a wilderness permit system. His "ivory tower" advisor told him that no wilderness permit system would ever work – it was incongruous, and no one would accept it. A while later, after implementing the same system at Mount San Jacinto State Park and having the "real world" system work exceedingly well, Jerry told his advisor about his success with the program. Jerry chortles that his advisor never spoke to him again.

Jerry's goal was to use his newly minted M.A. to become a state park resource ecologist. The job of ecologists was to manage the natural resources at a variety of state parks. They were to supervise resource management programs like prescribed burning, ecosystem restoration, non-native plant removal, and endangered species habitat projects.

According to the departmental rumor mill, however, State Parks was looking to hire only people with degrees in forestry. Jerry called the personnel section, and they reassured him that the Department was, indeed, looking for people who were capable of managing a broad range of ecological programs, as outlined in the job description.

With that encouragement, Jerry applied for the ecologist exam, and he and wife Pat started thinking about which regional office location would suit them best – Santa Barbara, Monterey, San Diego, or Santa Rosa. Not surprisingly, Jerry scored very highly on the written and oral examinations. He was one of the very top candidates for the job, according to the posted test results.

Then Jerry was called to a final interview, and one of the people asking the questions was the Department's licensed forester. Every question had to do with identifying hazardous trees, rather than managing a resource management program. After it was clear that the Department was actually looking for people who would go around removing dangerous branches and entire trees, Jerry said that, in his opinion, that was technician level work and should not be a major component of an ecologist's workload. He did not score well on that final interview and was never hired as a resource ecologist.

Unfortunately, the results of that exam really discouraged Jerry about his prospects for a career at the State Parks Department. He had just finished a master's degree while working full-time, had just implemented an incredible set of innovative wilderness policies and procedures in a very short period of time, and was ready to move up in the organization to a position where he could really use his talent and experience.

This setback convinced him that he should leave the State Parks Department and seek greener pastures. Soon, he left for a job with the federal government – the Young Adult Conservation Corps – in Ashland, Oregon. He returned to state service in California some years later, but his career with State Parks had ended forever.

Jerry credits his time with the Boy Scouts in the '50s as giving him the motivation to become a park ranger. In addition to being a scout, he worked for that organization for six years at Boy Scout camps during the summer and weekends, where he enjoyed teaching classes in how to use ropes and an axe. All this scout work, in addition to his fondness for visiting state and national parks, got him thinking about a job that would allow him to work outdoors for a career. He also recalls working on and hiking near his grandparents' ranch at the 9,000-foot level in Colorado as giving him experience at, and an appreciation for, wild places.

Then, when he started college at Long Beach State in 1960, Jerry took an elective class in law enforcement. The instructor handed out a flyer on all the jobs that a degree in law enforcement could lead to. To Jerry's amazement, one of the jobs listed was park ranger. Not too many people were connecting law enforcement and being a park ranger in the early '60s.

Jerry still had a sense that he wanted to work in the field of conservation, so he transferred to Humboldt State University in the fall of his senior year. Once he started there, however, it became clear that Humboldt State would not accept all his credits and it would take an extra two years to graduate. He began to plan his return to Long Beach State. In the meantime, Jerry was broke, so he lived in a tent behind the university football stadium – he called it "Tex's Hotel."

While at Humboldt State, however, Jerry had one of those experiences that would help him find his career pathway into State Parks. He became friends with a fellow student named Carl Chavez, who would go on to a long and distinguished career at the Department. One day Carl, Jerry, and two other guys went to the local Mad River Beach in Jerry's old military surplus Jeep. On the drive back, they passed four young women who were walking back to campus from the same beach, when Jerry's black cowboy hat blew off. One of the women grabbed Jerry's hat and teased him, saying she would not give it back unless they all got a ride home in the Jeep.

Jerry laughs and says they told the women they did not have room for them, and now realizes how dumb that reaction was. When the women threw the possibility of a homemade blackberry pie into their smiling offer, Jerry finally gave in. These women were trying to pick up the four guys, and the guys were arguing! One of the young women in the Jeep, Margaret Elmore, spent most of that day talking to Carl, and eventually married him. They are still happily together over 50 years later!

Although Jerry did transfer back to Long Beach State, he and Carl kept in touch. Jerry, like many others in this book, claims that he was shy and quiet in his youth. This is hard to believe. Blessed with a huge smile, he also has a booming laugh and a welcoming, friendly demeanor. He lights up the room when he enters –

everyone knows that Jerry is "in the house."

One evening there was a spring dance at Long Beach State. Jerry reluctantly went – he describes himself as an unaggressive suitor back then. Normally, if he saw an attractive woman, nothing would ever happen, unless the woman initiated a conversation.

When he first noticed the lovely and vivacious Pat Stevens, five guys had surrounded her, all vying for her attention. Atypically, Jerry just walked up, took her hand, told her he would like to dance with her, and led her to the dance floor. Jerry chuckles, "I never let go!"

Jerry likes to ponder about how little decisions can have results with such large implications. Had he not gotten his courage up to ask Pat for a dance, his world would have been very different. Their children would not have been born, and he would not be living out a charmed retirement in the foothills of the Sierra Nevada.

Soon after graduation from Long Beach State in 1964, Jerry joined the U.S. Marine Corps and served in Vietnam, beginning as a second lieutenant. For six months, as a Marine officer, he led search-and-destroy missions and night ambushes. After completing an assignment manning a combat outpost with a reinforced rifle platoon, he was pulled into Da Nang. There, Jerry was tasked with traveling around southeast Asia purchasing recreation equipment for 30,000 of his fellow Marines on R & R. After 3½ months of that assignment, Jerry was re-assigned to combat again – this time with the 2nd Battalion 4th Marines, which was operating in the Demilitarized Zone. Jerry was awarded the Navy Commendation with a Combat "V" for his service in Operation Prairie. Thank you for your service!

After his discharge, he was offered a job – an exciting prospect, no doubt – with the CIA! He had his airline tickets to go to Washington, D.C. to start work, but he still had to fill out some papers in Los Angeles. Pat and he drove to L.A., and Pat waited in the car while Jerry went in to fill out the final paperwork.

A light came on in his head, however, and, by the time he got back to the car, he had decided not to start work with the CIA. That decision changed their future and left them uncertain about what to do next, but they have no regrets. When asked what caused him to change his mind, he laughs and says, "Well, I really wanted to be featured in this book about park rangers!"

In the spring of 1967, Jerry visited Carl and Margaret Chavez at Bodie State Historic Park – a ghost town high in the desolate rolling hills east of Bridgeport. Carl was a ranger there, and he was surprised one day to receive a radio call from the sheriff's office telling him that a Mr. Jerry Henderson was there, looking for a ride to Bodie. Carl fired up the park's SnoCat and gave Jerry a ride up the hill. Jerry spent the night with Carl and Margaret, and came to the logical conclusion that Carl had a terrific job. Before he left, Jerry asked Carl to let him know if a civil service exam for park ranger ever came up.[1]

Some time later, Pat and Jerry visited Carl and Margaret in Southern California. Carl had transferred to Pt.

---

[1] Chavez, Carl S. *A Pathway Through Parks – A Park Ranger's Reminiscing.* 2004.

Jerry visits Ranger Carl Chavez at Bodie State Historic Park. This visit resulted in Jerry getting serious about a job in State Parks.
Courtesy Carl Chavez.

Mugu State Park, and the young couple was living in an apartment in Oxnard – a far cry in almost every way from Bodie. Jerry remembers, "Carl and Margaret were living in this tiny little apartment in town, but they were happier than all get-out. I kept thinking that maybe there must be something really special about being a park ranger. I reminded Carl to keep his eyes open for a ranger exam."

That decision to visit Carl and Margaret was to have major implications. Soon afterwards, the current hiring freeze ended, and Carl sent Jerry an application to become a state park ranger. Remarkably, only six months later, Jerry was on duty as a ranger trainee at Big Basin Redwoods State Park. "One day," Carl says, "I answered the phone, and Jerry was yelling to me that he was now a ranger trainee at Big Basin – he was so excited!" That was the first of his assignments as a ranger, followed by stints at Huntington State Beach and Mount San Jacinto State Park.

Although Jerry majored in law enforcement in college, served as an officer in the U.S. Marines, and had eight years' experience as a peace officer, he has a surprisingly negative outlook on the Department's current emphasis on law enforcement.

One of the outstanding park aides at Mount San Jacinto State Park, Frank Padilla, went on to become a state park ranger. Jerry stopped in to see Ranger Padilla at Leo Carrillo State Beach, near Malibu, and was led back to the "ready room" to see Frank. Jerry recalls, "In the ready room, there were rows of shotguns and assault rifles, and all the rangers were cleaning their firearms. I asked Frank, in all seriousness, if they were getting ready for a riot, and he said 'No, this is just routine activity.' I was truly shocked."

Jerry also recalls his days as the wilderness ranger at Mount San Jacinto State Park. "The first winter I was there, I noticed that the rawhide base of all the snowshoes had rotted, and the snowshoes were unusable. I was in the ranger station by myself one day, and there was a raging snowstorm outside, so I built a fire and spent the entire day using parachute cord to repair all the snowshoes. I realized that this is what rangers should be doing – fixing snowshoes and the like. I remembered the huge unruly crowds that were the norm at Huntington State Beach and thought, 'Wow, I gave up all that fun for this wilderness gig?'

"I went back to the Long Valley Ranger Station a couple of years ago and noticed those snowshoes still hanging up in the ranger office. I doubt they get used anymore, especially since aluminum snowshoes are now the norm. I mentioned to the ranger on duty that I had restrung those shoes in 1973 and asked him a few questions about how the wilderness management was working these days. He could not have cared less about the wilderness, but he was sure to be wearing his sidearm and bulletproof vest. He was probably plotting how to get transferred to Huntington State Beach so he could get more action."

Jerry also believes the emphasis on law enforcement, almost to the exclusion of the other parts of the job that serve the Parks Department's mission, makes it difficult for the "traditional" generalist ranger to rise up to positions of leadership. He believes there are park units, like Huntington State Beach, where law enforcement skills are important. But he is discouraged that "real parks for real rangers, such as Mount San Jacinto and Anza–Borrego, are being staffed by cops now."

One of the greatest legacies that Jerry created is the inspiration he gave to those who worked for him. Park aide Jon Anderson and his wife take fuel-efficient and low-emission stoves to Haiti to donate and install them. Mike Hamilton went on to earn his Ph.D. in biology and, for many years, managed the UC Riverside science field station just north of Idyllwild.

Then there is Rick Sanger, another former park aide at Mount San Jacinto State Park. That park is where Rick learned the skills of wilderness survival, tracking, and emergency first aid. Rick was featured in the book, *The Last Season,* which is about a massive search for a lost seasonal backcountry ranger at Sequoia Kings Canyon National Park. The book mentions that Rick got his training at Mount San Jacinto State Park.

Jerry attends lunch with a regular group every Friday near his home in the Sierra Foothills. One day, in walked a guest, and it was Rick Sanger. Now no one becomes wealthy as a seasonal backcountry ranger, but it was abundantly clear that Rick loves the work and the parks where he works.

Muses Jerry, "If we could all inspire just one person to carry on the work of conserving wilderness, our country would be in great shape." Jerry Henderson inspired many, many people – both inside and outside of the State Park System – to love and protect wilderness.

When Jerry arrived at Mount San Jacinto State Park in 1972, he got out his router, created a wooden sign, and nailed it up at the Long Valley Ranger Station for all to see –

MAY THE PEACE OF THE WILDERNESS BE WITH YOU

It is safe to say he never asked permission to do this.

For more information —

Huell Howser. Mt. San Jacinto State Park. Huell talks to Ranger Eric Hansen about the features of the state park.
https://blogs.chapman.edu/huell-howser-archives/2017/11/08/mt-san-jacinto-palm-springs-week-33/

Huell Howser. Palm Springs. Huell discusses the construction and usage of the Palm Springs Aerial Tramway.
https://blogs.chapman.edu/huell-howser-archives/1997/01/08/mt-san-jacinto-californias-gold-804/

Blehm, Eric. *The Last Season.* Harper. 2006

DAVID AND JANET CARLE

Save Mono Lake

Mono Lake is a stunningly beautiful lake in the high desert east of Yosemite National Park. The lake – which lies at the base of the eastern escarpment of the Sierra Nevada – is one of the oldest and most ecologically productive lakes in North America. More than 6,300 feet above sea level, this lake is part of the Great Basin hydrographic province, and has no connection to any ocean.

Fed by rainfall and snowmelt from five significant streams, Mono is a very large and natural lake. Although the water in the lake is very salty, four of the lake's feeder streams have been diverted, to some degree, as a source of fresh water for the City of Los Angeles, some 300 miles to the south. The lake also supports an amazingly large and diverse biota – qualities that make it worthy of protection. The battle for its water –

should it be siphoned off to help spur the needs of a remote city, or left *in situ* to help provide sustainability for its biotic communities – was epic. This conflict was ultimately decided in the courts and by the California State Water Resources Control Board – after several decades – and helped set legal precedents for other, similar struggles.

When Janet Broughton was growing up in the San Francisco Bay Area community of Alameda, she had never heard of Mono Lake – at that time, it had not yet been designated as a state park. Some years later, as a young ranger in Sacramento in the late '70s, Janet began to notice an increasing number of vehicles with the bumper sticker, "Save Mono Lake." For her, these bumper stickers were to become, in just a few years, a call to action.

The man she later married – Dave Carle – and Janet were destined to become key players in the permanent protection of Mono Lake. In addition to this important conservation accomplishment, together they created a successful new model in the Department of Parks and Recreation for married couples who worked and lived together, raised a family, and developed policies and procedures for a brand new unit of the State Parks System. For Dave and Janet, Mono Lake became their life's work.

Courtesy of David and Janet Carle.

In the early 1970s, Dave Carle had a newly minted degree in biology and decided he wanted to be a field biologist for a government agency – most likely the California Department of Fish and Game or the U.S. Department of Fish and Wildlife. While undergoing the process to become hired by one of those agencies, Dave got a seasonal job as a park aide at Doheny State Beach in southern Orange County in 1973. Seasonal work at Doheny meant life in the entrance station – selling day-use tickets, assigning campsites, and providing visitor information at an extremely popular Southern California beach. One of the bright spots at Doheny for Dave was becoming friends with a rookie ranger named Dick Troy, an idealistic young Army veteran and recent college graduate.

The following season, Carle and Troy both moved a few miles south to San Onofre State Beach, which was a bigger, more natural, park. According to Dave, "I was so impressed with this fresh, idealistic young ranger – Dick sucked me into ranger work through his energy and upbeat outlook. He had such an interest in all aspects of park work. Working with Dick and other idealistic rangers at San Onofre convinced me I should become a park ranger, rather than a biologist for a fish and game agency."

Looming on the horizon was the first major environmental battle of Dave Carle's life. Southern California Edison and San Diego Gas & Electric – major utility companies in the Southland – were planning a significant expansion of the San Onofre Nuclear Generating Station (SONGS). Unfortunately, Edison and SDG&E wanted to place the new facilities, Units 2 and 3, on the marine terrace overlooking the state beach. The proposed plant would have significant negative impacts on the park's dramatic bluffs, canyons, and associated biological communities.

A fairly new player in these environmental issues was the California Coastal Commission. It was clear that this commission was to be the main avenue to derail, if possible, the expansion of SONGS. The environmentalists were given hope when the commission's executive director, in the staff report on the project, stated that destroying the cliffs and canyons of San Onofre State Beach would be tantamount to "cutting down our cathedrals for firewood." Strong words, indeed!

Dave took photographs of that beautiful part of San Onofre that would be destroyed, documented the biological impacts, and put together a dramatic slide show. He showed these slides at a regularly scheduled commission meeting, where the proponents of the nuclear plant expansion expected the project to be approved swiftly and unanimously. Dave's impassioned presentation caught Edison and SDG&E off guard, and the commission actually declined to approve the project!

The power companies, though, were like a heavyweight boxer facing a much smaller opponent. The lightweight had delivered the first blow and sent the heavyweight to the canvas. However, once the larger boxer got up and cleared his head, he was angry and determined. Both U.S. senators for California were called in for support, along with a boatload of other elected and appointed officials, while the director of State Parks got an earful about "his guerrillas" at San Onofre State Beach. A lot of behind-the-scenes lobbying and arm-twisting took place over the next few months, and the project was ultimately approved at the very next commission meeting.

About 40 years later, San Onofre Nuclear Generating Station was decommissioned due to safety concerns. Of course, the damage to the bluffs and canyons of the state beach is irreversible, and the decommissioned reactors still mar the landscape. Meanwhile, the radioactive waste that was generated at the plant is still in need of a safe repository.

Slight of build, quiet in demeanor, and author of several serious books – Dave does not present the image of a rabble-rouser. However, Dave Carle's passion and determination, combined with his scientific background and natural ability to build a coalition, make him extremely effective when he believes he is on the right side of a controversy. The willingness that he demonstrated at San Onofre to take on the big issues served him and the Parks Department well a decade later, when he and Janet became involved in the effort to save Mono Lake.

Janet had wanted to become a park ranger from a very early age. She remembers one family camping trip to Calaveras Big Trees State Park when she was about 12 years old. She got the courage to ask one of the rangers there, "How do you get a job like this?" He was kind enough to take some time to extol the virtues of being a park ranger, and Janet decided at that moment that becoming a ranger was her career goal.

Several years later, she was still living in the East Bay, when the State Parks Department developed a program to get "urban kids" to work in state parks. Janet was hired to work at Patrick's Point State Park on the north coast of the state, about 30 miles north of Eureka. This was quite a change from the urban bustle of Alameda, but having a family background in camping helped her adjust to living in a remote location. Although she would later have some trepidation about moving to and raising a family in the Mono Basin, she now was able to get some idea of what that life could be like.

After several years of seasonal work at State Parks, Dave and Janet, independently, applied for seasonal work with the National Park Service – arguably the largest and best park agency in the world. So, their tale of meeting and beginning a life together is a park story.

In 1975, they were both hired to work at the Cedar Grove area of Kings Canyon National Park, in the Sierra Nevada. Janet had just graduated from UC Davis with a degree in environmental planning and management. Although Dave had also graduated from Davis a couple of years earlier with a B.S. in wildlife and fisheries biology, their paths had never crossed.

So, here are these two young seasonals, single, working and living in a remote and beautiful national park. Dave's job was to issue wilderness permits at Roads' End trailhead, while Janet was a seasonal campground ranger at Cedar Grove. The long and winding road into Cedar Grove ensured that the seasonal staff did not leave the park too often, and their entertainment was usually provided through low-key parties and potluck dinners.

Dave and Janet met at the first party of the summer, and recall dancing together to some Beach Boys tunes. A few days later, Dave was relaxing at his cabin late in the day near the Roads' End trailhead, when Janet rode up on a bicycle to visit him. Dave, ever alert to subtle clues in nature, interpreted this as a positive sign.

After talking to Dave longer than expected, Janet realized it was getting too late and dark to ride back to her cabin safely, so she borrowed a sleeping bag, told Dave good night, and walked into the woods a short way to spend the night sleeping under a tree. In the morning, Dave took her a cup of coffee – a cup they both laughingly recall as the worst coffee she has ever tasted in her life.

But it was an important step to a lifetime together. They both recall the summer of 1975 as "magical," as they explored the extraordinary Kings Canyon through hikes and backpacking trips. Dave and Janet chuckle at the memory that, ostensibly, the purpose of these hikes was to get to know the backcountry of the park better – that enhanced knowledge would improve their ability to explain the wilderness' geography, geology, and

Janet and Dave at Kings Canyon National Park. *Courtesy of David and Janet Carle.*

biology to the public, right?

That fall, Dave's career took a leap forward when he was hired by the State Parks Department as a ranger trainee and assigned to the Mendocino District, which is composed of several absolutely gorgeous redwood, headlands, and coastal state parks. He put all his energy into learning the ropes of being a ranger through the Department's training program.

Meanwhile, Janet returned from a European trip, and came home to spend the holidays with her family in the East Bay. Memories of the wonderful summer with Dave at Kings Canyon, and time at home where she could sort out the priorities in her life, led to a trip to see Dave in Mendocino. Just as with her bicycle trip to his cabin at Roads' End, her visit to Mendocino lasted longer – a lot longer – than she had planned.

Having had a taste of Kings Canyon – a large wilderness park – Janet had developed a vision of being a ranger for the National Park Service. It was large iconic parks, such as Grand Canyon or Denali, that appealed to her. However, Janet decided that a life with Dave Carle was more important to her than working at the Grand Canyon, and she could still fulfill her dream of becoming a park ranger if she worked for California's park system. Shortly thereafter, she was hired by State Parks as a ranger trainee, and soon both Dave and Janet were working as full-time state park rangers.

After Dave and Janet married, they tried to work in parks that were near each other so that they could live together in the same house. For a while, Dave was at Auburn State Recreation Area – an intense and heavily visited recreation park – while Janet was the volunteer coordinator at the Sacramento District.

One of the advantages of working for a state agency in Sacramento is that, if you are doing a great job, you come to the attention of managers who can help you achieve career goals and advancement. Janet was attracting a lot of notice at the Sacramento District, in a good way. Effervescent, extremely competent, and upbeat, she was adored by the park volunteers. She was also very organized and efficient – traits that are very valuable when training, scheduling, and managing volunteers.

Although volunteers are technically employees of the state, they are not paid, and therefore are motivated by other factors, such as love of the park, desire to "give back," and passion for the subject matter. One of the jobs of the volunteer coordinator is to understand and nourish those motivating factors for each individual volunteer – a task that became more difficult as Janet successfully recruited more and more park volunteers. She was getting a lot of positive feedback – from the volunteers, as well as from her supervisors and managers.

Her work experience at Kings Canyon and Patrick's Point, though, gave Janet reason to be conflicted about her future. She remembers sitting in her office in Sacramento, looking out her office window at nothing but a brick wall. Her mind drifted back to Kings Canyon, while she shook her head. She recalls wondering, at the time, whether someone were slashing the tires on her car parked outside – a concern she never had to deal with at Patrick's Point.

On the one hand, she recalls that she could have been sucked up into the Sacramento dynamic and perhaps promoted rapidly up the career ladder. While she was contemplating her job (and life) situation, an opportunity arose in 1982 that the Carles could not dismiss or ignore – they saw a bulletin for a ranger position at the newly created Mono Lake Tufa State Reserve. It seemed ideal for Dave and Janet on many levels – it was a remote, sizable park, it was a "generalist" ranger job (that is, the ranger would do patrol, enforcement, interpretation, education, resource management, and even some maintenance), and it was a new position at a new park. This last factor was appealing, because the first ranger assigned there would be able to really define that assignment – the tabula rasa of ranger jobs!

On the other hand, there were negatives to consider. There was only one ranger position budgeted for Mono Lake, and there were no other nearby state parks. The closest was Bodie State Historic Park – 45 minutes away if conditions were perfect, and several hours away if it was snowing or the roads were impassable.

The remoteness probably appealed to Dave a little more in the beginning. Janet recalls that it was a "big step for a city girl." Although she had worked in remote parks, she had always left a trail open to get back home – seasonal work lasted a few months, and then she could return to civilization. She recalls being a little scared of a permanent move to the Mono Basin – the boondocks – from a comfortable job in Sacramento. Plus, it was a new park with few other staff and an undefined job – the conditions of the job that made it attractive also made it daunting.

Dave and Janet also wanted to start a family. A traditional approach would have been for Dave to accept the ranger position and Janet to take maternity leave or resign, and raise children for several years. Then, when the kids were a little older, the family could move to a less remote location and Janet could return to work.

The couple had other ideas. They approached the managers of the Tahoe District and proposed the notion of job-sharing the single ranger position. Fortunately, Bob Macomber and Bob Tardiff, the superintendent and the chief ranger, respectively, at the district, were very willing to give it a try. Dave recalls his amazement and gratitude that management was willing to give this crazy idea an opportunity to succeed.

This was a first for the State Park System. Couples had worked together before, but always in two separate, funded positions – sometimes as peers, sometimes as a permanent and a seasonal. If management had not been willing to be creative and give this arrangement a try, this would be a much different story. It was important to Dave and Janet that they both work as rangers while they started a family.

The Carles had to be creative and flexible as well. Janet gives Dave a lot of credit for being a pioneering stay-at-home dad several days a week. In

A TV station interviews the Carles about their unusual lives.
Courtesy of David and Janet Carle.

the early '80s, this practice was uncommon enough that a Sacramento TV show did a piece for the evening news, showing Dave baking a pie and Janet driving up in the ranger truck.

Of course, decision-makers at State Parks must have believed that this job-sharing arrangement would be advantageous for the Department – having two people thinking all the time about how to make this new park unit a better place. Also, Dave and Janet each had different interests and skill sets to bring to the park. The Carles also felt a responsibility to future couples who would want to share a ranger job. It is a testament to their character that they carefully considered all the long-term ramifications of this arrangement – consequently, they set their own bar high. Naturally, they wanted the Department to view this experiment as a success.

In spite of the trepidation she felt at the time, Janet now looks back with satisfaction after having worked at the park for 21 years, living through the Mono Lake court battle, and raising two sons. She will forever be thankful that Dave "dragged her" to Mono Lake. She acknowledges that Dave recognized the potential it had for them as individuals, as a family, and as professional rangers, much earlier than she did.

So the Carles swallowed hard and accepted the transfer to the new park unit – officially named Mono Lake Tufa State Reserve. They also faced the certainty of adding significant costs while halving their income – it is easy to understand why Janet was a little nervous about this move on more than one level. They would have children to raise, and there was no "park housing" available – they would have to find a place to rent or buy in the nearby town of Lee Vining. Again, looking back, Janet is very thankful it turned out the way it did. She got to spend most of her career in a "real" park being a "real" park ranger.

When Dave and Janet arrived at Mono Lake in 1982, they were excited about a lot of things. They were about to start a family; they were going to manage a brand-new state park unit; they were going to be setting a Departmental precedent by sharing a position; and they were moving to a remote, breathtakingly beautiful slice of the state. With all this to look forward to, they had no idea how their lives and work would become part of the fabric that ultimately helped to rescue Mono Lake. It is hard to envision the Carles without their Mono Lake experiences, and it is difficult to picture a sustainable Mono Lake without the contributions that Dave and Janet made.

When they first drove into the park, the only informational sign was near the turnoff for Mono Lake Tufa. Someone at the Mono Lake Committee – the local support group for the lake – had painted the sole word "Tufa" in green, along with a directional arrow, on a piece of plywood. They drove past that sign down to the lake, only to discover a cow carcass on the shore. What a welcome to their new ranger assignment!

Janet recalls being terrified of getting stuck on the sandy dirt roads on the back side of the lake. She would drive faster than normal – like a bat out of hell, in her words – to keep the momentum of the truck going through the soft sand. In addition to wanting to set a good example of two rangers sharing one job, she also was determined not to be calling for help all the time. She does recall the time, though, that she got the state truck stuck in the snow. Rather than radio for assistance, Janet (a petite woman) spent three hours digging the truck out by herself. She now recalls that just about every staffer there over the years has been stuck in the soft sand or snow at least once – it is the nature of the park, as well as a rite of passage.

In fact, when the district superintendent delivered the first patrol truck to the park, shortly after the Carles' arrival, he also had business in Bodie State Historic Park. He invited Janet and Dave to come along and learn "the back way" into Bodie. Well, the back way had a lot of snow and mud that year, and after burying the brand new truck in the mud, they all had to hike about five miles to the paved road. Janet recalls that all the rangers wore their Stetsons the whole way. It took three weeks for things to dry out enough to drive the new truck again. With no patrol vehicle available, Dave and Janet went back to Sacramento on temporary assignment for that entire stretch.

The entire infrastructure for the park at the time the Carles arrived was that one sign inherited from the Mono Lake Committee. While there was a lot to do, there was no office, no gates, no fences, no phone, no housing, and only that one lonely sign. They were given the keys to the park's sole truck and told, "Here is your new park – go forth and protect it!" For communications, they would drive to a phone booth on Highway 395 to make calls. They eventually were able to rent a little storefront office in Lee Vining. Dave and Janet regard the park's current office space in the large U.S. Forest Service visitor center as a huge improvement!

Lee Vining Creek, one of the freshwater streams that is being "siphoned off" by Los Angeles.
© *Sbrockman, Dreamstime.com*

Maintenance staff had never been assigned to the Mono Lake unit, and Dave and Janet spent a lot of time picking up trash and cleaning the toilets in order to improve the experience of the park's visitors. It took years to see progress in some areas, but steady work and a good vision have produced a wonderful park experience today.

Of course, they had no way of knowing that their first winter – the winter of 1982-83 – would be record-setting in terms of snowfall. In fact, it turned out to be the biggest snowfall winter of the 20th century. The water level of Mono Lake, which was at 6,372 feet above sea level when they arrived – its lowest elevation in centuries – actually rose nine feet that spring as the snowpack fed the streams that flow into Mono Lake.

Janet and Dave had their first son, Nicholas, that winter. He was born on Christmas Day, and Janet remembers hearing the snowplows operating all night, as she fed the baby at odd hours. Son Ryan soon followed, and the trials of raising two babies, while sharing a job, presented some unusual challenges. If the baby would get hungry while Janet was on duty, Dave would pack up the boys in their personal vehicle and find Janet so that she could nurse. The Carles do not even refer to these challenges as barriers – they fondly recall the many and varied situations for which they had to find solutions in their groundbreaking role as job-sharing parents and rangers.

Dave and Janet are very careful not to take the credit for saving Mono Lake. They prefer to say that they were part of a larger effort among attorneys, environmentalists, advocacy groups, consultants, and the media to conserve the lake. They give a lot of the credit to the Mono Lake Committee (MLC), which was formed in 1978 for the express purpose of saving Mono Lake by restoring it to a functioning and sustainable condition.

A few years earlier, a teaching assistant at Stanford, David Gaines, had led the first major effort to study the ecology of Mono Lake. Those studies led to the publication of a report that highlighted the potentially catastrophic ecological impacts of the falling surface level of the lake. The report drew a straight line from the declining lake level to the diversions of water from four of its five largest tributary streams. Los Angeles aqueduct diversions from Mono's streams began in 1941 to bring fresh water to that city, about 300 miles to the south.

David Winkler, who edited the report, along with David Gaines and UC Davis student Sally Judy, found allies at the Santa Monica chapter of the National Audubon Society. These three activists were able to demonstrate not only how the water diversion was dropping the lake level, but how that lowering of the lake level was creating a land bridge that would allow predators new access to islands in the lake that provided breeding grounds for California gulls. Their evidence was so compelling that the National Audubon Society made the permanent protection of the lake a high priority nationally. Ultimately, a legal, legislative, and educational approach was developed to help garner support for their mission. This was about the time that Janet saw those "Save Mono Lake" bumper stickers begin to appear in Sacramento.

If the lake were drawn down to a level where these islands would be connected to the mainland, it would be devastating for breeding bird populations.

Part of the legal approach was for the Mono Lake Committee and the National Audubon Society to file suit in Mono County Superior Court, charging that the diversion of water to Los Angeles did not comply with the public trust doctrine. This doctrine states that government has a duty to protect navigable bodies of water for the use and benefit of all people. These benefits include fish, wildlife, habitat, and recreation. A few years later, another suit was brought against Los Angeles, charging that its diversions were in violation of the California Department of Fish and Game codes. These suits were ultimately combined.

The court's decision was to require the State Water Resources Control Board, which allocates California's water, to hold hearings to determine how the city's water licenses for the streams that fed Mono Lake should be amended. Wisely, the MLC had argued FOR securing adequate water supplies for Los Angeles. The committee realized that it could not win a case that advocated elimination of all diversions into the lake. It took a pragmatic approach – one that attempted to meet the highest priorities of all parties, including those of lake recreationists. This court decision was appealed several times by the City of Los Angeles, but the MLC and the Audubon Society prevailed at every level of appeal. The battleground ultimately became the hearings held by the Water Resources Control Board, and this battle lasted a while.

Another step the MLC had taken was to lobby a state senator – John Garamendi – to pass legislation creating the Mono Lake Tufa State Reserve. Once signed into law, this bill made it possible for the Parks Department to avoid some of the often cumbersome steps involved in establishing a new unit of the State Parks System. The new law made it possible for the Department to obviate the need to justify the park's acquisition, go through a lengthy and contentious planning process, and a classification exercise. This enabling legislation passed in 1981, and it tied the unit boundaries to the demarcation of state-owned lands below the elevation of the lake before the water level had dropped. The combination of filing lawsuits against the City of Los Angeles and giving the lake greater protection by creating a new state park reserve proved, eventually, to be a very effective strategy.

Written into the legislation was the proviso that the creation of the reserve would NOT affect the water rights of the City of Los Angeles. The Carles were told explicitly not to express their opinions publicly about the issues involved, and to explain that the Parks Department did not have an official position on the controversy. State Parks maintained that its role was solely to operate the reserve in the best interests of the reserve's resources and its visitors.

The state reserve includes all of the lake – which makes it a big park, consisting mainly of water – plus those exposed lands. The fact that the park was created through legislation had the effect of making the legislative process the forum where arguments were made and compromises were forged, rather than the more traditional setting of the Parks Department's planning process and concomitant public meetings.

So, there was a perfect storm of a brand-new state park unit, new staff, a boiling controversy with huge statewide implications, and a precedent-setting model of job-sharing – definitely a worthy challenge for Dave and Janet.

What then was the role of the Carles in this legal process? As state park rangers, they had to remain officially neutral on the many issues. At the same time, they became local experts on the biology, ecology, politics, laws, land use issues, and water rights surrounding the process. As rangers, they became adept at dealing with the outside experts sent in to investigate the local issues.

The courts, the State Water Resources Control Board, the City of Los Angeles, and the environmental groups all had attorneys, biologists, and subject matter experts pawing and sniffing around the lake, developing

In January, 1982, legislation went into effect establishing the Mono Lake Tufa State Reserve. Shortly thereafter, the ranger assigned to the park arrived for duty -- Janet and David Carle.

"We interviewed for the one available position as a two-person job-share," explained Janet. "It was the first time that two rangers were allowed to fill one position, splitting both the work and the salary. It's a rare situation; to this day, we're the only married couple working like this in the state park system."

The Carles met in 1975, when they both had summer jobs as campground rangers in King's Canyon National Park. They were married a year later, while David was a ranger doing night security at the Hearst Castle State Historic Park. They both decided on a career with the state park service, even though they realized the odds of working together were slim.

"Life can be tough for a married couple who are park rangers," David allowed. "When Janet and I met, the state would try to assign couples to locations somewhat close together. But now it's much more difficult. Today assignments are made solely on the basis on seniority. Married couples can be given assignments hundreds of miles apart."

"Our sharing the one Mono Lake ranger position has worked remarkably well, both for us and for our employers," said Janet. "It has allowed David and me to raise a family while we both continue our careers. We have two boys -- Nick, now nine years old, and Ryan, seven.

"For the state, the arrangement has been extremely cost effective; for one salary, the parks department has gotten the equivalent of a ranger and a half. Both David and I bring different skills to the job."

Janet graduated from the University of California at Davis with a degree in Environmental Studies, while David majored as a wildlife and fisheries biologist. He agrees that their different specialties have helped them at the State Reserve.

"This is the old type of ranger job that goes back 40 years,"

Good news! The Mono Lake Tufa State Reserve is safe for another year!

Faced with severe budgetary problems, the California State Department of Parks and Recreation had threatened to close it as early as this summer.

We thought you should know more about Mono Lake's state reserve -- and the two people who have managed it for over ten years.

The Tufa Reserve's Ranger Carle -- Both Of Them

by Bob Schlichting

he explained. "Today, most state parks have specialized staffs, with people to do maintenance, people to do law enforcement, and people to do interpretation or administration. The tufa reserve has only one position. Janet and I need to be 'jacks of all trades.'"

"We do everything from cleaning chemical toilets to leading nature hikes, from cutting down and eradicating tamarisk trees to aiding researchers who are studying the ecosystem," Janet added. "We present programs to numerous school groups that travel here each year from all over California."

"We also built and maintain two board-walks at Mono Lake, one at Old Marina along highway 395, and one below the county park. Those two locations are visited by about half of the more than 200,000 visitors to Mono Lake last year. South tufa accounts for the other half," Dave explained.

Another important part of their job is studying and commenting on Environmental Impact Reports. "David and I are the ones representing the state's interest in environmental matters here at the lake. Protection of Mono's public trust values of is one of the reasons the legislature formed the Reserve back in 1982."

As tufa rangers, David and Janet have carried out numerous search and rescue operations over the years. They also carry guns; as fully empowered peace officers, they enforce all state laws, both inside and outside the Tufa State Reserve. They protect the park from vandalism, and try to educate the occasional tourist who tries to take some tufa home.

"We've had to track down people who take tufa as souvenirs," said David. "One man -- a teacher from the Central Valley -- had a pickup truck full of tufa. We convinced him to return it."

What would have happened if the Mono Lake Tufa State Reserve had been closed by department budget cuts? Who

A rare moment when both rangers are on duty at the same time – *a tufa one deal?*
Courtesy of David and Janet Carle.

Janet leading a nature walk of the Tufa Towers. *Courtesy of David and Janet Carle.*

arguments, and collecting data to support their points-of-view. The media visited often, since it was a hot environmental topic for 20 years (and remains so today, in light of climate change impacts). Janet comments that one of the more challenging parts of the job was keeping up with sharp legal minds during many long phone conversations.

Dave and Janet, as state park rangers, were trained in interpretation – the art of making facts and figures interesting to and relevant to listeners. They were also educated – they eventually received a joint master's degree – in relevant fields. Janet and Dave are both low key, intelligent, knowledgeable, well-respected, and immensely likable. They loved the reserve and understood its ecology and seasonal and daily nuances.

This is another way of saying they were the perfect people to represent the Department of Parks and Recreation on this major issue. They could listen to and understand the biologists, attorneys, and subject matter experts, synthesize their information, and explain their points in terms the general public and the media could grasp. More importantly, they were able to explain these key points to others, on all sides of the issue, in a way that all could understand. Probably like no others involved, they had the big picture, and could

The unusual looking sand tufas just above the level of the lake.

explain that image to others in a meaningful and relevant manner.

Public consciousness of the issues surrounding the lake grew over time. Dave and Janet geared their park interpretive programs to deal with these issues, maintaining neutrality all the while. They allowed the facts to do the talking. They would explain the processes at work – natural, legal, and political – and visitors could draw their own conclusions. More than once, visitors would get testy with each other over these issues while on a ranger-led nature walk, requiring Dave and Janet to be diplomatic peacemakers.

They discovered early on, while interpreting the lake and describing the legal battles, that the breathtaking landscape of the Mono Basin sold itself to people. As a result, those people wound up caring about it and would go buy a bumper sticker at the MLC office. Visitors could easily see the beauty of the reserve and what was going on there. Dave and Janet did not have to tell visitors what to think – they just had to show them how special a place it was and how endangered it was, and visitors drew their own conclusions. In large measure, this tactic worked well on politicians, agency staff, legal investigators, and the media.

Janet chuckles when she recalls that there was one weird phenomenon that really helped their effort. "Every time, seriously EVERY critical time, that a politician like Garamendi, or agency bigwig or member of the media showed up to see Mono Lake, the weather and the skies cooperated to create a spectacular day. Someone was up there saying, 'I need to create a remarkable day today, because the lake really needs this person's support.'"

The Carles went about the business of opening and operating a unit of the State Park System, raising a family, and being part of the effort to rescue the lake. Dave recalls that the reason they decided to stay longer than they had originally anticipated was that, for a long time, the lake had not been "saved," and they wanted to be stationed at Mono Lake when the major decisions were rendered. They also realized that the real key to the lake's long-term sustainability was the implementation of those decisions, if they turned out to be favorable.

As the hearings progressed, Dave and Janet's particular and unique knowledge provided answers to questions – questions that, literally, no one else could answer – about recreation and visitors' opinions and desires. For example, "Where were the tufa towers that would be re-submerged as the lake rose again, and what had happened to them due to the diversions?" It was very gratifying to be considered subject matter experts and to be asked questions that, truly, they were in a good position to answer. They testified several times in various court and water board hearings.

In 1994, Dave and Janet planned a family vacation to Yellowstone National Park. There was no definite date for when the final decision of the water board would be issued, but it looked like mid-1994 was the likely time frame. The Carles kept postponing their vacation, until it became clear that they had better go, or they would have to postpone their trip until the following summer. Naturally, they really wanted to be in Sacramento when the decision was announced.

Of course, just as they finally arrived at Yellowstone in the fall, the favorable decision was made public. The Los Angeles Department of Water and Power – the entity responsible for siphoning off the fresh water from the streams – was ordered by the state to allow the lake to rise to an elevation of 6392 feet. This was 20 feet higher than Mono Lake's lowest level, which had been reached in 1982. Janet recalls walking among the geysers that morning and seeing a small group of bison frolicking in the stream. Dave and Janet took comfort in the belief that the bison were sharing their joy regarding the Mono Lake decision.

Dave retired in 2000 (six years after that decision). Janet is three years younger and, right on schedule, retired in '03. They still are in the home they lived in while they were working, which has a splendid view of Mono Lake. Dave and Janet remain active, committed members of the local community and continue to contribute to the lake's health and sustainability.

Twelve years after she retired, Janet was still coordinating the volunteers for all the agencies. All during their stay at the reserve, they were able to work with the U.S. Forest Service, the Bureau of Land Management, and the Mono Lake Committee on interpretive activities and programs, along with State Parks' efforts. In addition to managing this important interpretive program, for years, Janet also produced the newsletter for the California State Park Rangers Association.

After retirement, Dave has written more than a dozen books. Ever the Renaissance Man, his published titles include a children's book, historical fiction, a murder mystery, history, water policy, technical books on scientific topics, and, with his charming co-author Janet, a documentary of their trip around the world examining water issues on the 38th parallel. They also have taught community college classes in the Mammoth Lakes area.

Dave credits his time working at the lake and on the politics of saving the lake with giving him the knowledge to be able to write some of these books. He did so much research on water issues, water rights, and water law that he was able to author his most successful book, Introduction to Water in California.

After more than 40 years of marriage, Dave and Janet very naturally project the attributes of a satisfied and well-matched couple – they are quick to give the other credit, laugh a lot, and seem the happiest when together.

In 2015, Dave volunteered to lead a nature walk for a small group at South Tufa. It was easy to see why his knowledge base was so vital to those collecting information for the court battle 25 years earlier. The subtle changes in the color of the lake, which were not obvious to first-time visitors, were very evident to Dave, along with the probable scientific explanation. It was very enlightening. Dave and Janet are truly experts on all aspects of Mono Lake, and are eager to share their passion.

The major concern at that point for the Carles, and indeed all those who had helped to save the lake, were the effects of climate change and drought. The recent four-year drought in California had had the unfortunate effect of drastically lowering the lake level again – how discouraging after all the hard work of the 1980s and '90s! Janet also became involved in helping to form a climate action group in the Mono Basin to encourage movement toward a renewable energy future.

Another deep concern of theirs vis-à-vis resource protection and visitor service has been budget and staffing cuts at the reserve. Ironically, there are few better places to tell the story of water in California. Politics, law, economics, public trust doctrine, recreation, and ecology – they all come together at Mono Lake.

How about those two sons who grew up with job-sharing ranger parents at Mono Lake? Nick went to work in the Mono Basin for the U.S. Forest Service caring for the visitor center facility, doing air quality monitoring, and managing water deliveries to a historic ranch. An artist, he paints with oils whenever possible.

Ryan became a bird scientist for Oikonos, a nonprofit dedicated to protecting wildlife and habitat through scientific knowledge and research. He is a seabird specialist, working mainly with rhinoceros auklets, pink-footed shearwaters, and other pelagic species.

Asked if working at Mono Lake during this critical period in its history had provided lasting feelings on their part, Dave Carle responded, "People asked us over the years, 'Don't you get bored working at the same job for so long?' On the contrary, we both remain passionate and hopeful about Mono Lake and its lessons, as well as its future. It takes a while to grasp the nuances of these complicated issues. I am not sure we would have been effective if we had not stayed here so long.

The California State Water Resources Control Board established the goal of having the surface of Mono Lake restored to a level of 6,392 feet. California's drought has slowed progress.

"It was gratifying, challenging, and interesting to be involved with such a big and important issue, and to learn enough about water to feel confident to write books about travel, water policy, and water law."

Janet adds, "Mono Lake was a magical, ever-changing place. Lake level, light, politics, and wildlife were a constantly changing mosaic. The job required us to patrol places few people are privileged to visit, that were hard to get to, and needed driving skill and sand tires. Working at Mono Lake taught us patience as the court cases dragged on, and an appreciation for all the hard work being done toward a water decision. We started the job with a ton of idealism when we were in our late 20s and early 30s. As we continued to stay at this assignment, we became new parents, raised our kids, eased into middle age, dealt with an empty nest, and retired, all in the embrace of our favorite place in the world. Together, we have still have never lost that idealism.

"Mono's message is one of hope – hope that environmental challenges can be met with intelligence and compromise for a better future for the land and the people. Our kids will live their lives in a world dominated by such challenges on a daily basis. The lessons of Mono will help sustain us all."

For more information on Dave's books, visit the author's "Books by David Carle" webpage.

Books by David Carle:

Non-fiction:

Traveling the 38th Parallel (with Janet Carle)

My Visit to Mono Lake (a children's book)

Introduction to Water in California

Introduction to Air in California

Introduction to Fire in California

Introduction to Earth, Soil and Land in California

Mono Lake Basin (with Dan Banta)

Bodie's Boss Lawman, by Bill Merrell with David Carle

Burning Questions – America's Fight With Nature's Fire

Water and the California Dream

Mono Lake Viewpoint

Fiction:

The Spotting Scope

Mono, a Novel

I would also like to acknowledge and thank the Mono Lake Committee – its board, employees, and volunteers – for their efforts to "Save Mono Lake" and for the use of information on their website – monolake.org.

Huell Howser filmed two episodes on Mono Lake Tufa State Reserve – 16 years apart – featuring Dave and Janet Carle. Huell was able to articulate the differences that the implementation of the court decisions had on the lake and its environs between the first airing in 1992 and the second in 2008.

Huell Howser – 1992.
https://blogs.chapman.edu/huell-howser-archives/1992/12/10/mono-lake-californias-gold-311/

Huell Howser – 2008
https://blogs.chapman.edu/huell-howser-archives/2008/11/01/mono-lake-today-138-californias-gold/

CARLOS PORRATA

El Guardabosques

When Carlos Porrata walks the streets of the small town of Inverness, California, it is not uncommon for a townsperson to approach him and say, "Ranger Porrata, I will never forget the night I camped at Tomales Bay State Park as a fifth-grader! You taught me how the Coast Miwok made kochas (tule-covered shelters), as well as how to craft obsidian arrowheads, make fire, and prepare acorn mush so that it was edible." Or they will comment on how one of their children had that same experience.

After all, Carlos, who arrived at the park in 1980, taught the Environmental Living Program (ELP) at Tomales Bay for 24 years, until his retirement from State Parks in 2004. He remembers that his former

chief ranger, Jeff Price, did the math one day, and concluded that Carlos had touched the lives of more than 17,000 fifth-graders from public and private schools throughout Northern California! For many, that spellbinding, two-day experience at Tomales Bay State Park, listening to Ranger Porrata speak of the Coast Miwok traditions, culture, and crafts, was the most memorable experience of their entire elementary school education.

For someone who was born, raised, and educated in Puerto Rico, it has been a remarkable journey. Carlos lived the first 19 years of his life in Puerto Rico, and then moved to New York as a teen. It was there that he met his fetching wife Rebecca, who was a registered nurse in a private psychiatric clinic at that time. He chuckles, "I know what you are going to say, Dave, and NO, I was NOT a patient there!" Shortly, the couple moved to Puerto Rico, where they got married, and Carlos finished his bachelor's degree in psychology. They eventually returned to New Jersey, where Carlos went on to graduate school to earn his master's degree in education.

How does a young man from Puerto Rico, New York, and New Jersey wind up as a state park ranger in Northern California? Carlos says with a grin, "Well, the smartest thing I ever did was to lie on my application to become a park ranger!" The shock value of that statement must have achieved the desired result, for he was quick to fill in the backstory. Unlike those who pad their resumes, tweak their curriculum vitae, and create a few alternative facts, Carlos' "lie" was actually one of omission – he intentionally left off the fact that he had earned a master's degree. "I will tell you later why I lied," he smiled.

When Carlos was working on his master's in education in the '70s, his emphasis was on counseling youth. His first job was to work with juveniles in the urban core and take them out to the local forests, mountains, and lakes. He quickly observed that the dynamics of the group would often change quickly. The kid who was

Kochas constructed as part of the Environmental Living Program. *© 2008 California State Parks (Image 090-P77905).*

real tough in the city would be scared to death of what he would encounter in the woods. At the same time, some of the gang members who were lower on the pecking order would feel very natural and comfortable in the outdoors. One constant, though, was that the behavior of his charges would improve in these more natural settings. That intrigued Carlos, and he began to think that his life's calling might be to introduce kids to nature.

That personal revelation coincided with the couple's desire to move to California. Rebecca was from Southern California, but she had gone to New York to get her education in nursing, where she met Carlos. She followed him to Puerto Rico, where they married and had their first daughter, Alex. But the whole time they were in the East and in Puerto Rico, Rebecca remained anxious to move back to the West to be closer to her family.

She must not have been too anxious, since that 1976 journey from New York to California took two months! Carlos and his family often stayed at national and state parks on their cross-country camping adventure. As Carlos recalls, "Every time we would meet a park employee at the entrance station, in the campground, or at a nature walk or campfire program, I would realize that here is this person in green talking about the plants and animals, and how everything interrelates. I kept looking at my wife and remarking how great it would be to work in the outdoors all the time, and how rewarding it would be to find a wonderful niche in the park profession. On that trip, I committed to changing my career and life path. I decided to quit being a counselor in order to become a park ranger."

Carlos recalls that upon their arrival in California, the stars really aligned for him. The State Department of Personnel Administration had determined that the State Parks Department was not hiring enough women and minorities into the state park ranger trainee classification. The Parks Department responded by creating a new classification – state park technician – that required 60 college units rather than a bachelor's degree as the minimum educational standard. The Department believed that by changing this educational standard, it would be more successful in attracting women and minorities.

Carlos bristles at this concept and is convinced that the best approach to recruiting a more diverse workforce would have been, and remains today, to establish a long-term recruitment program. "You have to start long before the exam announcement comes out. The Department needs to have good recruiters visiting colleges and extolling the virtue of being a park ranger. Even better would be to start developing park management programs at community and four-year colleges. That is how you get the best people. I got excited about a park career when I observed and talked to park staff in the field – not when I saw a flyer about a ranger exam."

"That," Carlos chuckles, "is why I lied on my application and 'toned down' my résumé, at least as far as education was concerned." He believed that having earned a master's might count against him in the exam process. He was quickly hired as a state park technician and assigned to the Channel Coast District along the Ventura coastline for his first year. "Here is the interesting thing – once I got to the training center and met my fellow technicians, we all started comparing notes on formal education. Out of the class of 20, six of us had master's degrees, 13 had a B.A. or B.S., and one had a two-year degree. Collectively, we probably had more formal education than almost any former class, back when a bachelor's degree was required."

After his initial year at Channel Coast, where he completed the formal and on-the-job training, Carlos was assigned to Samuel P. Taylor State Park in Marin County. He and Rebecca now had two daughters, and they all fell in love with the parks of the region north of San Francisco. Having been raised in the tropics, Carlos was initially unfamiliar with the natural features of Marin County – the redwoods, salmon in the rivers, and oak woodlands.

Not surprisingly, Carlos began a process of self-education. He got a daypack and other hiking essentials, bought a number of books on the local natural and cultural history, and taught himself all about the local ecosystems and the Coast Miwok way of life. He recalls that his formal educational background was in psychology and education, and he knew little about the natural and cultural sciences.

This great desire to learn and to become a local subject matter expert came naturally to him. He had already been inspired – not only by the National Park Service rangers he had encountered on his westward migration, but by the state park rangers at Channel Coast. This inspiration, along with his background in education, helped to make Carlos an excellent interpreter. That is the part of the ranger job that appealed to him most. Through interpretation, he believed that he could protect the resources of the parks, improve the experiences for park visitors, and, most importantly, inspire young people to become stewards of the lands that Carlos was coming to love.

After three years at Samuel P. Taylor, Carlos transferred to Tomales Bay State Park. Tomales Bay was a much smaller operation than Taylor – there was one ranger and one maintenance worker, plus a few seasonal workers. So, the ranger job was more of a generalist, out of necessity. When Mike Coronado, the maintenance worker, was off, Carlos had the responsibility for trash pickup, cleaning restrooms, fixing trails, and minor repairs. Conversely, the maintenance worker was willing to engage with park visitors – answer their questions, provide directions, and remind them of park rules and regulations.

Carlos had found a park home that would provide him nourishment for the next 24 years. He recalls that the park was like a church for him, and he tried to create that feeling for visitors. "When they entered the park, I wanted them to feel safe and to be in a thoughtful and inspirational setting – where they could think about nature and their place in it. I wanted the park visitors to become protectors of that park and fall in love with it, just as I had."

He quickly got involved with the park's Environmental Living Program (ELP), which was set up for fifth-grade students at local and nearby schools. This was the second ELP program in the Bay Area – the original ELP program was started at the Tall Ships in San Francisco Bay. (This unit was subsequently transferred by State Parks to the National Park Service.)

From the state park featuring the Tall Ships (shipboard life) and Tomales Bay (Coast Miwok way of life), the concept spread to other park units – Fort Ross State Historic Park (Russian history), Sutter's Fort State Historic Park (California Gold Rush), Angel Island State Park (Civil War period), and Old Town San Diego (local culture). It is a brilliant concept that ties in to the fifth-grade curriculum approved by the State of California's Department of Education.

In addition to the positive feedback from former students who remembered their experiences, Carlos also heard back from former students who were now fifth-grade teachers and who could not wait to bring their classes to the ELP. A few even mentioned that they chose the fifth-grade to teach in because of their inspirational experiences at Tomales Bay State Park with Ranger Carlos Porrata.

The basic concept of the ELP was for children to be able to live and learn from the culture that had been in place locally, and to be able to make their own culture in that setting with the materials and tools available at that point in history. The children had the opportunity to live under those conditions for two days and one night. ELP relies heavily on role-playing among the students. The interaction and the interdependency of people and their environment is a key concept of the program, and it serves to improve problem-solving abilities in those students.

Over the years, Carlos kept thinking of ways to improve the program. It became clear that the success of ELP would be enhanced by training teachers, developing relevant resource material, and communicating well with the schools and the parents of the students.

Again, it is important to recognize that the ELP meshes with the state's fifth-grade curriculum. The program at Tomales Bay actually helps the teachers meet core curriculum requirements – it is not an additional workload. The understanding with the fifth-grade teachers was that they would prepare the students before the visit to the park, and would follow up with review of key concepts well after the students returned to the classroom.

Teachers were provided with a resource handbook, which helped them get the students organized into "tribelets," in addition to letting the teachers know what to expect during their visit. The students, before they came to the park, would designate family tribelet elders who would lead discussions and make tribal decisions. Carlos recalls that the teachers who came to the park early in the school year often appreciated this tribal structure so much that they would use it the rest of the year for other subjects. It was a great decision-making tool.

Included in the resource handbook that Carlos, Chief Ranger Price, and Interpretive Specialist Tom Lindberg enhanced are equipment lists for each student, sample letters to the parents, detailed schedules and maps, suggested follow-up activities after the program, behavioral guidelines, and a request for an evaluation of the program by the teachers.

After setting up the annual schedule, updating the material, and holding a two-day workshop for the teachers, it was time for the students to come to the park and fully experience the ELP. For many of them, it was their first night away from home, or at least away from their families. For others, including some of the teachers, it was the first time they had ever camped. The program required a steady hand at the helm, and that hand belonged to Carlos Porrata.

Although the teachers were supposed to have prepared the students by describing the ways of the Coast Miwok, there is no substitute for hands-on activity. In the classroom, the teacher may discuss how to make a fire, collect plants for food, build a pump drill, or create brushes from the soap root plant, but the experience of actually doing these activities in the wild can provide lasting memories. In their role-playing, the students know that performing these tasks properly could, in the lives of the Coast Miwok, make the difference between the success or failure of the tribe.

Upon arrival at the park, usually around 10:30 a.m. on a Thursday, the students and teachers initially had to walk about a half-mile from the parking lot to Indian Beach, where they would camp for the night. Along the hike, they learned to identify native plants, including those that would be useful as food sources.

For the next 24 hours, the students would collect and cook food, build shelter, make tools, play games of chance, eat, have an evening campfire with storytelling, take a night hike, and have some great discussions about how the lives of the Coast Miwok differed from their own. In the middle of all this was Carlos, doing what he did best – inspiring fifth-graders to gain an understanding and appreciation of living closer to nature.

For all this, Carlos not only created these memories for two generations of fifth-graders, teachers, and families, he was also recognized by the Parks Department. In 2001, Carlos received the "Director's Olmstead Award" for his excellence in managing and improving this program.

Carlos adds, "I am very proud of the ELP. But a lot of people have a misconception of what we were accomplishing. They thought my goal was to teach about the Coast Miwok and their culture. What I was really doing, though, was using that Coast Miwok culture to establish trust with these kids. I thought if they could trust me, personally, this would be a huge step towards getting them to respect my views. Once I had gained their confidence, I could encourage them to respect the profession of state park ranger, treat the land and its resources properly, and preserve the culture and traditions of the local prehistoric people.

Ranger Pete Orchard helping fifth-grade students learn how to prepare food.
© 1965, California State Parks (Image 090-S32917).

"Looking back, I tried to connect with 17,000 fifth-graders during my stay at Tomales Bay. I have to believe that a fair number of these kids got turned on to state parks, to being a ranger, and to being an interpreter – all through the ELP. They also gained an appreciation for the culture of the Coast Miwok. I was not just talking about making an arrowhead or stringing a bow – I was showing them how to do it themselves.

"Then I could talk about the culture of these native people – the original stewards of this land. These stewards used this land for thousands of years, and they always kept it in great shape and never abused it. They set an example that I tried to instill in the students.

"So what I did was environmental education, through this great learning tool – the culture of the Coast Miwok. I tried to impart to the students the responsibility they, the kids, have for stewarding the lands, as well. These natural areas that surround us feed our desire to experience open spaces, and they serve us spiritually. When we need to recharge our batteries, we can go to areas like Tomales Bay that are maintained in a beautiful and wild condition. My hope is that many of those kids are still living their lives accordingly today."

Carlos gives a lot of credit to State Park Historian Glenn Burch and Ranger Pete Orchard for creating the ELP at Tomales Bay State Park. Glenn was very willing to pass on to Carlos the skills of the Coast Miwok that he had learned. One day, in 1981, the two men had a contest to see who could make a fire from scratch the fastest. When Carlos won the contest, Glenn smiled and said, "Great, I don't have to come back here – it is now your program." Carlos felt good that he had demonstrated to his mentor the fact that he was taking the program seriously, but he was sad that Glenn walked away and never returned. Twenty-seven years later, Carlos taught that skill set to a young interpreter, showed her how to operate the program, and walked away himself. He followed Glenn's example and stayed away. Maybe that is the way of the Coast Miwok.

Carlos became involved in the community in other significant ways. He became the first Latino ever elected to the local school board and served on several other nonprofit boards as well.

He also represented the state park on the Tomales Bay Watershed Council – a coalition of about 30 governmental agencies, nonprofit corporations, advocacy groups, private companies, and the University of California. The goals of this council include improving water quality, habitat conditions, and water supply reliability for the watershed. An outcome of this cooperative effort is protection of the local salmon, birds of the Pacific flyway, biodiversity, and several threatened and endangered species. Carlos eventually became chair of the council, and added these thoughts – "The Tomales Bay watershed's abundance and beauty fed the bodies, spirits, and souls of the native people for thousands of years. The protection and appreciation of these irreplaceable natural resources is a responsibility that we all need to share for the benefit of generations to come."

His commitment to public service was further rewarded when he was asked to join the board of the Marin Community Foundation – the fourth largest foundation of its type in the United States.

The foundation has well over one billion dollars in assets, and approves grants of over $50 million annually. After serving on the school board and local nonprofit boards, Carlos recalls his shock at the significant size of grants he was approving as a board member of the Marin Community Foundation. As Carlos puts it, "At first, I couldn't believe how many zeros were involved in the dollar amounts. I am a regular guy, and it took me a while to get used to approving grants of that size, which of course had the potential to make huge changes in local communities. The recipients included the arts, affordable housing, education, the poor and needy – this was a great way of fulfilling my need to be of service to others. It was just in a different way. Oh yeah – I was the first Latino on their board, too."

Carlos had a passion for interpretation, but he could be a fierce protector of the park if necessary. A neighboring landowner of a remote area of the park came to Carlos one day and asked if he could build a portion of his proposed new house on state park property. Of course, Carlos denied his request.

Then, some months later, Carlos was patrolling that remote site and there was the guy's house – 25 feet of which was on park property. State surveyors were called in, and they confirmed that the neighbor was trespassing on parklands. The neighbor's first response was to offer the state an easement through "his" property! When Carlos informed him that he had to remove his house, the neighbor started going the "political route." He had his legislators put pressure on the State Parks director to relent. Carlos recalls, "I felt totally supported by State Parks management, all the way to the director's level."

Through his decades as an active and respected member of the local community, Carlos had built up an excellent reputation with local reporters. The press came out totally on the side of the park staff on this highly charged issue. As Carlos can proudly state today, "Now there is no longer a house on park property."

Although being a tough ranger on the trespass may seem at odds with the caring instructor he was at the ELP, Carlos disagrees with this assessment. "One thing that makes park rangers different, especially in the field of law enforcement, is that they have a whole box full of tools at their disposal. The good rangers become adept at deciding which is the right tool for each situation.

"Here is a perfect example. When I started at Tomales Bay, there was a natural area in the park where no parking was allowed. This regulation was in force because parking was impacting – and compacting – the natural resources. But it was open and inviting, and cars kept parking there. There were NO PARKING signs all over the place, but many people just ignored the signs. So I wrote a bunch of parking tickets every weekend. Nobody was happy about getting a ticket, and the result was a lot of bad feeling towards the park and the ranger – me.

"I got together with Mike Coronado, the maintenance worker at the park, and we brainstormed ideas that would solve this problem. Mike got the park tractor and moved several large boulders onto the perimeter of the natural area, so parking there became almost impossible. Mike also broke up the soil that had become compacted, and we planted some native trees there. All the NO PARKING signs came out. The result – I never wrote another parking ticket there – ever!

"What I am trying to say is that Mike and I saw ourselves as problem solvers. I wore a badge and carried a gun, and sometimes I needed those tools. But we also could use a tractor as a way to solve a problem. One of the ranger's most effective tools is the ability to explain the reason for a regulation in an interpretive manner. If the visitor understands the reason for the regulation – especially ones designed to protect natural and cultural resources – they are more likely to abide by the rules in the future. I also like to think that the ELP was a proactive way to head off problems – if I could make park supporters of these kids at an early age, that positive energy would go a long way."

He experienced what he calls his most ironic (and heart-felt!) experience in the mid-'80s at the park. It was Valentine's Day, February 14, when Carlos received a call for medical assistance at Heart's Desire beach. It was low tide, and a recently retired man and his wife had been clamming on the beach, when the man suffered a massive heart attack. Maintenance Worker Mike Coronado and Carlos performed CPR on the man for what seemed like a very long time. Carlos' wife, Rebecca, an RN, came down from their park residence to lend a hand. Finally, the paramedics arrived and decided to stop CPR – the man had no signs of life.

Then two weeks later, the late victim's wife came by to deliver a thank you present for the heroic efforts of Carlos, Mike, and Rebecca. The present was See's chocolates in a box shaped like a heart – a heart-shaped box for their efforts to save a heart attack victim at Heart's Desire beach on Valentine's Day. Carlos adds, "If that is not irony, I do not know what is!"

Not surprisingly, Carlos can also make a bad situation into a positive outcome by being creative and using the interpretive approach. He recalls, "One time, a couple of guys came in and knocked down an osprey nest in the park, just because they wanted to set up a duck blind for the hunting season. I wrote them citations, but that did not solve the problem for the osprey.

"Then I got in touch with Jules Evens, who wrote THE book on the natural history of the Point Reyes peninsula. Together, we went to the local school and told them the osprey now do not have a nest, and it will take a whole lot of sticks to rebuild their nest. Our idea was that if each student brought a stick, and we

Heart's Desire Beach. *© 1965, California State Parks (Image 090-S13339).*

placed it near the duck blind, the osprey could build their nest more easily. They wouldn't have to expend so much energy on nest building, and they could have it ready by the time the eggs were due to be laid.

"The students thought it a wonderful idea, and every single kid brought a stick to school. We put the whole pile in the state park boat and finally scattered all the sticks around the area. Sure enough, the osprey did use those sticks and rebuilt their nest in time. The students felt such an ownership of the nest after that, and I would see them out there occasionally checking on the progress. I know the teacher helped by keeping the project alive in the classroom. So the bad guys were punished for their misdeeds, but we also got to reach a bunch of students in a positive way. The local kids were excited about helping, as well as learning about the local natural history. We need to be on the lookout for opportunities like this one to provide public service, help local native species, and make kids feel good about their assistance on a cool project."

Carlos was able to take a different approach after a large fire burned through Tomales Bay State Park in 1995. The Vision Fire gained fame as one of the largest wildfires in California's recorded history. The three boys who started the fire were identified almost immediately, but it took a while to piece together the chain of events for that conflagration.

The local fire marshal asked for Carlos' help, not only because he was the local park ranger, but also because he was so well-respected and trusted in the local community. It took them four days to put together the account of what had happened.

The boys admitted building a campfire in the park, so Carlos did write them citations for that. But they vehemently maintained that they had totally extinguished the fire before they went to sleep in their campsite – at least they thought they had. Upon awaking the next morning, they checked the fire, and it still appeared to be cold and totally out, so they left. Unbeknownst to the boys, fires can creep underground through duff and roots. When a 45-mph wind came through the next day, it flamed the smoldering fire to life. The Vision Fire eventually burned 28 homes.

The fire marshal and Carlos decided to create the tone that the boys had made a terrible mistake with horrible consequences, but they never had any criminal intent. Says Carlos, "There was no doubt about it – the kids should not have camped there and built a fire – but they were not bad kids. There were no winners – the people who lost their homes, the boys, or the families of the boys. The boys and their families were embarrassed and rightly felt responsible for a lot of grief and destruction. They also felt threatened by others, and not without reason.

"If there was a positive side to this story, it was this. One of the teenagers came to me and asked me if he could go with me and give talks at local schools about fire – its effects and dangers. He was not required to do this, but he wanted to do it. I felt good about the outcome, odd as that might sound. I am not trying to diminish this awful situation and its results. Many homes were lost, and many lives were irrevocably changed. But given the media frenzy, the public's cry for justice, and the pressure from insurance companies, I believe we came up with the best post-fire outcome possible. Again, I think I used the right tool for that particular situation."

Carlos was proud of the fact that he and Rebecca, a public health nurse, were closing in on 50 years of marriage. "We are very happy. Although we have dealt with some incredibly difficult family health issues, we are a very strong couple." Rebecca and Carlos are both fluent in Spanish, and they tout their language skills as huge attributes during their 40-year stay in Marin County. As a registered nurse for the county, Rebecca was able to reach out to the local ranch hands and their families to provide assistance with their health needs.

During that same time period, Carlos observed that there were no Latinos visiting the state park, so he began an outreach program to those same locals. "It took me about two years to get the local ranch hands to understand that I did not care about whether they were documented. They were welcome at the park – just like everyone else. But I did want them to use the park responsibly – to be respectful of the park and other visitors.

"In just a few years, the locals were coming to the park for birthday parties, picnics, and family reunions. It probably helped that I speak Spanish, my native language, better than I speak English!" Carlos gets a big smile as he adds, "Rebecca and I made a good team at work, as well as at home. We both were committed to 'helping' professions. Marrying a nurse is a very smart idea!"

When it came time to retire, Carlos was able to walk away from the Parks Department. Although he had spent a good portion of his life – an extremely rewarding portion at that – at Tomales Bay State Park, it was time to leave the work at the park to the next generation. "When I retired, I really retired," Carlos says with a knowing smile. "I took off the uniform for the last time, and I was done wearing green. I felt it was time for me to move on and do other things, although all my new interests were still related to this place.

Photo by Carlos Porrata

Photo by Carlos Porrata

"I really appreciate the opportunity I had to work as a park ranger, especially at a place like Tomales Bay. When I first got here, I was so impressed by the beauty of this place and the quality of the local community. I knew my family had found home. There I was, in a pontoon boat, patrolling beautiful beaches and an incredible bay. That first year, I actually felt guilty for getting paid to work at the park."

Carlos feels fortunate that he and his family were able to retire without having to leave the area. His house, not surprisingly, has a terrific view of Tomales Bay. Although he does not spend a lot of time in the park, he is often found hiking and boating in the surrounding natural areas.

Several family health crises rocked his world soon after retirement. Although he saw his new job as helping his family get through these crises, he realized that he also needed to develop healthy pursuits. Carlos soon became a skilled nature and wildlife photographer. The pursuit of bobcats, coyotes, osprey, owls, and all sorts of animals provides him the opportunity to spend time in the natural haunts of his beloved Tomales Bay.

"Photography has allowed me to keep connected to my community and to keep healthy," he says. "I get to hike, haul my gear around, and sometimes go out in my kayak looking for photo opportunities.

"For me, personal success is measured by the quality of your life, and Tomales Bay and my experiences here have provided me with a remarkable and extraordinary quality of life. When I first arrived there, I realized how fortunate I was to be the ranger at this park, and I decided right away that I would become the best ranger possible at Tomales Bay. Surrounded by beauty, I am rich in spirit. I don't have much money, but my heart soars like an eagle – a very delighted eagle!"

Photo by Carlos Porrata

MIKE TOPE

A Benevolence of Tenacity

One of Mike Tope's first tasks as district superintendent of the State Parks System's Orange Coast District was to help lead a public meeting to discuss the future of one of Southern California's most incredible beaches – the magical and iconic Crystal Cove State Park. Mike had no idea that when he arrived at the meeting, he would be facing an angry and vociferous crowd of almost 1,000 people! Looking back, though, he believes that this meeting, and the chain of events that ensued as a result, composed the most difficult, but satisfying, period of his career.

In 1999, Mike had been named the new superintendent for this sprawling district of beaches and parks. Stretching from San Onofre State Beach up the coast to Huntington and Bolsa Chica State Beaches, this district is one of the state's busiest in terms of visitation, crime, and political pressure. Crystal Cove State Park, nestled between Laguna Beach and Corona del Mar, lies smack dab in the middle of the district.

Gray Davis had just been sworn in as the governor of California, and he had tasked Mike and newly appointed State Parks Director Rusty Areias with the job of implementing a $25 million, 60-year contract at Crystal Cove. This binding contract had already been approved and signed by both the developer and the state, and it called for the construction of a luxury hotel, three swimming pools, and several restaurants in the footprint of the Crystal Cove historic district. A public meeting had been

Mike Tope, Superintendent of Orange Coast District.

Crystal Cove – a rare gem of open space along the coast of Southern California.

scheduled so that State Parks officials could explain these new plans to the public.

Prior to the meeting, Director Areias and Mike had met with the editorial boards of several local newspapers. As they explained the Department's plans and answered questions from these boards, there was still no reason for the two of them to anticipate the reaction from concerned citizens at that evening's public meeting.

When Mike and the director arrived at Abraham Lincoln Elementary School in Corona del Mar that evening, they were shocked to see the size of the crowd. The public had shown up to voice their opinions about the contract and its potential impacts on Crystal Cove State Park. Mike and Director Areias learned shortly that these opinions were exceptionally strong, and generally not supportive of the state's planned development and operations at the park. Mike recalls, "We thought there would be a lot of public input, but we did not expect the strength of passion on this issue. We were both new in our jobs and got caught off guard."

It soon became clear that the public really only had three complaints:

- The planned development would absolutely destroy the quaint, charming, and beautiful character of the park's historic district.

- The state had purchased the property for the park in 1979, and 20 years later, the public (which owned the park) still was not being allowed full access to it. This attitude of public exclusion would prevail in perpetuity if a luxury resort were built on park property – lands that had been acquired with public funds.

- In the opinion of the public, the design plans for the historic district had been developed without adequate public input. Many of the leaders in the crowd believed that the process the state had employed was inappropriate, immoral, illegal, and, well, just plain stupid.

"Wow," Mike recalls with a chuckle, "only three minor complaints!"

At the school meeting hall, there was standing room only. There were several TV news trucks there, and it was clear that not everyone would be able to fit inside. Folding chairs and a public-address system were set up outside so that everyone could hear the proceedings.

Director Rusty Areias had a background as a state assemblyman and as a California coastal commissioner, so he was no stranger to testy public meetings and hearings. He is also a gifted public speaker with an uncanny ability to connect with his audience. However, the director was able to feel the mood of the crowd and the media, and he knew he was between a rock and a hard place. He was neither a strong opponent nor strong advocate for the project, but he also knew that there was a binding legal contract between the state and the contractor.

The director opened the meeting by welcoming and thanking people for attending. He outlined in general terms the plan for the park and the agenda for the meeting. However, when he introduced the developer, who was going to present more specific details about the development plans for Crystal Cove, the response from the crowd was intense. They booed loud and long, and would not even let the developer speak.

It did not take Mike and Areias long to figure out that they needed to change the dynamics of the meeting. More importantly, they needed to consider re-opening the public process for determining the long-term future of the park.

They decided to let everyone who wished to speak take their turn at the microphone. They were willing to listen to hundreds of speakers, if necessary. Dozens of people actually spoke, and the meeting went long past midnight. A combination of the late hour and the realization that just about every meaningful comment had already been made finally led to winding down the meeting.

That evening, Mike and Director Areias learned – and many speakers made this point – that the process that had led to the contract with the developer was fatally flawed. The Department had put the cart before the horse by making binding decisions without consulting its customers – the people of California – who cared a great deal about the unique setting and ambiance of Crystal Cove and whose tax dollars were used to buy the park in the first place.

One of the main factors that provided hope for changing the direction of this plan was that it had been conceived and approved under the previous administration. Governor Pete Wilson had created a blue-ribbon commission to explore the concept of public-private partnerships in the State Park System. Recognizing that State Parks did not always have the capital to develop facilities, nor the funds to operate those facilities once constructed, the commission's job was to recommend state parks in which these partnerships could be established and nurtured.

That commission's number one priority for such a partnership turned out to be Crystal Cove State Park. The commission had recommended the development of visitor-serving facilities at the park, especially since it was situated in an ideal location in a part of Orange County that was still remarkably undeveloped. The governor's office had approved the concept, and a developer had been selected to build out the new facilities. This plan also included razing several of the historic cottages in the park. A contract was drawn up, and both the state and the developer had approved its terms. However, since there were new players now at the state level, the possibility of re-negotiating that deal was deemed at least worthy of exploration.

After the public comment period at the meeting, Director Areias let the audience know that he and Mike had definitely heard them, and that they understood the concerns. More importantly, they would attempt to get the support of Governor Davis to amend the process and development plans. They set up another public meeting for the following month to reveal the progress they had made.

As Mike recalls, "I was so glad that Rusty was there at the first meeting. Here am I, the new superintendent, and this is by far the biggest and most raucous public meeting I had ever attended. I had held some meetings with companies that wanted to stage a surf contest, but I had no experience with something like this. I knew that after this initial meeting, I would be THE guy who would carry the effort forward. There were some real heavyweights there to try to influence the decision – the Natural Resources Defense Council, Friends of Irvine Coast, Coastkeepers, and Joan Irvine Smith.

"Not only did Rusty get us all through this first meeting, but he made it clear that the local superintendent – that would be me – would be the main person handling the planning process going forward. He basically told the group that it was a very important issue, but he had 279 other park units to pay attention to, and that he had full confidence in me to be in charge of running the planning process for the next two years. That was huge for my credibility and my confidence, and I felt empowered to step up and guide the whole process towards the best result possible."

To his credit, the director was able to convince the governor to allow the State Parks Department to attempt to cancel the existing contract and re-open the entire park planning process. The developer, of course, had in his possession a legally binding contract, but he was wise enough to realize that his project would likely become tied up in the courts for many years. He was, therefore, open to some level of compensation in exchange for terminating the contract.

In short order, the state and the developer agreed to a $2 million buyout to repay him for the investment he had already made. While this was going on, Mike was busy setting up another meeting, as promised, at the same school.

Director Areias was also a very good evaluator of talent. He had already recognized attributes in Mike Tope that he felt would be successful in carrying out the planning process for Crystal Cove with the supporters of the park. At this next meeting, Mike, along with staff from State Parks headquarters in Sacramento and the Department's service center in San Diego, again were greeted by 1,000 members of the public. Mike relayed the good news – the governor had agreed to re-open the planning process, and the large-scale development had been scrapped.

Although most of those in the crowd were delighted and relieved to hear this news, many were also dismayed

Crystal Cove started to become known as a beautiful beach. *Courtesy of California State Parks (Image 090-19853).*

to learn that the director would not be able to attend the second meeting. Mike assured them that Director Areias had done the hard work necessary in Sacramento to turn things around. It was now up to Mike, the support staff, and the public to develop the new plan for Crystal Cove. This time, the public was deeply involved, had a stake in the outcome, and after two years' effort, produced a plan that would, upon implementation, serve the public well.

"After all," Mike now recalls, "it is a public park, paid for by the people of California. It did not make any sense to build a hotel with rates of up to $700 per night, and remember – this was years ago. People justifiably wanted a state park that was affordable, accessible, and available. Of course, I also realized that planning would only be one phase of making the park available to the public. Difficult work would remain after the plans were finalized – many of the cottages were falling apart, we still had private residents in a lot of those cottages, and there were over 270 occupied mobile homes in a different section of the park. All the occupants of those cottages and mobile homes would have to be removed, and the state simply did not have the capital to solve all these problems right away."

Crystal Cove really gains popularity in the 1920s. *Courtesy of California State Parks (Image 090-19856).*

This incredible effort that Mike orchestrated definitely was the key step in making the Crystal Cove area – including the historic district, bluffs, cottages, creek, restaurant, campground, backcountry trails – a public oasis amid the development of Orange County. In the prior hundred years, however, lay an unusual series of events that led to the development of what is now the historic district within the park.

Around 1917, workers on an enormous ranch, owned by James Irvine Jr., began to camp overnight at the mouth of Los Trancos Creek – right in the heart of what now is Crystal Cove State Park. Irvine had inherited the ranch from his father, and in 1894, incorporated his land holdings as the Irvine Ranch. It was around this time that Orange County was officially formed, splitting off from southern Los Angeles County. By charging his workers a small fee to camp there, he condoned the usage of the beach and its environs. A road was established between the bluffs and the beach, through the normally dry creek canyon, and this access opened the cove up to other uses.

It was not long until artists, known as "plein air painters," from Laguna Beach and other communities in Southern California discovered the delights and inspiration that Crystal Cove provided. And, in short order, movie producers from nearby Hollywood capitalized on the public's taste for movies with a Polynesian theme by filming outdoor sets – replete with imported palm trees and thatched-roof huts – at the cove.

In 1925, Irvine hired E. Roy Davidson to manage the influx of campers, movie directors, and artists. He allowed Davidson to build a small office, complete with living quarters in the back, in a strategic location in the canyon. The popularity of the beach and cove increased with campers, and a couple of additional wooden cottages were built.

In 1927, another occurrence spurred the rapid growth of "vernacular architecture" now extant at Crystal Cove. A large schooner was destroyed nearby, and a huge amount of wooden scrap washed up on the beach at Crystal Cove. People who had until then been campers seized the opportunity and, without permission or building permits, built a number of small cottages using the sea's bounty of lumber. Nobody really had a set of building plans or a building permit, and there was no real sewer system. Each cottage was unique, and outhouses became prevalent. The number of cottages grew over the years. Meanwhile, the campers became more sophisticated – every summer they would build temporary wooden frames for their canvas tents, situated between the cottages and the ocean.

The original cottages were built in a style now called "vernacular architecture."

It was a haphazard community, but it seemed to work. The campers formed close bonds with the residents of the 45 cottages, and the years leading up to World War II were an idyllic time. It was these mid-century decades that defined Crystal Cove, and they form the "historic period" – 1935 to 1955 – that the State Parks Department wants to preserve. Visiting Crystal Cove today, it is not difficult to picture the beach community of 70 to 80 years earlier.

Since it was such a wonderful location and lifestyle, some of the residents decided to make their summer cottages more suitable for year-round living. Electricity and plumbing were installed, without permits of course, along with insulation and improved roofing material. These improvements attracted the notice of the Irvine Company, which still owned the property, and in 1940, the tenants were required to sign 10-year leases. The residents had no claim to the land or the buildings – they were living on company property, and almost all of them signed these leases.

After World War II ended, usage picked up again dramatically, and for a while, it seemed like the cove was one big summer party. There were volleyball games on the sand, luaus at night, body surfing and fishing in the ocean, and the camaraderie of "living the good life," celebrated over an adult beverage or two as the sun was setting over the Pacific Ocean. One of the quotes in the book *Crystal Cove Cottages* stands out – "Every night was Saturday night, and Saturday night was New Year's Eve."

The Orange County Board of Supervisors terminated tent camping on this beach in 1962, and that altered the "vibe" of the cove. The 1950s and '60s were also a time of great change in general for Orange County. Disneyland had opened in nearby Anaheim, and Southern California had become a major destination for tourists and new residents. The sleepy days of Crystal Cove were numbered.

In 1979, the state reached a deal to purchase almost 1,900 acres at Crystal Cove from the Irvine Company. This tract included the historic district, where the cottages were located, but that area was only about 13 acres. The new park also had three miles of beach. Today, it is hard to imagine that, in the '70s, the state was able to add a unit of this size and quality to its park system. Three miles of beach and 1,900 acres of new parkland in the heart of bustling Southern California – priceless!

A few years later, State Parks acquired an additional 900 acres from the Irvine Company to add to the park. The state park now had a backcountry area where hiking and mountain biking were to become popular, once it was opened to public access.

Also included in this new unit was an underwater park. Established for the enjoyment of skin divers and scuba divers, the underwater park stretched the entire three-mile length of the beach and extended to a depth of 120 feet. Crystal Cove originally was named because of the extremely "crystal clear" ocean water there, and the "underwater community" soon began to appreciate this addition to the Department's roster of underwater parks. One unusual feature for divers is the presence of a World War II era Corsair fighter plane, found at a depth of about 60 feet.

The state now was also the proud owner and landlord for 45 cottages and over 270 mobile homes. The residents who occupied these cottages and trailers were, shall we say, more than a little reluctant to give up their homes on the beach.

Mike says now, "Of course, I get it. Everybody gets it. Let's say you are lucky enough to be one of the residents of a cottage in the historic district, or you are living in a mobile home on a small bluff overlooking the beach at the park. You've got it made! For a very reasonable monthly cost, you got to live in paradise. During the summer, there was a beach party every night with a bunch of your friends.

"Right down the road, in Laguna Beach or Corona del Mar, you pretty much have to be a millionaire to afford to live this close to the beach. You have an ideal climate, and the beach areas are really not too crowded. The residents of Crystal Cove did not want to give up their homes without a fight."

Although it was the long-range goal of State Parks to have residents move out of these homes, this issue became a political football for almost the next 20 years. Once again, there were a lot of factors in play, but eventually it would fall on Mike to put into effect the evictions of hundreds of people.

Mike looks back now, "I don't think I ever saw the task 'evict hundreds of residents' in my duty statement. When these evictions were running hot and heavy, I sure spent a lot of time in the Orange County courthouse dealing with this issue. I guess for a superintendent this is covered under 'other duties as required.'" Of course, those evictions were still years down the road.

Meanwhile, as mentioned previously, Governor Wilson had chartered his blue-ribbon commission to look into public/private partnerships. This commission identified Crystal Cove State Park as a high priority for creating this type of relationship, and the controversial contract with the developer to build the luxury hotel was the result. This led to the contentious public meetings discussed before, as well as the pledge that State Parks would re-visit the general plan for the park.

Over a two-year course of calm and mission-driven leadership, Mike led the process that converted that near-mob into a cadre of strong park supporters – supporters who developed an excellent and innovative general plan for this amazing open-space slice of the Southern California coast.

As Mike thinks back, "Crystal Cove is one of the most unusual, most highly fought over, most expensive, least widely known, and most remarkable state parks in California. I recognized that I had the unique opportunity to help conserve, in perpetuity, the amazing Crystal Cove State Park – truly one of Southern California's most beautiful beaches. I had to make sure I did it right."

Mike and departmental staff spent the next two years – right after those two initial public meetings – conducting public workshops, both large and small, soliciting and recording everyone's ideas. "Basically, we took the original general plan, which was very 'bare bones,' and updated the whole thing. The new general plan was very specific in its goals and how those goals would be achieved. We wrote the operations plan that identified how each cottage would be utilized. Some would be used for public rentals, while others would be re-purposed for disparate functions, such as employee housing, office space, interpretive centers, and research centers.

"During this period, one of the first things we had to do was to get an interim plan approved by the State Park and Recreation Commission as well as by the State Coastal Commission. There were still people living in some of the cottages, but all the 'septic systems' – and I used that term loosely – had become a real issue. The State Regional Water Quality Control Board had issued a 'cease and desist' order for the cottages – in other words, this regulatory agency was saying that the effluent from the residents of the cottages was creating an unsafe water quality issue, and the use of the existing septic systems would have to be terminated."

The water board had also established an "Area of Special Biological Significance," or ASBS, for the ocean waters just offshore from the park. According to the state, an ASBS is "an area monitored and maintained by the board and is an area of California's coastal waters. ASBS are basic building blocks for a sustainable, resilient, coastal environment and economy."

Mike continues, "As the land owner, the Parks Department could not just evict residents on short notice. Not only would it be inhumane and unfair, but the residents had some powerful political allies pleading their case. The residents of the cottages had already received extensions to their leases with the state for the use of the cottages, but the order from the water board brought matters to a head.

"That board was telling State Parks that the Department essentially had to get rid of all the tenants, all the culverts, and all the septic systems – no water or effluent would be permitted to go into the ocean or into Los Trancos Creek, which runs through the middle of the historic district and into the ocean.

"Fortunately, there was a park bond act that had just been passed, and we were able to tap into that for funding. We also had the public saying loudly that this had been a state park for 20 years already, and there still was not much public access to those beaches.

"At the same time, we were hearing from the tenants, through their legislators, pleading their case to be allowed to stay in the cottages while the Parks Department solves some of these problems. Their point was that the cottages would be maintained while occupied, but once they were vacant, cottages would deteriorate more quickly. It was a good point, but the cease and desist order from the water board left us – the Parks Department – with little choice other than to require the tenants to vacate the cottages.

"When the Parks Department had extended the residents' leases for the cottages in the late '80s for another 10 years, the tenants, in exchange, had agreed to waive the awarding of relocation costs. The new leases also specified that the tenants waived their rights to all structures, including the cottages. So at least those sticky legal points had already been decided. The cease and desist order from the water board really convinced the residents, as well as their elected representatives, that the time had come for the residents to move out. These septic systems could not be upgraded – they all were pretty much 'home-made' septic systems. Let's just say that licensed professionals had not been utilized to design or construct the septic systems there – some of which were right next to Los Trancos Creek. The bacteria readings in the creek did not meet acceptable standards. Los Trancos flows into the sea, while kids frequently swam in the creek and the adjoining ocean.

"The interim plan had to take all that into consideration. We not only had to shut down the septic systems and remove the cottage residents, but we also had to manage asbestos and lead paint abatement in the cottages, as well as the issue of bluff instability.

"The first order of business was to design and install a new sewage system. When the initial land acquisition was going through in 1979, Tom Miller (the superintendent at that time) had a stroke of genius and foresight and had the Parks Department pay the sewage connection fees at that time – roughly $240,000. Of course, that was when there was bond funding available. More than 20 years later, we were able to get all the runoff diverted to the new sewer system and get a sewer line down into the park from a connection near the coast highway. The interim plan was designed to get us through two years of operations.

"We were in the middle of the interim plan becoming operational, but we still had to come up a solution for the BIG PLAN – how to restore and operate 45 cottages. The public had spoken – they did not want some fancy resort in the Crystal Cove historic district – they wanted us to implement actions that preserved the vernacular architecture and re-purposed it for affordable public use, education, and research. Now all we had to do was find the capital for this.

"While considering different scenarios and making our plans, we at State Parks knew it would be very unlikely to get a budget approved that provided for additional staff or new operating funds. Although park bond money was available, those funds could not be used for operating the park. We knew that running a cottage rental operation was beyond our capability. The capital available through the park bond could, however, be used to restore and remodel the cabins and construct the infrastructure necessary, such as the sewage system, upgrading the electrical service, and improving roads, trails, and safety features.

"Other factors were in play in shaping our plans in the historic district. One of the outcomes of the public process was the desire to retain the traditional 'look and feel' of the site. State and federal laws mandated that we preserve the historic integrity of the district and the buildings. We wanted the historic district to look pretty much the way it did during the mid-20th century. As an example, we left the electrical wires in the district on overhead poles. These days, it is tempting, and it is much more attractive, to bury electric and phone cables, but that look would not be authentic vis-à-vis the historic period.

"In addition, we had to ensure that the new and restored facilities were in compliance with the ADA – the Americans with Disabilities Act. Essentially, ADA required us to make the facilities accessible to people with disabilities. This is not just the law – we at Parks have a strong commitment to providing a 'big tent' for all Californians. We want all people to have access to our extraordinary parks and beaches."

Looking back, Mike laughs at the situation the planners found themselves in. "At first, I kind of felt sorry for the engineers, architects, historians, and ADA consultants who were trying to come up with a plan that would accommodate all these seemingly diametrically opposed requirements. How could they possibly agree?

"For example, let's say we are planning for the rehabilitation of one of the cottages. When it goes operational, it has to be authentic enough to look like it did in the 1950s (both inside and out), it has to meet modern building codes, it has to be modern and comfortable enough to attract paying customers, it has to be safe in terms of asbestos and lead paint and earthquake standards, and it has to be accessible to disabled customers. To my astonishment and pleasure, it turns out these folks were, without exception, very excited about this project.

"Their response was something along the lines of, 'Gee, anybody can design a standard park restroom or a park road or figure out how to put a wheelchair ramp next to a park office. Working on the rehabilitation of Crystal Cove was the opportunity of a lifetime – we got to design stuff that no one else will ever have

State Parks has gradually been restoring the cottages and the historic district.

the opportunity to work on.'

"These designers all came in ready to defend their particular discipline, and then wound up working very well together as a team. Each of them was very proud of the final design. They were all able to have the goals of their separate areas of responsibility met, while the plan they came up reflected a true synergy of creative thought and teamwork."

Mike deserves a lot of the credit for creating an atmosphere that engendered and rewarded this collegiality. However, once he got these teams working on the physical plan, he still had to figure out how to operate the cottage rentals when they came on line.

Unlike the deal with the developer who had the previous contract, there was no need for a 60-year contract this time. Since State Parks was capitalizing the construction, rehabilitation, and infrastructure costs, there would be no need for a developer and operator to amortize those costs over that long of a period. Mike figured he would still have to offer at least a 30-year concessions contract, though, in order to attract interested parties.

Typically, the state will "go out to bid" when there is a concessions opportunity of that length and magnitude. There was another constraint in the mix, however. One of the conditions of approval from the coastal commission was that the Parks Department had to commit to keep the overnight rates at the cottages low. That commission had heard from the public that rent for the cottages should be kept affordable to the majority of Californians – the true "owners" of the park. The overnight rents were capped at $179/night. (That was the rate established in 1999 – rental rates are adjusted annually in conformance with the Consumer Price Index.)

This rate cap made operation of the cottages unattractive to most potential concessionaires. However, one of the nonprofit organizations that had formed to help guide the Parks Department's plans for the park was the "Alliance to Rescue Crystal Cove." The Alliance reorganized itself into the Crystal Cove Alliance under the leadership of Laura Davick, Joan Irvine Smith, and Meriam Braselle, and they proposed that they be allowed to operate the cottage rentals under the auspices of their nonprofit corporation.

The Crystal Cove Alliance became an official cooperating association with the Department. However, since the Alliance would also be operating a cottage rental concession (something that cooperating associations are typically not allowed to do), special legislation would be required.

Mike recalls that, at first, he had some concerns about this formal relationship with the Alliance. "It was not your typical cooperating association contract, and we had some concerns about how it would work out. Looking back, however, this partnership was key to the success of the park. We could not have accomplished all the things we did without the outstanding assistance of the Alliance."

Since this relationship would have the result of retaining more funds locally to support the state park, this concept was supported at the State Parks Department. Mike credits not only the three leaders of the Alliance, but the State Parks headquarters staff, in particular Donna Pozzi and John Mott, for having the creativity, foresight, and talent to make this concept a reality.

From the park bond act, $12 million was appropriated, and that got the ball rolling on cottage rehabilitation, bluff stabilization, and construction of a modern sewer system. There have been subsequent phases to the rehabilitation plan, but it was important, for many reasons, to get at least a few cottages open to the public for overnight use. The public had been patient for 20 years waiting for "their" cottages to become available, and State Parks wanted to meet their needs.

The initial appropriation was not sufficient to provide for the rehabilitation of all the cottages. Sixteen cottages are currently available, and several of them are large enough so that more than one overnight space is available in that cottage. A lot of the infrastructure expenditures have been completed, however, and the

Many of the cottages are now available for overnight stays for the public.

Cottages at Crystal Cove that have been renovated.

plan is to continue to work on making the remainder of the cottages available for public use.

The progress on the park infrastructure was key, since it solved the some of the water quality issues with the Regional Water Quality Control Board. The cease and desist order, at least for the historic district, could be lifted.

An agreement with the University of California, Irvine was approved so that this partner could help with research and the operation of the education center. The events center also came on line, and that improved the ability of the park and the Alliance to market the park to new audiences and new park supporters.

Mike now says, "When I look back, I realize how much fun it was. We were doing something really 'out of the box.' There is no place like Crystal Cove anywhere else in California – or anywhere period as far as I know. Community champions, fund-raising events held by partners, auctions by local artists, donors large and small – it seems like everybody pitched in to raise money to help the operation of the cottages."

Mike adds, "Working for State Parks, at least as a district superintendent, can be frustrating at times. And don't get me wrong – the process of getting Crystal Cove on line had more than its share of discouraging moments. But here, you got to see the fruits of your labors. Today you can go to the park and see school kids on a tide pool walk, a group of friends eating at the restaurant, or look up at a cottage on the bluff and see a family relaxing on the patio overlooking the beach. That makes me feel good, and it makes all the effort worthwhile.

"There is another unusual aspect to being a parks professional. When you work for an agency involved in conservation, success can often be measured by a 'lack of progress' – at least in the traditional sense.

That is a hard concept for some to understand. On occasion, some might even view success in parks as 'moving backwards.'

"Let me give you an example. As progress was continuing on getting the cottages in the historic district in operation, the issue with the El Morro trailer park was starting to get intense. This trailer park was part of the state's acquisition at Crystal Cove, so it became part of the state park there.

"There were 70 mobile homes on the small bluff on the west side of the coast highway, right next to the beach, and there were another 200 or so mobile homes on the inland side of the highway. State Parks was the landlord, but again, the goal was to return these lands to the public for whom the state bought this parkland. The residents would have to vacate these homes, and then the trailers would be removed. This is what I mean by 'moving backwards' – a developer or a city planner might see the removal of 270 homes as a step backwards. But at State Parks, we see it as providing valuable recreational opportunities for all Californians to enjoy. These residences were available to only a few people, and our goal was to open up these lands to all visitors."

Unlike the residents of the cottages in the historic district, the occupants of the mobile homes at El Morro still had valid leases – and they had a little time before the leases would terminate. However, the Regional Water Quality Control Board had issued the cease and desist order for the entire park, and that order included these 270 mobile homes. Their sewage was not being treated properly, and there were negative effects on the water quality of that particular area. Mike and his team at State Parks knew that they had to comply with the water board's order. They also knew that getting the residents of 270 beachfront and ocean view mobile homes to vacate their premises would be a tall order.

There was an election at the state level right around the time that the El Morro residents were being notified that they would have to vacate their homes in a reasonable period of time. A new assemblyman was elected for the district that included Crystal Cove State Park, and it immediately became clear to the park staff that one of his highest priorities was to extend the leases of the trailer park residents. The assemblyman introduced legislation that would provide residents with 20-year extensions of their leases.

Mike knew that the state budget included funds for removing the mobile homes, and he had to keep that process moving forward, even as the legislation was introduced to extend the leases. The press, of course, loved this conundrum, and they kept asking Mike what he was going to do about it. As always, Mike was the straight shooter. "State Parks has an approved project with funding behind it," he would say. "We cannot control the legislative process, so we will keep making as much progress as possible in a timely fashion."

The state assembly eventually rejected that legislative bill, and the eviction process continued. Mike felt good about the fact that the Parks Department – mainly through the efforts of Park Superintendents Ken Kramer and Rich Rozelle – was able to donate a lot of those mobile homes to nonprofit organizations and to needy low-income families at other locations. It cost a little extra money, but Mike was always determined to do the right thing.

After the trailers were removed, the process of putting in facilities that served the public began. The Department's plans for the El Morro area included 60 campsites, a day-use parking lot for 200 vehicles, a new lifeguard headquarters facility on the beach side of the coast highway, picnic sites, an interpretive center, and, of course, all the necessary infrastructure – including roads, trails, signs, and restrooms. These are all in place now, and Mike is very happy with the results.

He adds, "It was quite a journey, but it was well worth the effort. We had a lot of challenges to deal with – meetings with the residents who had to give up their sweetheart deals, the cease and desist order, legislative pressure, getting budgets submitted and approved, designing and building one of the few new campgrounds in the state in the past 40 years, rehabilitating a historic district with so many conflicting mandates, leading contentious public meetings, vacating and paying for the unwinding of a huge and binding contract, hundreds of evictions, the California Coastal Commission, the Regional Water Quality Control Board, legal actions, fighting for bond funds, developing a partnership with UC Irvine, and finding a partner to operate the cottage rental concessions – just to name a few.

"It was very satisfying to see the winds of political pressure change over the course of this time period. The local politicians began by trying to help the cause of the residents with their desire to stay in their beach homes. But then the drumbeat of public sentiment kept getting stronger and stronger and louder and louder – the people of that region, as well as the people of California, had paid for this park, and they wanted it opened to the public. The elected officials heard this message and ultimately supported the Department's efforts to provide public access at Crystal Cove."

In his determination to do the right thing during this crucial period in the history of Crystal Cove State Park, Mike demonstrated extraordinary tenacity, along with a spine of steel. All the while, however, he relied upon park staff at many levels to provide him with the data he needed, and to this day credits those staff planners, attorneys, technical specialists, field rangers and lifeguards, and administrators with being the key to the Department's success in turning Crystal Cove from a rather private enclave to a unique and popular public park.

It took the incredible fortitude and integrity of Mike, along with the actions he took (as well as those of his predecessors and successors in the job of superintendent of the State Parks Department's Orange Coast District), to ensure that this gem of a state park would not only be conserved, but available to the people of California for recreation and enjoyment in perpetuity. A key factor leading to this remarkable success story was Mike's unwavering commitment "to support the Department's mission."

The story of how Mike even wound up in this position as superintendent of the Orange Coast District contains many twists and turns. Mike recalls his first rather inauspicious contact with a state park lifeguard supervisor – Jack Roggenbuck – who would have a very positive influence on Mike's career over the span of several decades.

"I was in my early 20s, working at a City of Riverside swimming pool as a lifeguard. At the time, a couple of friends from my water polo team at Riverside City College were working at nearby Lake Perris State

Recreation Area as seasonal guards. I owned a Hobie Cat (a small catamaran sailboat), and on Fridays I would take it out to Lake Perris to sail. One of these friends and I were sailing one day, and as we cruised by the Perris beach, he looked over and said, 'Shoot, there's a rescue going on. They're looking for somebody who just went under. They have a recovery line set up and they have lifeguards doing surface dives looking for the victim. We had better see if we can help.'

"As you can imagine, young lifeguards think they can do just about anything, so I sailed my Hobie right on to Perris beach. We landed near Tower 5 and it seemed like everybody else was surface diving at Tower 4. We asked a state lifeguard what was going on, and he told us a 12-year old African-American boy had just disappeared under the surface of the lake. So my friend and I got right to work surface diving and looking for the boy. Visibility was horrible – only about 24 inches.

"Almost immediately, though, I saw a black arm under the water. I was so excited that I grabbed the arm with a death-grip and kicked as hard as possible to reach the surface and save the life of this boy. I remember thinking, though, that this boy was awfully heavy for a 12-year old.

"It turned out that I had 'rescued' Jack Roggenbuck, the state lifeguard supervisor – I mistook the black wetsuit he was wearing for the arm of the victim! We did not have time to even talk at that point – we just kept on surface diving until dark, when we finally had to give up our search. Jack came back over to talk to me. He was discouraged that we had not found the victim, and we both knew that this search would not have a happy ending.

"However, Jack told me that he admired my initiative, and asked if I would be interested in being a seasonal lifeguard at Lake Perris. The next year I did take the state test for seasonal guards, did well, and got hired on there. I had been a swimmer and water polo player in high school and at Riverside Community College, and really liked being around the water.

"At Lake Perris, I quickly got in tune with everything about lifeguarding for the Department there. I liked the whole atmosphere. It was a new park, with a young enthusiastic staff. This was back in the days when everybody in the field got along – lifeguards, rangers, and maintenance workers. It was like we were one big family – we had potlucks all the time, and just about everybody would show up. It was so fun, and I remember telling myself – hey, this is what I want to do for a career.

"I would talk to Jack, the local lifeguard supervisor, and I would just ask him, 'Who would want to do anything but this?' I loved the park and my job there. I just fell in love with the Parks Department and the idea of making a career out of being a lifeguard. In California, some beaches and lakes have heavy visitation nearly year-round. Once I found out it was possible to have a permanent, full-time civil service appointment as a state park lifeguard, my career path was set!

"A couple of the permanent lifeguards at Lake Perris started mentoring me, and once they realized I was thinking about a lifeguard career, they told me, 'If you are really serious about this, you need to work on the beaches of Southern California. A lot of the culture for the state's lifeguard program is based on the surf, the waves, the swells, rip currents, and reading the water – things you do not find at a man-made lake. Frankly, a lot of those coastal guards do not take our work at the reservoirs very seriously. You really have to work at the beach for a while – if you work there and do a good job, you will be noticed by the lifeguard supervisors who really can make things happen.'

"I worked with Jack on a transfer to Huntington State Beach, but I had to re-test and re-train over there. All my testing and training had been at Lake Perris, and the beach guards wanted to be sure I was capable and trained for ocean guarding. After my first season at Huntington Beach, the state offered the exam for permanent lifeguard. I took the test, came out in the first rank, and was hired as a permanent guard at – you guessed it – Lake Perris!

"I eventually promoted to be the lifeguard supervisor at Lake Perris. After four years in that position, I promoted again – back to the coast, to serve as the chief lifeguard for Huntington State Beach, Bolsa Chica State Beach, and Crystal Cove State Park. I was there three years, took the Lifeguard Supervisor III test, did well on that, and became the aquatic specialist for the southern region in San Diego in 1987.

"Since Southern California provided the vast majority of aquatic programs in the Department, the aquatic specialist at the San Diego office really had statewide responsibilities. I had been serving in that position six years when the Department went through one its major re-organizations. When this 're-org' was finalized, not only had my position been eliminated, the whole concept of regional offices had been vaporized!

"I took several departmental promotions exams so that I could have some options on where I would land when the dust of the reorganization began to settle. Once again, I followed Jack Roggenbuck into a job when he promoted to superintendent of the new and expanded Orange Coast District, and I was able to move into his old position as the visitor services chief for that district. A few years later, Jack retired, and I was promoted into the role of superintendent of the Orange Coast District. It was a terrific job, and I pretty much knew that was the job I would have for the rest of my career.

"It was a wild time for several years following the re-organization. In addition to a lot of people having to change jobs and relocate, the Department started doing business in a whole new way. We adopted a style of Total Quality Management – we called it Park Quality Management – that was in fashion at the time. That meant that we collected a lot of data – data that were then used in our decision-making process. There was also a focus on customer service, the use of teams, and continuous systems improvement.

"But the biggest, best, and most important change was the 'empowerment' of the field staff. Giving decision-making authority, as well as the trust and responsibility that accompanied that authority, to the district superintendent – well, that change was simply huge.

"Empowerment came at a critical time. I was empowered to deal with elected officials, the residents of Crystal Cove, agencies such as the State Coastal Commission and the State Water Resources Control Board, local municipalities, and the media. I became the guy all of those entities went to for decisions – I don't think we would have had as good an outcome at Crystal Cove State Park if things had been handled in the old way. Instead of all the local entities going 'over my head' to a staff person or a manager at State Parks headquarters, they learned that I was the person they needed to go to for advice or a decision. It was kind of overwhelming at first, but then I kind of grew into the role.

"Looking back, it was crazy that the re-organization and all the challenges it provided led me right into the most politically charged issue I had ever dealt with – the whole ball of wax at Crystal Cove. Parks employees throughout the state had all these dangling wires and no wiring plan to figure out how to reconnect them. At Orange Coast District, we were fortunate to have a great staff. We all worked hard, had to be creative, learned that we needed to stow our egos away, and we got through it and made it work. We wound up with an amazing district. Some people say we made Crystal Cove successful despite the re-organization. I have to think we made things better because of that re-org. We were being required to think 'out of the box,' and I think that helped us in the long run.

"We did catechism on the whole park quality management thing – empowerment, the big bucket budget model (Mike laughs that although the budget bucket may have been bigger, it was less full than before), big nails, little nails, blue rules, red rules, and even purple rules. We rebuilt everything, and everything kept working.

"After a few years, I thought I had finally made it through all the hard stuff – getting Crystal Cove State Park online and surviving the statewide re-organization, when another huge issue arose – the proposal to construct a toll road through the heart of parcel 1 at San Onofre State Beach."

Parcel 1 is the inland portion of San Onofre. The Department leases all of San Onofre State Beach from the U. S. Marine Corps at Camp Pendleton. This lease goes back to the Nixon years. The "Western White House," where President Nixon would go to relax in the late '60s and early '70s, overlooked what is now the Trestles area of San Onofre.

Meanwhile, a local agency exists – the Transportation Corridor Agency, or TCA, in Orange County – whose job it is to plan, finance, construct, and operate toll roads in the county. Not surprisingly, when an agency has as its only reason for existence the creation and operation of toll roads, they spend a lot of time, money, and energy trying to build and run toll roads.

As the population of the region has grown, there has been a corresponding increase in traffic on the existing freeways. So the TCA looks at the routes where there is the most congestion and tries to find a way to put in a toll road to help alleviate that congestion. Traffic on Interstate 5 through the communities of San Clemente and San Juan Capistrano has become one of those notoriously congested areas.

In response, the TCA has proposed, for more than 20 years, the construction of a toll road around these two cities, to be routed through the backcountry. Projects like this in California must undergo environmental review, and those in the state's defined "coastal zone" are also required to obtain a permit from the State Coastal Commission.

The California Environmental Quality Act (CEQA) mandates the full consideration of a whole array of options to solve a problem before the project proponent may select the "preferred alternative." In what amounts to less than shocking news, the local TCA, when it was considering alternatives to the construction of a toll road through the backcountry of southern Orange County, decided that widening the existing I-5 freeway or adding carpool lanes was, perhaps, just not as exciting as building an entirely new toll road. After all, where is the fun in making an existing freeway more efficient and effective?

Unfortunately for State Parks, the route of the "preferred alternative" toll road was designed to go right through the heart of Parcel 1 at San Onofre State Beach. The State Parks Department, and parks agencies throughout the United States, face this dilemma over and over. Open space is seen as the path of least resistance for infrastructure projects. Proponents of roads, power lines, gas pipelines, solar and wind farms – you name it – they almost always reckon it is easier to put their project on parkland. No matter the legal protection that the park enjoys, it is seen as an easier pathway to get a project approved through a park than through a housing community or commercial district.

There were a few factors in this proposal that helped the cause of State Parks in resisting it. The new toll road could negatively impact the "Trestles" surf break, widely recognized as a world-class surfing area. The surfing community, led by the Surfrider Foundation, rose up to fight the toll road.

Also, it came to light that the proposed toll road would occupy 300 acres out of an 1100-acre park, not to mention the other effects – noise, runoff, erosion, and pollutants. The Department operates a very popular 157-unit campground right next to the proposed road, and it could be argued that these negative impacts would ruin the camping experience there. All of a sudden, this parcel would not be of state park quality any more – it would be bifurcated by a multi-lane, extremely busy road.

Probably most importantly, Parcel 1 is being leased by State Parks from the U.S. Marine Corps. The Marines have, to date, opposed the TCA's proposal as well. As the landowner, they rightly have a big say in the future of that piece of prime real estate.

Mike thought he had seen a serious public outcry when a major development was proposed at Crystal Cove State Park. He recalls, however, that the public meeting of the California Coastal Commission at which the fate of the toll road through San Onofre State Beach was being voted on was even more controversial. "The coastal commission staff told me that it was the most heavily attended meeting in their 40+ year history," Mike recalls.

The commission had to hold the meeting at a very large room in the Del Mar Fairgrounds in order to accommodate the public who wanted to attend the meeting. Heavyweight players, such as the Natural Resources Defense Council, weighed in against the proposal, and the coastal commission denied the permit request of the TCA at that meeting.

By that time, Mike had decided to retire. "The Orange Coast District was lucky enough to have a terrific set of superintendents along the way. Crystal Cove State Park was purchased when Tom Miller was superintendent in 1979. He made some very smart moves in those days, including paying for the sewer connection in advance. For a while, you had a run of 'water men' in charge. Jack Roggenbuck, Rich Rozelle,

World-class surfing is available at "Trestles."

Ken Kramer, and Brian Ketterer all promoted from the State Parks lifeguard series to become the district superintendent. They all did a tremendous job of protecting the parks and beaches that compose the Orange Coast District."

Mike recently met with the current superintendent – Todd Lewis. Although Todd was never a state park lifeguard, he is a surfer, wave skier, boater, water skier, and has served on the Department's scuba dive team. Mike chuckles, "I guess we could make Todd an honorary lifeguard, since he loves the water and fits right in as superintendent."

Todd expressed his gratitude for the excellent work that Mike and the others mentioned above accomplished in fighting successfully for the integrity of San Onofre State Beach and, in particular, Crystal Cove State Park. Mike, in typical fashion, turned the discussion around.

"Todd, admittedly it was difficult work – Crystal Cove was a monster. But we had the fun job of making the plans for the park. You have a much more difficult task – converting those plans into operational reality.

"The trouble with some of these big environmental issues is that they really never go away. Traffic is still congested on the I-5 through San Clemente, there is still a local Transportation Corridor Agency, and they still want to build a toll road to help alleviate congestion. The freeway has since been widened, but you have to remain vigilant, Todd, and stick to the Department's mission."

Todd added, "You and the other superintendents who had responsibility for Crystal Cove (Miller, Roggenbuck, Kramer, Rozelle, and Ketterer) created what is now viewed as a model of excellence, in many ways, for other units in the State Parks System. That model includes not only the preservation, public access, and public lodging pieces, but also that ground breaking concession/non-profit public private partnership."

Mike responded, "We lucked out, because we had very talented and committed State Parks people and some incredible partners – members of the public who really loved the place. Joan Irvine Smith and her whole family played a huge role in our success there.

"There was only so much that I could do politically from my role as a public servant who works, ultimately, for the governor. Joan was very skilled and adept at the political game, plus she had a good platform to operate from. She knew how to finesse the politicians at all levels of government."

Mike takes a minute to reflect back on his career. "When you think of lifeguards, you usually think of recreation. When you mention the Orange Coast District, most people visualize these iconic Southern California beaches – Huntington, Bolsa Chica, Doheny, San Clemente, and the 'Trestles' at San Onofre.

"But what I am most proud of is the conservation work we accomplished at Crystal Cove State Park. However, it really does tie back in, because by conserving the historical cottages, making the open space available to hikers and bicyclists, building a new campground and picnic area, and ensuring access to the beach there for millions of Californians – it really is recreation. People who visit Crystal Cove are going to fall in love with it, and that means that they will fight to protect the park long after I am gone."

Footnote 1 "El Morro" is the spelling of both trailer parks that used to occupy portions of the south end of Crystal Cove State Park. State Park historians concluded, through their research, that "Moro" is the correct spelling. Since the former spelling was in place when the events in this chapter were unfolding, that spelling is used in the chapter. The Department named its campground that was constructed in the same vicinity "Moro" in order to remain historically accurate.

For more information —

Huell Howser – 1995. Crystal Cove State Park.

Huell interviews the residents of the Crystal Cove cottages while they were trying to remain in the cottages.

https://blogs.chapman.edu/huell-howser-archives/2016/12/07/crystal-cove-visiting-421/

Huell Howser – 2007. San Onofre State Beach.

Huell interviews District Superintendent Rich Rozelle about the potential impacts of the toll road on San Onofre State Beach.

https://blogs.chapman.edu/huell-howser-archives/?s=san+onofre

Steen, Karen E., Laura Davick and Meriam Braselle.

Crystal Cove Cottages – Islands in Time on the California Coast.
2005. Chronicle Books.

GARY STRACHAN

Bird Nerd, Surfer, Hero

Many park people with a degree in wildlife biology or botany would consider promoting into a job as a state park scientist in beautiful Monterey, California, a dream come true. The role of the scientist there – the civil service title at the time was "state park resource ecologist" – was to manage the State Parks Department's effort to protect and restore the natural resources of dozens of parks in the state's Central Coast. These included such gems as Point Lobos, Pfeiffer-Big Sur, Julia Pfeiffer Burns, Big Basin, and Año Nuevo State Parks – truly some of the state's crown jewels. Gary Strachan, however, calls accepting this promotion

Gary and Resource Ecologist Gary Fregien discuss the advantages and disadvantages of being a field ranger. *All photos courtesy of Gary Strachan.*

"potentially, the biggest mistake of my life. It did not take long for me to make the correction and demote back to a ranger position."

In the 1970s, park managers and scientists had begun to question the Department's laissez-faire approach to the oversight of natural resources. State Parks leaders recognized the importance of scientifically and actively managing the Department's vast array of priceless natural resources, instead of "allowing nature to take its course." Of course, the administration of these programs requires staffing and funding. An effort was initiated to populate the regional state park offices with these scientists. The exam was offered for state park resource ecologist, and Gary, based on his education and experience in wildlife biology, easily qualified for and passed the exam. A job opened up in the Monterey office, and he was selected to fill that vacancy.

Although Gary was good at this ecologist work, he chafed at the constraints he was now living and working under. He'd come from being a ranger in a remote park at the Gold Bluffs Beach unit of Prairie Creek Redwoods State Park, in Northern California – miles away from any office. This remoteness required that his supervisors trust him to act independently and to make good decisions. After five years there, he heeded the advice of many colleagues and opted to take a position as a full-time natural resources manager.

However, instead of residing in a rustic house in the redwoods, or on a remote and beautiful beach, he and his family were now living in the semi-urban and expensive community of Monterey. Although the move to resource ecologist was a promotion, Gary's personal happiness has never been measured by a big salary or by moving up the career ladder.

"I was ripped out, by my own choosing, of something that I love – living, working, and recreating at the beach, in the redwoods, and being a 'hands-on' manager of resources and visitors. I could see where I could have an effect in protecting natural resources in this new ecologist position, but you have to realize – I had wanted to be a park ranger since the age of 12. In my new job as an ecologist, I enjoyed working at the many beautiful parks in the Central Coast, and I still got a kick out of teaching resource management to the ranger trainees. But I really missed the camaraderie of being in the parks with other staff, along with the ability to mingle with, educate, and inspire park visitors.

"Being a resource ecologist involved a whole lot more paperwork. As a ranger, you always feel like you are getting something done – giving a nature walk, performing first aid or CPR, and taking care of visitor incidents, both large and small. In my ecologist office, it seemed like I spent a lot of time moving a big pile of paper from the in-basket over to the out-basket all day long. And an eight-to-five job with weekends off did not fit well with my desire to be in the ocean on a frequent basis. When I did get to the beach, all the good surf spots were already too crowded. If you are a ranger, on the other hand, your regular days off, typically, are weekdays, when there is nobody else on 'your' wave.

"After I had been in Monterey for a couple of years, a 'supervising ranger' job came open at Año Nuevo State Park – north of Santa Cruz and right on the water. In fact, there is also a small island just offshore – Año Nuevo Island. Living and working there appealed to me in many ways – the surfing and kitesurfing, the birding, the elephant seal ecology, the big ol' farmhouse we would live in, and the ability to be the manager of

Park residence, circa 1986.

this splendid and diverse park. I thought this job would be a really good fit for my family and me.

"So one day I got up the nerve and went into the regional director's office and told him I really wanted that job at Año Nuevo. Dick Felty, then the regional director, stared at me for what seemed like two full minutes, then chuckled and said, 'Are you sure? You are probably not aware that there are currently three huge problems at that park, and the park supervisor will be expected to make all of those problems go away.'

"I did not get up and immediately walk out, so Felty continued, 'First, I want you to stop the war between the park staff and the surfers there – it's like a war zone. The damned surfers think THEY are running the park.'

"'Then I want you to get the University of California under control. The professors and students from nearby UC Santa Cruz, who are doing research on the northern elephant seals at the park, have been led to believe that they are the sole academic group there. So, they have come to believe that THEY are running the park.'

"'Finally, the Año Nuevo Interpretive Association (ANIA – although Gary has conjured up other, shall we say, more colorful and descriptive four-letter acronyms) is the local natural history association. They were created to support the park, but have now been led to believe that they have free rein in spending money – funds they made at the park – on projects that often are of no value to us. They have been allowed, even encouraged, to set their own priorities and ignore the park's priorities. They have moved into park buildings and are ordering around park employees. They refuse to listen to our requests or opinions. They think that THEY are running the park. Actually, now that I think about it, THEY ARE running the park! The previous park management failed to deal with these problems, then retired, and left us with a huge mess.'

"I told Felty why I thought I would be a good fit for this job. First, I was a surfer, so I could talk their talk and walk their, well, walk. Next, I had a background in wildlife biology, and this would be very useful for the interface required with the scientific researchers at the park. And finally, I knew I could outmaneuver the natural history association. If that didn't work, I could just go about becoming their worst nightmare, and they would eventually choose to go away of their own volition."

Gary has never been accused of being a weak leader, so he was selected to relocate to Año Nuevo State Park and work on these difficult issues. Although technically it was a demotion, Gary could not have been more thrilled with the move. He knew he would love the work, and he was excited that his family would be in a much better situation. The presence of excellent surf nearby was also extremely exciting to him.

This part of the beautiful coastline between San Francisco and Santa Cruz includes a renowned surf break at

Año Nuevo Island in the background; elephant seals hauled out in the dunes.

nearby Waddell Creek. Año Nuevo is also famous for its population of northern elephant seals. Every year, females give birth to pups, and at some point those seal pups are going to have to enter the ocean – their natural habitat. This annual phenomenon has not gone unnoticed by the seals' least favorite predator – the great white shark. So surfing an area infested by hungry, fanged predators certainly has risks.

When I mention this to Gary, he just smiles and shrugs. "When I recall fighting with angry surfers, arguing with smug scientists, and ousting arrogant natural history association board members – well, them 'fangy thangs' just did not seem so threatening."

The relationship with the local surfers was very strained at that time. The park staff favored the idea of banning surfing within the park. Their reasoning was that surfing was harmful to the elephant seals' reproductive behavior. Also, the surfers were causing other problems – they would let their dogs run free, camp illegally, build fires, and leave trash behind. Gary was the right guy to work with this user group – he was an excellent surfer and communicator, and he stood a good chance of improving the relationship between the surf crowd and the park staff. He understood the often-rebellious members of the surf subculture like no non-surfer ever could.

The University of California at Santa Cruz had set up a major strategy for conducting research on the northern elephant seals at the park. As with many programs, if a partner agency is not managed properly, things can get out of control. And that is what had happened at Año Nuevo. The professors and the students had developed this feeling that they were running an exclusive research program – and they were actively keeping other academic entities and organizations from performing any research in the park. The position of State Parks was that the Parks Department, through its local staff, was in charge, and that the requests and activities of the university researchers were subject to review and approval by the park supervisor. Not surprisingly, the researchers at UC Santa Cruz did not support this entirely appropriate and reasonable approach.

Gary'a mates captured him surfing with a bird.

The other, even more difficult issue at the park was the relationship with the Año Nuevo Interpretive Association. The staff and the board of directors of the association believed that they had been, based on the overt encouragement of previous state park management, empowered to run the park. These were the very early years of the partnerships between local interpretive associations and State Parks, and many issues that needed resolution were beginning to bubble to the surface.

The groundbreaking progress that Gary really set out to accomplish was to re-define and re-shape the relationship with the natural history association. Nature abhors a vacuum, and there was a dearth of strong leadership at the park before Gary arrived there. Quite naturally, ANIA moved to fill that vacuum. And, because the association supported the park volunteer program financially, their board members came to believe that they should direct the activities of the park volunteers and, in general, run the volunteer program.

Gary had a number of secret weapons at his disposal. At first, few knew that Año Nuevo was one of Gary's favorite surfing spots when he was growing up in the Santa Cruz area in the mid-'60s. He had often camped at Año Nuevo Point or on one of the nearby beaches, occasionally in a driftwood shack. He would pay the Steele family – they had owned and farmed the property and built all the historic buildings before it became a state park – a dollar to spend the night on the beach. Gary knew this territory like the back of his hand.

Gary did not hesitate to tackle all these issues – surfers, elephant seal research, and ANIA – together. The UC scientists were in agreement with the park staff – they also want surfing banned from the park. Reasonably, Gary wanted to know more about what the surfers were actually doing that was creating these negative impacts.

The scientists said that one of the primary activities they had issue with was the dogs that surfers would bring with them and leave loose to run on the beach, while the surfers were in the water, far from their dogs. The beach and nearby dunes were exactly where the elephant seals would "haul out" of the ocean to rest, mate, and reproduce. Naturally, the dogs were curious about these strange marine mammals – they would innocently hassle the seals and affect the bacular ministrations of the alpha males.

Although surfers were causing these problems, Gary concluded that surfing was not the impactful activity – it was the dogs, camping, litter, and fires that the surfers brought with them. As a surfer, he knew that those four activities were not necessities for the surfers. Gary also knew that the rumors of potential eviction from the park had reached the surfers, and they had responded with acts of vandalism in the park. So he set out to fix the problem.

Gary met with the surfers and laid out his plan – he would allow the surfing to continue, but he needed the cooperation of the surfers on their associated activities. He told them he was going to come down hard on loose dogs on the beach, littering, illegal camping, and campfires. Of course, some of the surfers thought they were giving up too much in this deal. But cooler heads prevailed, and Gary was able to convince them that, under this possible scenario, they could continue surfing in the park if their associated deleterious activities were eliminated. In short, if they wanted to keep surfing at Año Nuevo, the surfers would have to clean up their act.

It never does any good to reach a deal and then not follow through. Gary and his staff patrolled the beach and, through an approach of educating the surfers and issuing citations to those who did not want to be educated, began to see improvements.

Gary was also able to take this agreement to the UC researchers as proof that he was "the new sheriff in town." These issues with surfers had been festering for years. Although the scientists had lodged dozens of complaints, local management had totally ignored the situation. Gary was able to gain compliance from the surfers in a remarkably short time. Needless to say, the folks at UC were both impressed and a little bit nervous. To them, the good news was that some of the surfers' activities that were harmful to elephant seals had been curtailed. The bad news was that they knew they were probably next on Gary's "to-do" list.

Getting the UC scientists into compliance with park policies was not really too difficult. The researchers needed the park, because, um, that was where the elephant seals were. The park needed the researchers, because protection and management of natural resources is a key part of the Parks Department's mission. And the researchers were best able to inform the park staff, on not only the ecology of the elephant seals, but on recommended management actions – actions that only the park staff could take – in order to sustain and grow this pinniped population in a healthy condition.

At a meeting that included Gary and the researchers, they easily and quickly agreed on the joint management goals of protecting this population and educating the public about the elephant seals. Of course, this visitor education had to be done in a manner that did not threaten the seals. Gary was able to articulate protocols and procedures that would ensure the success of the program. The only issue became whether the UC scientists would be able to adhere to this program.

Change is often difficult. The researchers had enjoyed pretty much free rein for many years – they had received little oversight from the park staff. Now they attempted to bypass State Parks and went to a state assembly person – seeking their help in providing UC Santa Cruz with exclusive research rights at Año Nuevo State Park. The Parks Department had anticipated this maneuver, however, and had already given the assembly member a heads up.

When Gary next met with the UC researchers and explained that the program he was initiating would meet the goals of all parties, the scientists readily agreed to hold up their end of the bargain – they had already heard back from their local elected official. Gary's changes would involve more paperwork for the UC folks, but at the same time they would be encouraged to continue their vital work on the northern elephant seals.

Then Gary faced his biggest challenge – getting the ANIA back into compliance with Departmental policies, procedures, and protocols. The disparity between how the association was operating in the park and how the program was designed to work was becoming a real problem for the park staff and for the Parks Department in general.

The association, however, was not the only entity at fault. The former park management had allowed them to take liberties, and the problem kept growing larger. And ANIA was not alone among its peers – the same factors that allowed this problem to develop at Año Nuevo were at work in other parks, too.

The problems at this park were really a harbinger of troubles throughout the Department, and Gary's work was the first time these issues had really been addressed in a major and direct manner. The fact that a park supervisor was given the responsibility for dealing with an emerging statewide problem speaks volumes for Gary's abilities, as well as for the high regard State Parks managers had for him.

In order to understand this issue, it is necessary to be aware of the history of these relationships. In the early '70s, the idea of creating natural history associations to assist a local state park really started getting traction. Based on the model initiated in the National Park Service, local park supporters and park staff would typically get together and decide to start their own natural history association. The paperwork would be prepared to form a nonprofit corporation, which would be submitted to the IRS for approval. A governing board would be elected, and the association would be up and running.

One of the main goals initially was the ability to purchase equipment and materials for the park staff to use, mainly in interpretive programs. The park budget for interpretation was, and remains, pretty skimpy. Rangers really wanted to improve their ability to inspire park visitors, so the natural history association model appealed to park staff, park volunteers, and park visitors.

In most cases, the model would be to have the natural history association sell books, maps, and other interpretive materials out of a visitor center, or even a park entrance station, to generate revenues. For example, a park visitor would buy a map, the association would book the profit, and its board of directors would approve how to spend the income for the benefit of the park.

In the beginning, nearly everything would be run by park volunteers, with some assistance from park staff. Often, their bank would literally be a shoebox or something similar. A common purchase in the early years of these associations was a slide projector, a good camera, a pair of binoculars, or slide film. With these items, the local park ranger could readily develop a decent slide show for an evening campfire program or a nature walk.

One of the problems at the inception of these relationships was that the board often included park staff – sometimes even the park supervisor. Of course, if the park employee made a request for funding for one of their priorities during a board meeting, it was pretty automatic that those requests would be granted. At some point, everyone agreed that the relationship needed to be a little more "hands-off," and now park employees are not permitted to serve on the association boards.

As these support organizations grew, they became more sophisticated and wealthier. Instead of funding a slide projector, boards started to think bigger – why not build an entire visitor center? The lines kept getting fuzzier on what the association could and should fund.

Then, at some point, many boards would raise the question of whether it made more sense to hire an executive director, rather than continue with volunteers doing everything. Of course, hiring paid staff is a big and expensive step, and funding a staff takes away capital that could be directly spent on park priorities. It is a tough decision. It can be argued that a talented executive director would be able to develop relationships with donors, write grants, and manage their board – and all these could greatly enhance the ability of the association to directly assist the park.

In some cases, however, hiring a paid staff and strengthening the financial position of the association led to significant problems. Suddenly, the association might start believing it was independent of the park, or even more important than the park. Controlling the funds created a sense of power on the part of the nonprofit. Another new issue that arose was the management of the park volunteers and their programs.

Ask any park supervisor, and they will usually rave about the park's volunteers. These people are the backbone of the customer service that parks provide to their visitors. And, in the nearby communities, they are advocates for local state parks. As staffs have shrunk in the past few decades, volunteers have been asked to accept greater workloads. They work in the visitor centers, give nature walks, keep an eye on valuable park assets such as archeological sites, assist with resource management projects, and perform a large share of campground management tasks. Our state parks would truly be poorer places without these terrific park ambassadors.

One major responsibility that natural history associations are usually asked to assume is the support of the park volunteers. The association provides funding for volunteers and their programs, helps to train them, and hosts volunteer appreciation events. This relationship usually works very well. The problem arises when either the association or the volunteers themselves fail to understand that the volunteers officially work for the state. Park volunteers are state employees, even though they are not compensated financially for their work. They do receive workers' compensation benefits, along with other perks, as unpaid staff.

Because of the financial support of the association, however, some of the volunteers believe they are working for that entity rather than for the park. The park staff has always had to be careful to ensure that the volunteers know and remember that their supervisor is a state park employee.

Almost inevitably, all the problems that could happen with an association did happen at Año Nuevo State Park. The association believed it was so independent that park priorities were being ignored. The volunteers were made to feel allegiance to the association, not the state park. The association took over all the nicest historical ranch buildings at the state park, so that the rangers were forced to work in tiny, out-of-the-way offices. The association was selling items in the park visitor center that the park did not feel were appropriate. As Regional Director Felty had stated, "THEY ARE running the park!"

Gary truly had his work cut out for him with this situation. The association had the money, the allegiance of many of the volunteers, and momentum – no one had ever tried to slow down their march into areas that were beyond their scope. Gary's attempts to gain legal compliance on the part of the association were snubbed. When he tried to get his priorities funded, he was ignored. The idea of a meeting with the association to attempt to agree on common ground was anathema to the board members. Gary was left with few options.

After several years of wrangling, Gary had to oust the association from the park. They were not allowed to occupy state park buildings, and they were not permitted to sell materials on state park property. Of course, this caused upheaval in the community, among the park volunteers, and in the press. However, Gary was doing the right thing and had the backing of State Parks management. The association eventually went out of business, and a new, more cooperative association – the San Mateo Coast Natural History Association – was established to assist the park.

So, what was the path that led Gary to be a "person of place" at Año Nuevo State Park?

He gives his mother a lot of credit for his interest in the natural world and in parks. "Mom was a naturalist in Santa Cruz, where I grew up. I wrote a two-page paper in pencil when I was 12 years old. My mom kept it, and it says that I really wanted to become a ranger. It's a trip!

"My family came to Santa Cruz County in 1858. They built a beautiful wooden house in the Santa Cruz Mountains near Zayante Creek, and Mom was born in that house in 1920. Then I came along in 1950, and all I wanted to do was have fun in the redwoods or down at the beach.

"My mom taught me about birds – all about birds. She knew the name of every species, as well as its call. She taught me how to use an old pair of binoculars, and I spent hours learning the birds of the redwood forests and the local beaches.

"After high school, I went on a surfing safari to Mexico with some friends. We were surfing the beaches of the western coast of mainland Mexico, and I was also birding at San Blas – just north of Puerto Vallarta. When we returned to the States, I picked up a newspaper and it listed all the numbers of that year's military draft lottery. It was a 'torpedo' to my existence at the time. I don't remember my exact draft number, but it was somewhere between the numbers one and three! So, I knew I was going to be drafted, especially since I was not in college at that time and did not have a student deferment.

"Then I went surfing in Hawaii – long enough for that state to become my official state of residence. I received a notice to report to Fort DeRussy (Gary calls it Fort Watusi) in Oahu for my draft physical. There were 30 young guys who showed up for the physical – out of those 30, there were 28 Tongans, Hawaiians, and Fijians, all of whom said they wanted to go into the service and kill the Viet Cong. There were two skinny white guys, and I was one of those. I was pretty sure I really did not want to kill anyone. Anyway, I don't know if it was the 'surfer's knobs' or what, but the doctor informed me that I flunked my draft physical because of bad knees.

"I spent another year or so surfing and birding, then I decided to get serious – yeah right – and I wound up going to Humboldt State. I met my beautiful life partner Terry there, and we got married in '74. I earned my bachelor's in wildlife biology in 1975. All that time I worked seasonally for State Parks. I really had a passion for ornithology (he calls it the study of ornies), and kept spending as much time as possible learning new birds and bird calls. I became a real 'bird nerd.'

"The Parks Department hired a lot of ranger trainees in the mid-'70s, so I guess my timing was good in that respect. Like everyone in those days, I spent a year in training, and then my first permanent assignment was at Gold Bluffs Beach – a remote beach that was a part of Prairie Creek Redwoods State Park. Terry and I just kept growing closer – she is the best thing that ever happened to me. We had two children – Morgan and Kelly – and we all lived together in this remote park for the next five years. We had elk, bear, and mountain lions in our backyard all the time. It still seems like such an amazing time at an extraordinary park."

Gary was the only ranger at this beach, which stretched for 12 miles. One ranger for 12 miles of beach does not sound like a very good level of staffing. However, it is remote and the weather can be wet and cold a lot of the time, so visitation is light for most of the year. When people do make it to the beach, however, they can get into trouble in the water in very short order.

Gary flourished there. He is what's known as a "waterman." He loves being in the ocean, whether it is surfing, kayaking, free diving for abalone, swimming, or kitesurfing. He is an expert at reading the water, and is always up-to-date on the tide charts, fish runs, and marine mammal behaviors.

He also knows that the ocean harbors inherent risks. Besides the cold temperatures, riptides, and "sleeper waves," the waters of California are also habitat for the feared great white shark. When asked about surfing or kitesurfing in waters favored by these top-tier predators, Gary says with an infectious grin, "It's like driving a car on the highway. If it is your day to die, that car next to you or that shark underneath you can cause some serious, even fatal, damage. You cannot live your life without taking risks – it is part of the beauty and richness of our existence here on Planet Earth. I have a wife and family I love, and I am not going to do anything stupid. Well, okay, nothing REALLY stupid!"

It was an ideal assignment for young Ranger Strachan – family, redwoods, birds, the ocean, surf, and little close supervision. The beach was remote, so Gary had to learn to be a self-sufficient ranger quickly.

It was in 1980 that Gary performed the rescue for which he was awarded the Governor's Medal of Valor for saving the lives of three swimmers. Paraphrasing that citation:

"Ranger Strachan risked his own safety and life in saving the lives of swimmers caught in a riptide off Gold Bluffs Beach at Prairie Creek Redwoods State Park on May 16, 1980. While on routine patrol, Strachan received an emergency call and was directed to respond to an emergency situation at Gold Bluffs Beach. Upon his arrival at the beach, he observed two men struggling in the waves. One man was approximately 100 meters off shore, and the other was much further out. The water temperature of the ocean was 43 degrees, and waves six to seven feet high accompanied a strong riptide that was carrying the two swimmers out to sea.

"Strachan radioed for back-up help and quickly removed his boots, peace officer protective equipment, and clothes. His wife, at their nearby state house, heard his call on the park radio. She ran to tell the park's maintenance worker, who grabbed a longboard and headed to Strachan's location on the beach. In his underwear, Ranger Strachan entered the frigid water, swam to the victim farthest from shore, and tried unsuccessfully for several minutes to bring the cold and exhausted swimmer closer to shore. Anxiously looking toward the beach, Strachan noticed that the second swimmer had somehow been swept safely ashore, and a bystander was entering the surf with the longboard to provide assistance to Strachan and the swimmer. The bystander was not a surfer, and he was soon in trouble in the waves as well.

"Ranger Strachan (a very accomplished surfer and a strong swimmer) left the first troubled swimmer, retrieved the surfboard, and instructed the second swimmer to cling to a floating crab pot. Now cold and exhausted himself in the very cold and rough water, Strachan returned to the first swimmer. Using the surfboard as flotation, he was able to push the first swimmer to the beach. With all the remaining strength he could gather, Strachan then returned to the second man and brought him through the treacherous riptide and waves safely to shore."

At the awards ceremony, State Assembly Speaker Willie Brown presented Gary with his well-deserved Medal of Valor.

I first met Gary when I was the duty-ranger at Refugio State Beach, near Santa Barbara, in late 1980, while he was still working at Gold Bluffs Beach. It was just after his heroic rescue of the swimmers.

Gary drove up to the park entrance station wearing faded jeans and a well worn aloha shirt, with a surfboard strapped onto the roof rack of his beater truck. I did not take him, let us say, for a Northern Californian. Gary did not know me, so of course he immediately started giving me a bunch of grief over local park policies and asking me a lot of technical questions about the surfing conditions that day. All the while, he had this huge grin. It was that smile that gave him away. "Nobody who seems as upset as this guy," I thought to myself, "would be grinning like this."

When I called Gary on his act, he stomped on the accelerator, pulled over into the parking lot, and hopped out. Tall and lean with a sparkle in his eye, he kept talking to me but I could see that he was keeping one eye on the waves. I started giving him back some sass on whether he could handle the monster two-foot waves that day. He started guffawing, and we hit it off right away.

When I met him at Refugio, I had just been asked to teach a class at Asilomar on natural resource management. I accepted, and also asked if I could team-teach the 16-hour class. I did not have a co-teacher in mind at that point, but the prospect of standing in front of 30 trainees for two solid days seemed overwhelming. Gary and I corresponded over the next few months, and he agreed to help me teach the class. We turned out to be a good team – we were both just crazy enough to keep the students awake most of the time – okay, some of the time.

Gary spent another couple of years in Northern California redwood country – living the good life – before he made the Big Mistake and promoted to Monterey. One nice thing about working in the regional and headquarters offices was that, if you were talented, you quickly came to the attention of the regional director and their staff. Regional Director Felty saw that Gary was a terrific parks employee on many levels and could succeed in any number of assignments. So when Gary asked Dick Felty if he could demote and become the park supervisor at Año Nuevo, Felty made it happen. Gary was the right guy to handle all those touchy issues. He and his family also became embedded in the local community, and the locals soon grew to respect him as an outstanding ambassador for the park.

After Gary had improved the status with the surfers and the UC researchers at the park, and had helped ANIA decide to go away, there was still a lot of work to do. A natural history association can be a terrific ally for a state park, if the relationship is healthy – when both entities benefit from the cooperative partnership.

Gary soon recruited and helped to establish a new nonprofit group – the San Mateo Coast Natural History Association. One of the benefits of this new outfit was that it was designed to help all the local state parks and beaches – not solely Año Nuevo. He was able to get this association up and running, and he helped guide their early years so that the roles of each partner were clear. He is quick to credit this association, and the hundreds of park volunteers, with the incredible work they do to help the park. "Thousands of park visitors have benefited from the dedication of our volunteers and the support of the natural history association," he says.

Although Gary spent a lot of time and energy on the three major issues in his first few years at Año Nuevo, he still needed to manage the normal workload of a park supervisor. Facilities were in poor condition, the number of visitors coming to see the northern elephant seals was increasing rapidly, and there was always the constant inherent tension between protecting the park's natural resources and the public's desire for recreation.

As Gary recalls, "When I came back as the park supervisor in 1985, I perceived the Dickerman Barn – which was then serving as the park's visitor center – as a good example of 'Santa Cruz Rustic.' Only half the building could handle visitors, because the floors and walls were rotting away. The south wall was basically open to the elements – wind and rain came in freely. The staff was divided on its opinion on which disaster would happen first – either the barn would blow down in a strong wind, or it would burn down in a fire caused by the jury-rigged electrical system.

The Dickerman barn in 1985 before it was restored as the park's visitor center.

"Despite the barn's decaying condition, however, the park staff was determined to ensure that park visitors fulfilled their desire to see the elephant seals in their natural habitat. It was kind of funny – on a rainy day, visitors would enter the barn and take off their raincoats. It was not long before they put their raincoats back on – the weather conditions often seemed worse inside than outside!

"As the number of visitors increased, the amount of media attention grew as well. All the positive attention now being paid to Año Nuevo gave us the confidence to ask for financial help. Local State Senator Becky Morgan secured funding for us – we were able to upgrade the Dickerman Barn into a safer and more welcoming visitor center, while we maintained the historical integrity and 'fabric' of the barn.

"We also had award-winning restrooms available to the public – unfortunately, the award was for the stinkiest and most dilapidated restrooms on the coast! The ranger office, the visitor parking lot, the office for docents, the shack where visitors would 'stage' to begin their guided tour, and the entrance station kiosk – all these were in horrible condition. To call these our buildings 'shacks' would be an insult to real shacks.

"We just kept after it – eventually all these abominations were replaced and relocated. The old parking lot was even converted back to native habitat. All these things take a while. I think that is one advantage to having staff that sticks around for a while – not only is there 'corporate memory,' but there is also 'corporate momentum.'

"My favorite deferred maintenance project, though, was the park's 'equal access trail.' State Parks, over the years, has been attempting to provide access to its facilities and programs to persons with disabilities. This was a statewide endeavor, and was not limited just to this park. At Año Nuevo, the previous management had accepted the donation of a 3,000-foot long, rubbery conveyor belt. It was emplaced to wind up and down,

Son Morgan with an 18-foot great white shark at Cascade Beach. "Dad, could you please teach me to surf out in that shark soup? Please, Dad, please!"

over the dunes. It was okay when it was dry. On the other hand, when it was raining, no one could walk on it safely, and getting a wheelchair going up even the slightest rise required serious effort. The conveyor belt was very popular, however, with the seals – they loved to slide on it when it was wet. It was hilarious to watch.

"We enlisted the assistance of a volunteers group – the Telephone Pioneers – and they built a fantastic wooden boardwalk. They joked that building the new boardwalk was a lot easier than removing that funky old conveyor belt."

Meanwhile, Gary maintained his passion for surfing, while he added kitesurfing to his skill set. One day, not long after he moved back to Año Nuevo from Monterey, an 18-foot long, dead great white shark washed up on Cascade Beach. Gary, naturally, took his family down to the beach to take a look. Despite the fear that these predators inspire in most people, Gary taught both his children to become excellent surfers and kitesurfers in the local waters.

About 20 years after his move to Año Nuevo State Park, my wife and I visited Gary and his family at his park residence, situated on the coastal terrace. This idyllic 19th century farmhouse is just beautiful, and has a terrific view of the beach, bluffs, and Año Nuevo Island itself. On the top story of the old wooden farmhouse, Gary had set up an observation post – ostensibly to observe human activity, birds, and seals – but he could also check out the surf conditions.

Gary took us on a tour of the dunes where the seals were hauled out. It quickly became obvious that his

Gary became an expert on elephant seal ecology and behavior.

knowledge of the natural and cultural history of the park is profound. The history of the buildings, the call of every bird, the story of the island, and even the geomorphology that shapes the surfing waves – these were all part of our lesson plan for the day. Amazing, too, was Gary's expertise on the ecology and hierarchy of the elephant seals.

For example, we were observing a mixed group of about 20 males and females of varying ages. One of the younger, non-dominant males raised his head, vocalized loudly, and Gary instantly said, "Now keep your eye on that alpha male over there – he is going to show the young dude who is boss." Sure enough, the largest male raised his head and stared at the challenger. The younger male quieted down and pretended it was all a misunderstanding. Gary told us that if the challenger had not backed down, there would have been a physical battle between the two, with little doubt about who would be victorious.

Before dinner, Gary asked me if we liked fresh artichokes. Now, this region of California is renowned as the artichoke capital of the world, so we knew we would never get fresher or better artichokes than these. My wife and I said, "Sure," but Gary replied, "Well, we don't have any right now. However, the artichoke farmer right next door is a good friend of mine and he lets me pick as many as I want from his field." Wearing a big smile, Gary grabbed a sack, and the two of us started walking towards the artichoke farm.

We were walking through a small grove of eucalyptus that separated the state park from the adjoining private farm and began eyeballing the best-looking 'chokes. Suddenly Gary appeared to be startled and stage whispered, "Get down!" while he crouched behind a large artichoke plant. He put his index finger to his lips and stayed as low and quiet as possible. We waited quietly and anxiously for a few minutes, and then Gary poked his head up over the artichoke. He looked around, then harvested about eight of the best ones, and we scampered back to his house.

I had to ask the obvious question, "Do you or do you not have permission to take that guy's artichokes?" Gary just grinned while we hustled back to his home. He finally replied, "Well, I do have permission, but I think the artichokes taste so much better if I think I pilfered them!" To this day, I have no idea of the real answer to that question, but I do recall that they were the best artichokes I had ever eaten.

These are just a few sides of Gary. One day he would risk his life to save three swimmers who had no business being in the ocean. The next day he would be surfing the waves of central California, Costa Rica, or Baja California with his mates – "I have pretty much surfed without a long break since 1964." Gary strongly believes that surfing and kitesurfing have helped to keep him healthy. As he says, "It just goes to show – you gotta milk every day!"

On another day, as an expert birder, he would be assisting the U.S. Fish and Wildlife Service by doing bird surveys at Kilauea Point on the island of Kauai. The next day he would be teaching a class on resource management at the Parks Department's Mott Training Center at Asilomar. And yet another day, as a recognized expert on the northern elephant seal, he would be leading a group of scientists on a field trip at Año Nuevo State Park. And some of the best days were, and still remain, when he and his family all hang out together and surf along the Central California or Baja California coast.

Gary owned a 1950 Chevy fastback while stationed at Año Nuevo. He nicknamed it "Murrelet," after the marbled murrelet – a local, endangered bird species. He was a major part of the effort to discover its nesting habits and to implement its recovery plan. Gary recalls that, often, he would slap a magnetic State Parks logo on the side of Murrelet, and then he would patrol the park in her, giving out "living history" information.

Retired now, Gary and his wife live six months in Southern Baja and six months in the Santa Cruz Mountains. Adhering to the "you only do this once" theme, he is still surfing, kitesurfing, birding, volunteering at Año Nuevo State Park, and giving presentations on the "History of Protecting the California Coast."

Gary's zany humor, his incredibly deep knowledge base of the region, his ability to connect with visitors, and his passion for conserving parks – all these attributes made him an extraordinary, unique, dedicated, articulate ranger, and an amazing person.

For more information —

Huell Howser – 2003. Huell tours Año Nuevo State Park with Ranger Kevin Williams. https://blogs.chapman.edu/huell-howser-archives/2003/12/31/californias-golden-parks-111-año-nuevo/

MIKE LYNCH

◆

The Sultan of Swag – One Very Busy Chap!

In reflection, it is difficult to believe that Mike Lynch, one of the most articulate and ardent supporters – ever – of the rights of California's state park rangers, permitted an egregious error on the part of the Department of Parks and Recreation to slide by without a protest. Looking back, Mike now says, "Had I known then what I know now, or even what I knew five years after this screw-up, I would have fought as hard as possible to correct it. And I would have won."

This SNAFU could have cost Mike his chance at becoming a state park ranger. State Parks, and the profession of park ranger, throughout the world, would have been much poorer places for that loss of a

Foot patrol at Jack London State Historic Park. *All photos and images courtesy of Mike Lynch.*

ranger, author, historian, collector and producer of memorabilia, teacher, event coordinator, union activist, park superintendent, organizer, officer of nonprofit organizations, advocate for assisting rangers in other nations, and warrior for the improvement of his chosen profession and life's work. The creativity, dedication, and personal drive of Mike Lynch, combined with his ability to "think outside the box," have been, and will continue to be, very difficult to recreate.

In 1973, Mike was working as a seasonal ranger (State Park Ranger, Permanent Intermittent – or PI Ranger) in a State Parks district just north of San Francisco. He was filling in mainly for full-time rangers who were on their days off or on vacation. His degree in anthropology from Sonoma State University served him well, since he really enjoyed giving talks on the history and prehistory of the local region. For many young men and women, seasonal park work was a stepping-stone to becoming a permanent, full-time ranger, and for Mike, that was the case as well.

At the time, the Department was offering entrance exams for state park ranger trainee. Personnel Board rules provided eight additional exam points for PI Rangers. With 99 points as the highest possible score, eight additional points was significant. Along with his PI experience, devotion, and evident passion for ranger work, Mike came out at the top of the hiring list. His district superintendent at the time, Dick Menefee, liked the prospect of Mike becoming a state park ranger, and was making sure that the hiring process was being handled properly.

When the time came to select and hire a class of ranger trainees, Dick called Mike and asked if he had been scheduled for a final interview. When Mike said that he had not received a call, Menefee called up the personnel staff responsible for administering the exam and asked what was going on. Personnel told Menefee they would correct the oversight, and Menefee told Lynch to expect a call that same day. He also told Mike to be ready to go to San Francisco for his final interview the following day.

Still, nothing happened. The following Monday morning, Menefee called Mike to ask how his interview had gone, and was shocked when Mike told him he had never received any word from the personnel staff.

Menefee again called the exam administrators to express his dismay. It turns out there was another candidate named Mike Lynch much farther down on the hiring list. This Mike Lynch was living in Los Angeles, and he immediately flew up to San Francisco to take the interview. It was not until he walked into the interview room that the other Mike Lynch was told of the Department's mistake, and that he could not be interviewed.

At this point, the Department had finalized the hiring list and made commitments to all the candidates that would compose this class of ranger trainees. Personnel admitted their responsibility for the error to the district superintendent, and made the commitment to hire Mike in the very next ranger trainee class. Menefee told Mike that he could protest the Department's action if he wanted to, but Mike accepted the Department's promise to make things right in the near future.

That "near future" turned out to be nine months, but Mike did get hired full-time in the end. Now, however, Mike says, "Looking back, absolutely anything could have happened that would have resulted in me not getting signed up – a state hiring freeze, a decision to scrub the existing list and create a new one, a significant injury, a job offer at a different agency – who knows? It is not hard to think of scenarios that would have resulted in my not getting in as a state park ranger." State Parks – and thousands of its past, present, and future rangers – should be grateful that Mike Lynch was finally hired on.

In September 1974, Mike finally was selected to begin work as a state park ranger trainee at Samuel P. Taylor State Park in Marin County. It is hard to imagine in these days of severe understaffing, but the nature of the Department's "intake areas" created a situation where the local supervisors had, at times, too many staff! For 9–12 months, trainees were at their intake area, learning how to manage campgrounds and day-use areas, patrol, give campfire programs and nature walks, control traffic, manage natural and cultural resources, use radios, write warnings, take care of patrol vehicles, and, importantly, fill out the requisite paperwork.

Sometimes, halfway through the training period, a new crew of three or four ranger trainees would show up at the intake area for training. It was not out of the question to be assigned to a night shift – at a day-use picnic area! This on-the-job training was interspersed with many weeks of formal training at the Department's training center at the Asilomar Conference Grounds in Pacific Grove.

At the end of this training period, Mike received notification of his first permanent full-time assignment, at George Hatfield State Recreation Area – 45 acres of mowed lawn in a bend of the Merced River in the

Mike as a young ranger at Hatfield. Patrol vehicles improved over the course of his career.

state's Central Valley. Mike was surprised by this assignment, and not only because he had never heard of this park. Mike was the only ranger there, which seemed odd for a rookie ranger. Then he realized that many of his fellow trainees had had no experience as a seasonal park aide or seasonal ranger – ever. So, he was actually more ready than most to work without close supervision. It was also a measure of the respect in which he was held by managers in the Department – not too many ranger trainees straight out of the academy are entrusted with a park with no other ranger staff at the site to mentor and train them.

Mike recalls that it was a pretty quiet 2½ years at Hatfield. The park has a small campground and a picnic area, as well as a loyal following of fishermen. "My biggest resource issue was controlling the gophers that were ruining the mowed lawn," Mike laughs. "Hatfield was also popular with people 'tubing' the river during the heat of summer – a great way to cool off. As the only permanent staff person at Hatfield, it was a terrific opportunity for me to learn the administrative and maintenance programs – useful skills to stow in my ranger tool belt."

Not surprisingly, Mike took this "quiet" assignment as an opportunity for self-improvement. He started on a master's degree, earned his lifetime community college teaching credential, and started teaching a "park management" course at West Valley Community College. Mike remembers his teaching experience at the community college, "There was no textbook, but I was able to find an outline for a park management class somehow and developed a semester's worth of material from that. Of course, I oriented the class to the California Department of Parks and Recreation. It was a good gig – the college paid me $20 per hour, versus the $8 per hour I was making as a ranger." This proclivity to use every spare moment to enhance his own skills, while finding ways to serve and improve the ranger profession, was to typify Mike's career and, indeed, his life.

Mike also took this opportunity to get more involved in the leadership of the California State Park Rangers Association (CSPRA) – a professional affiliation of park rangers. Before the state of California unionized many of its employees, CSPRA was the primary outlet for rangers to connect with their colleagues and share experiences and mutual concerns. In short order, Mike found himself vice-president of the association. "I was kind of a joiner," he recalls. Thirty-five years later, he became interim executive director of the organization. Shortly thereafter, he was elected president of CSPRA, capping his more than 40 years of service to this professional association.

In 1977, Mike transferred to Auburn State Recreation Area, in the Sierra Nevada foothills – a newly established 40,000-acre park where he would spend the next 37 years as a ranger, supervisor, and superintendent. The construction of a dam had just been authorized for the American River, which, upon completion, was designed to create an immense impounded reservoir similar to Folsom Lake. This was truly an untamed place at a wild and woolly time.

The Department entered into an operating agreement with the federal government – the Bureau of Reclamation (BOR) – to operate the recreational and resource functions of the proposed lake. The federal government still owned the real estate, while the state would provide patrol, first aid, law enforcement, interpretation, and resource management. From the point of view of a park visitor, this would ultimately

Patrolling Auburn in 1977. Patrol vehicles are a little better.

become a typical state park recreation area, with a focus on water-oriented recreation.

Since it was a new unit of the State Park System, all the staff was hired about the same time – rangers, maintenance, district superintendent, chief ranger, and office personnel. There were no rangers, or anyone for that matter, who had experience at the new park unit. The new staff would have to create all the protocols, patrol sectors, training, maintenance schedules, and administrative procedures. Relationships would need to be developed with vendors, local agencies, park supporters and detractors, concessionaires, special interest groups, park visitors, and elected officials at every level of government.

According to Mike, "We were a bunch of young, hotshot rangers. We were ready to set the world on fire. We had raw earth to manage, a brand new park to work with, and we went at it pretty hard. Remember that this property used to be managed – actually mismanaged – by the federal government, but now it was a state recreation area. The first year, we rangers probably made over 500 visitor contacts just for the possession or use of firearms."

Another important factor was the appointment of a young, aggressive district superintendent named Ron Hanshew. As Mike recalls, "At that time, only rangers at certain state parks were authorized to carry firearms on their person, at all times. At the vast majority of state parks, rangers had to carry their guns in a briefcase in the trunk of their patrol vehicle! Our superintendent knew that the rangers at the nearby Folsom Lake State Recreation Area were allowed to carry firearms, so he authorized us to do the same. We were never sure if he got approval for this or if he did it on his own. Since it was the right decision, we never questioned it."

One of the most challenging assignments for a ranger is being assigned to a new unit that was previously managed under different – much looser – rules and regulations. Changes in management philosophy invariably cause a lot of headaches.

Often new parks have been established following the acquisition of private property, whether the land previously had been used as a cattle ranch, logging operation, or family retreat. Private lands typically did not allow public use, so the operational problems arise from conflicts with the previous owners. After the sale or donation of private lands to the state, the previous owners may feel that they still have the right to use the land as they did prior to the transfer of property.

The transition can be even more difficult when public or semi-public use was permitted prior to the transfer of the land to the State Park System. The public has become used to a certain set of rules, as well as to how strictly those rules were enforced by the operating agency.

When State Parks started managing Auburn State Recreation Area in 1977, on lands that had been previously managed by the federal government, there was a long and challenging period of, shall we say, "education" on the new rules. The rugged and remote nature of the park, combined with the lack of marked boundaries, added to the challenge – the public, and sometimes even the rangers, were seldom 100% sure of jurisdictional boundaries.

State park rangers, now responsible for managing the park, were not allowing activities that had been permitted under federal oversight, whether due to different rules or a different level of enforcement of the rules. Visitors who used to carry firearms and shoot at targets now were being told they were not permitted to do that anymore, and were having their firearms confiscated. The regulations against cutting up downed trees for firewood were now being enforced. Rafters and kayakers, along with commercial outfitters, no longer could go down the American River without some level of oversight from the state. The "hotshot rangers" of Auburn had their hands full of unhappy people. Restricting the freedom of Americans is not an easy task.

One incident that Mike recounts illustrates this situation. "My patrol partner, Tom Lindberg, and I rolled up on a couple of 'tree pirates' in a remote area of the canyon. These guys had just cut down a large, beautiful 'heritage' oak tree. They were in the process of loading wood rounds into the back of their one-ton junker truck. Of course, cutting wood on private or public lands is not legal without permission. To establish this element of the crime, we asked, 'Do you know whose property you are on?' One of the wood thieves looked around a couple of times and then blurted out, 'Isn't this government waste land?' We wrote both men tickets and confiscated the wood. This mindset became the Auburn rangers' favorite way of describing the motives of most resource violators. The 'government waste land' consciousness has not disappeared from some Americans' view of public lands to this day, no matter what agency at what level

At "The Quarry" overlooking Auburn.

owns and manages those lands."

It was this "interim" period that created havoc. Of course, the dam was never built, although it is still "federally authorized." In the early years of State Parks management of the area, many members of the public had the point of view that it should not matter that their activities were damaging the environment. Everyone, it seemed, knew where the proposed high-water line was for the lake. The entire area would soon be under water, and therefore, their impact on the environment was – in the minds of many visitors – temporary, insignificant, or both.

Although the dam is still an authorized congressional project, all the funding has been eliminated for its construction. Cost estimates, in 2015, were about $12 billion to build the dam. Also, the discovery of an earthquake fault in the dam site vicinity caused consternation. The Bureau of Reclamation stated that the fault would not affect the integrity of the dam, but further studies and events at other dam sites gave the Congress pause. Mike says now that, although the dam is still on the books, there is very little chance of it being constructed in the foreseeable future. He adds, "In 2012, the feds and the state signed a 25-year management agreement that recognizes that the dam is not on the near horizon and that the state will continue to operate the land and the rivers."

From the quiet days of running Hatfield, a tiny park on the Merced River, Mike got thrown into the maelstrom of Auburn State Recreation Area. The difficulties of managing a new park, the need to find solutions in the gray areas of this park in transition, and the opportunity to work with a tight-knit group of young aggressive rangers (under the direction of a young aggressive superintendent) all combined to forge the convictions of Mike Lynch. These formative years were crucial to his future work as an advocate for rangers' rights.

As has happened with many rangers, there is one incident that stands out that could have ended Mike's career quickly and unceremoniously. He made a mistake in judgment, but it turned out all right. As Mike tells it, "We got a report of an intoxicated young man who was causing a disturbance on a lake beach. I got to the scene, and saw this young man toss what I first thought was a beach ball into an open car window. Then I immediately thought, wait, that beach ball has arms and legs – it's a human baby!

"We moved towards the young man to place him under arrest, but before I could handcuff him, he ran into the woods. I ran after him and, after several minutes of searching, caught him. I arrested the man, handcuffed him, and put him in the cage seat of my truck. Right away, he started whining – 'I can't breathe; I can't breathe. It's so hot.' I was not paying very close attention – lots of people whine when they are cuffed. Then other visitors, and even one of our rangers, started saying that he did not look so good. I just kept saying that he was fine and not to worry. I had the air conditioning going on full blast in my patrol truck, so I knew it couldn't be extremely hot in there.

"This went on – back and forth. Park visitor – 'He really doesn't look too good.' Me – 'HE'S FINE! He's going to jail, so leave my prisoner alone.' I was interviewing some bystanders, when I happened to look back at the truck. Some other visitors and one of my backup rangers had dragged him out of the truck, called for an ambulance, and appeared to be performing CPR on him. My career passed before my eyes, because I had ignored all these people who were telling me this guy was in bad shape. Other rangers at the scene immediately took over the CPR and began administering oxygen.

"While he was being intubated, I was like 'Oh my God!' Finally the medics in the ambulance called on the radio and said they had arrived at the lake, but there was no one there. We kept yelling at them that we were at the lower lake, not the upper lake. At the time, it seemed like it took the ambulance several hours to make it to our actual location. It probably was really only about 25 minutes, but the man would stop breathing every few minutes, and time just kept stretching out. Each time he failed to inhale on his own, I was thinking 'Oh no!' We removed his cuffs so we could perform CPR more effectively. It was a crazy situation.

"Finally, the ambulance arrived, assessed the man, gave him something for heroin overdose, and rushed him to the hospital. We learned later that he had swallowed a whole heroin balloon. He survived, but I learned a huge lesson that day. We came to call that the 'Beach Ball Baby' incident."

During his first few years at Auburn, Mike took and placed highly on the ranger promotional exam. As he recalls, "I had never planned on staying long at Auburn. I was at the top of the Ranger II (supervisor) list, and in late 1979, I got an offer to promote to Pismo Beach as a supervising ranger. Unbelievably, I was the victim of another personnel SNAFU. I had my promotion letter and was making my final plans to move when I was notified that my promotion had been canceled. Then I discovered that they had moved someone else there in some kind of weird deal." Mike's experiences with the personnel system helped build in him a desire to fix that system. He developed a strong interest in making processes and protocols fair, transparent, and just.

He finally did become a supervising ranger – first at Carnegie State Vehicular Recreation Area for six months – then more permanently back at Auburn in 1980. These were turbulent times. The U.S. Bureau of Reclamation had traditionally provided most of the funding for the staff at Auburn. In 1982, however, due to budget cutbacks at the federal level, along with the uncertain future of the proposed dam and lake, the state park staff was downsized from 12 rangers to four. One of Mike's options was to demote in place at Auburn. He took this option, in order to stay there and continue his work in the newly formed ranger union.

In the late 1970s, the State of California had passed legislation to begin collective bargaining for rank-and-file state employees. Mike decided to become active in the early days of collective bargaining – at the time when the rules, protocols, and tactics were just being developed. He was the organizer, founder, and first president of SPPOAC, the State Park Peace Officers Association of California. By forming it around peace officers, and not just rangers, it allowed state lifeguards to be represented by the same bargaining unit. Tactically, those rangers who were organizing the effort in these early days believed that combining the rangers and lifeguards into one bargaining unit – one that was separate from other job classifications – would create a stronger bargaining position.

One benefit of Mike's demotion in 1982 was that it permitted him to become more active in union activities. He felt it would be more effective to do this union work from a rank-and-file position, and for the next five years, Mike was fully engaged in that effort – ranger benefits, training, pay, and legislation.

Mike was the negotiations chair for the first two contracts. Unit Seven, the bargaining unit for rangers, was able to make a lot of progress right away. Of course, as Mike says, "When you start at the bottom in terms of pay and benefits, there is only one way to go, and that is up. In our first two contracts, we received very good raises and many enhanced benefits."

Mike recalls, "Looking back from where we are now, it is hard to imagine how bad things were at the time for state park rangers in California. We were the lowest paid peace officers in the whole state, and we made roughly half of what field rangers at the National Park Service were earning. Patrol vehicles were inadequate for the law enforcement and public safety functions and were in very poor repair. Meanwhile, the transfer policy had become almost corrupt. The district superintendent could select whomever he wanted, and often that selection was predetermined. Officially, the system did not permit 'preselection,' so candidates unwittingly would prepare like crazy for a job interview, drive hundreds of miles for an interview at the park they wanted to transfer to, and later realize it was all for nothing. Sometimes the superintendent would select a clearly inferior candidate – a choice that no one could understand.

"Making seniority the criterion for transfer was not the highest priority for our bargaining unit, but it was the most complex issue. You could sit down with the state's labor negotiators and agree on a thousand rules on how it would work, and then management would come up with a million ways to circumvent those rules. It was very frustrating for our members.

"The determination to install Code 3 equipment (red lights and siren) on ranger and lifeguard vehicles had been left to the discretion of the district superintendent, as was the type and configuration of that equipment. As a peace officer on patrol, you might be assigned a vehicle with no Code 3 features – just a little yellow rotating light!

"When William Penn Mott Jr. created the ranger trainee classification, he insisted that these trainees possess a bachelor's degree. Reflecting back to those times, the trainees were used to thinking for themselves and changing conditions they did not like. So you had these bright and creative young men and women who were motivated to making the system more fair and just.

"Everybody we talked to would tell us a horror story and wanted the union to fix it. Rangers would be assigned to a park where the district superintendent was not a big proponent of, say, training. So the ranger would not be nominated for advanced law enforcement courses. Here you have this tremendous personal liability as a peace officer and you are not able to keep up even on required training. The whole system was very 'hit and miss.'

"There were huge issues to deal with at the time, and often we had to overcome the opposition of the Department of Parks and Recreation. For example, we felt that it was imperative to have rangers and lifeguards formally meet POST training standards and possess POST certificates. POST is short for California's 'Peace Officer Standards and Training,' and it is the organization that sets the bar for those peace officers who are trained to their standards and who hold their certifications. Thanks to the many efforts of SPPOAC and PORAC (Peace Officers Research Association of California), the legislature passed a bill that put these rangers and peace officer lifeguards under the POST certification program, against the wishes of the Department.

"So many things that rangers take for granted now were very stressful battles at the time. Back then, rangers and lifeguards were not included in state safety retirement, and they were not included in the insurance exemption. This exemption states that if you were to have a vehicle accident while on duty, it would not count against your driving record. However, the whole attitude among many at the time – even in our own Department – was that rangers were not 'real' peace officers.

"You can understand why I consider our biggest coup, early on, was officially gaining 'full' peace officer status legislatively – having the same authority as deputy sheriffs, city police, and the California Highway Patrol. Having rangers recognized as full peace officers was, and remains, a big deal. I could see why a lot of employee groups wanted that legal designation – all the way from poultry inspectors at the Department of Agriculture to school security guards. In the early 1980s, a major re-write of the Penal Code had been scheduled that would specify who was out and who was in, and we REALLY needed to be in.

"State Senator Robert Presley, from Riverside, was the chair of the select committee on peace officers. He had been a sheriff before being elected to the state senate, so he knew a thing or two about peace officer status. This was before term limits for state legislators, so these committee chairs really wielded a lot of power for a long time. The first draft of the re-write of the bill to amend the Penal Code came out, and rangers, lifeguards, and Fish and Game wardens were not included. PORAC represented virtually all the major peace officer associations in the state. They had a lot of legislative juice, much more than SPPOAC. They kept fighting on our behalf, but we just could not gain any traction.

"There were a lot of people working on this issue – we did a ton of research and produced excellent reports that made the case for rangers to be included as full peace officers. Finally, PORAC set up a small, yet key, meeting with Presley. From the senator's point of view, he was making a Solomonic decision for many groups – you are in, but you are out. He did not feel he could include all those groups in the peace officer classification, or it would become too diluted. PORAC, which also represented many of those other employees, finally told Presley that PORAC's highest priority was the inclusion of the rangers, permanent lifeguards, and Fish and Game wardens. Presley finally agreed to include these three employee classifications. As you can guess, we were ecstatic!

"Again, the Department was tepid in its support for its employees, especially the move to full peace officer status. But then the 'final' bill came out, and we were shocked – the rangers, lifeguards, and wardens were not in there, and nobody knew what had happened. We went back to scratching and clawing, and that version of the bill was amended one last time to include these three groups. Finally – we were included in 830.2 of the Penal Code. One big impact of this was that now there was language in the legislation about weapons and POST status for rangers and lifeguards. In order for the Department to change these conditions, it will have to do it legislatively, rather than administratively, and that is far less likely."

"For most of the '80s, I put my heart and soul into this union work," Mike recalls. "I felt strongly that, in order to attract and retain the best possible rangers, the Department should treat them fairly. It was also out of a sense of justice. Rangers and lifeguards were being asked to perform the law enforcement function, so they should have the right training, equipment, and authority.

"In 1986, though, things started to change. After incredible successes, like two 14% pay raises for rangers, and many other improved benefits for rangers and other peace officers in Bargaining Unit 7, the non-peace officer members of Unit 7, who had not made such dramatic gains, revolted. A tremendous amount of conflict began occurring between the groups that made up that unit. I felt the only long-term solution to these inherent conflicts was to create two bargaining units – one composed of peace officers and the other made up of non-peace officers. I led this one-year-long effort, but this proposal was ultimately shot down by the State Labor Relations Board in 1988. At that point, I was on the outs in Unit 7, so I sort of went back to focusing on ranger work and cut back completely on my union work."

Mike has an incredible affinity for other rangers and peace officers, whether they are state park rangers in California, a police officer in Australia, or the Yeomen Warders (who are special police constables) of the Tower of London. Mike had always traveled internationally, starting with his college study year abroad program to India in 1971-72 and continuing with many overseas trips to places like Australia, Great Britain, and Europe in the 1970s and '80s. As his union work ebbed, he continued to travel the world on his time off. It was during this time that he discovered the existence of the largest police organization in the world – the International Police Association (IPA), which has nearly 420,000 members in 63 countries. The IPA, whose motto is "Service Through Friendship," has all sorts of programs for members, including home exchanges, home stays, and insider tours.

For example, Mike recalls the insider Ceremony of the Keys tour he attended at the Tower of London, available to IPA members. "This ceremony has been held for over 400 years – the 'Yeoman Warders' invite IPA members to their private club (bar) inside the 600-year-old Tower for drinks and snacks. There, the special invitees get to take an after-hours night tour of the Tower and get to watch the closing ceremony when the site is shut down. Then you go back inside for more drinks. It was a tremendous and fun experience – one which I never could have had without the IPA."

While on an Australia trip, Mike got a tour of the famous bridge in Sydney Harbor. This IPA insider tour by the Sydney police included a climb to the top of the bridge, part of which included climbing on some metal rungs on the outside of the bridge structure, to get to the top, and Mike grimaces, "It was a long way down to the harbor!

"Of course, when IPA members from anywhere in the world came to my neck of the woods, I was sure to give them special treatment. Mostly, I escorted them around, coordinated home exchanges and home hosting for them, and helped them with tours of popular tourist spots in California. I was also able to take those who were willing on the catwalk tour of the 730-foot high Foresthill Bridge in Auburn SRA – not quite as spectacular as the Sydney Harbor Bridge, but taller and almost as frightening."

Finally, Mike helped form a local Northern California Region of the IPA and served as its region president for nine years. He also was elected to the national board of the IPA, where he remained for 20 years – serving seven years as the president for the United States section of the IPA, the first ranger to ever serve in this position. He organized about a dozen IPA conferences in the U.S. and attended international IPA congresses throughout the world. His love of travel, organization, and "swag" made him an ideal fit for this avocation. He was always collecting, trading, or giving away patches, hats, and pins all over the world.

It was one of those IPA trips, to South Africa, that provided Mike with one of the most unusual law enforcement encounters of his storied career. Mike, along with fellow ranger and IPA member Larry Warren, were on a KLM flight back to San Francisco after the conference, when they noticed another passenger acting very oddly. This young disheveled American was walking up and down the aircraft aisles, talking loudly and acting extremely agitated. He was begging money from some passengers and even crawling over others to get back to his seat.

The crew's attempts to calm down this passenger were not successful, and finally the airline captain came back to the cabin to see how to handle this situation. Mike and Larry realized that there was no sky marshal on board, so they offered to help the captain with this unruly passenger. The man just kept getting worse. After getting authorization from the captain, Mike and Larry were able to subdue and handcuff the man with the captain's handcuffs. They got him strapped into a crew seat, and he flew the rest of the way to San Francisco belted, handcuffed, and further restrained with plastic flex cuffs around his ankles. Upon landing, before anyone could deplane, federal agents boarded the plane to, as the flight captain announced, "take away our very special passenger." It turned out the man had been kicked out of the house by his European girlfriend, decided that drugs were the means of choice to help soothe his hurt feelings, and hopped on a flight home. But it was just another day at the office for Mike and Larry.

Mike says that he gets asked all the time where he found time to do all this extra work – union activity, IPA, the California State Park Rangers Association, and writing a lot of books. He laughs and says he was famous for not really having a day job. He almost always opted for the swing or late shift at Auburn – from mid-afternoon until 10 p.m. or midnight. That left a lot of time during the day for him to be productive on other projects. Also, the Department would not pay overtime, so rangers would accumulate compensating time off (CTO) when they did work past normal hours. It was this buildup of CTO that allowed Mike to travel and work on other interests while he maintained his high level of commitment as a park ranger.

Mike adds, "I also get asked if anyone recognized me for my efforts, and I respond that, of course, I did not do any of it for the recognition – any of it – IPA, SPPOAC, PORAC, CSPRA, contract negotiations, and so forth. My own personal philosophy is that you had better get satisfaction on a personal level for what you are doing, because no one is likely to pat you on the back.

"It is like writing a book – you are not going to make money, you are not going to get famous, you are not going to win any awards. So, you better make sure you are writing the book for the right reasons, whatever those reasons are.

"There was one exception, in 1985. It was in the middle of the union stuff – all the organizing and contract negotiations. But rangers, SPPOAC members, and the staff at PORAC got together and organized a party called 'The Lynching.' It was odd timing, because things were still evolving vis-à-vis my union involvement, but it was a terrific evening. Many friends and colleagues from all the organizations were there, along with department brass and even several legislators. I did feel very much at the Lynching that others were recognizing the effort I was putting in. Of course, as I mentioned earlier, a couple of years later I was on the outs. Looking back, I got 'Lynched' just in time!"

After Mike's union involvement started winding down in 1987, he became more active in the IPA. Of course, he still had his job at Auburn State Recreation Area – patrol, first responder, law enforcement, and other ranger duties. It was about this time that Mike also chose to get involved in the International Ranger Federation (IRF). It seemed to be a ranger version of the IPA, and he thought that looked promising. He and fellow park activist Bud Getty soon played a key role in getting CSPRA officially involved in this new movement. Mike wrote the application letter to join the IRF, and CSPRA was eventually admitted as a member "nation."

Mike recalls that in 1990, he also started what became the "ranger anniversary." He says, "I had always been personally interested in state park badges and patches – badges are great records of how departments evolve over the years. I started collecting them, and that is how I first came to be called the 'Sultan of Swag.' I began asking myself what was the original state park badge and patch.

"Finally, I came across an article on Galen Clark, who was appointed in 1866 as the very first guardian of Yosemite State Park, which had been created in 1864 (before it became what is now Yosemite National Park). Since Yosemite State Park preceded any national park (Yellowstone – the first National Park, was not created until 1872), that made Galen Clark not only the first state park 'ranger,' but arguably the first park ranger in the nation! It struck me that the following year, 1991, would be the 125th anniversary of the ranger." Typically, Mike decided something should be done to celebrate that occasion.

He organized, in his words, "a fantastic committee," which included Susan Ross, Bill Monaghan, Bill Berry, Dave Bartlett, Jackie Ball, Kirk Wallace, Paula Peterson, Nedra Martinez, and Don Murphy, among others. Bill Monaghan, a regional director for the Department at that time, was able to represent the committee in Sacramento and overcome any resistance from the Department. It turned out to be a terrific year of events honoring the profession of park ranger.

It also inspired in Mike the desire to formally record and celebrate the events he was coming across in his research. At that time, there was no history of state park rangers. Now Mike has written two books on that subject, and retired ranger Carl Chavez and others have published books on their park careers.

Mike now says that this research and writing became his main focus for a while. He realized that a lot of the Department's milestones and significant accomplishments had not really been well documented. The historian, author, and event coordinator sides of Mike came to life, and he spearheaded, with the assistance of many colleagues, the effort to organize other anniversary events.

This led to the celebrations of and the design, production, and distribution of commemorative insignia badges, pins, and patches for the following anniversaries: the California Resources Agency's 150th (2000), the State Park Lifeguards' 50th (2000), the Off-Highway Vehicle Recreation program's 35th (2007), the K-9 program's 50th (2009), the Firearms program's 40th (2011), the State Parks System's 150th (2014), and the Park Rangers' 150th (2016).

As a result of his passion for history and accuracy, Mike also strove to present a valid record of key events in the Department's history. For years, Big Basin Redwoods State Park was touted as the Department's first state park, created in 1902. Mike questioned this assumption. He knew that a state park had been established through an act of Congress at Yosemite in 1864. Joseph Engbeck, a well-respected writer for the Department, published a book under the aegis of the Parks Department, *State Parks of California,* to coincide with the Department's 50th anniversary celebration in 1978. However, the first chapter of Engbeck's book is "Yosemite, the First State Park."

Mike's research also revealed that parks at James Marshall Monument at Coloma and Sutter's Fort in Sacramento both preceded the establishment of a state park at Big Basin Redwoods. Mike chuckles, "I am still trying to figure out what happened in 1928 to cause anyone to think that that was when the first

Department was established."

Many have called the park movement that sprang up after this 1864 event and the flowering of the National Park idea "America's greatest gift to the world." Based on the importance of the park concept, Mike believed it imperative that the Department and the National Park Service should commemorate that momentous occasion. He began to spend a lot of time and energy trying to develop support for the staging of a 150th anniversary celebration, timed to roll out in 2014.

The Department was at a low point in terms of budget, productivity, and morale, and after a very frustrating couple of years of meeting after meeting and memo after memo, the event was not given much support initially by the Department. Mike still believes it would have been a terrific opportunity for the Department

Mike ... ved to collect badges, patches, and other memorabilia.

to rebuild public support, highlight the Department's many accomplishments over the years, reach out to tens of thousands of new visitors, and regain excitement for carrying out the Department's mission.

Things did improve, thanks to the involvement and support of Deputy Director Ted Jackson, who appointed Donna Pozzi – chief of interpretive services at the time – and Mike to head up a 150th Anniversary Committee. Supported by many organizations (including CSPRA), a wide variety of 150th activities were organized for the year, including many events with Yosemite National Park, in an effort called our "joint heritage" at Yosemite. Mike says, "I cannot thank Donna enough for her total dedication to the anniversary. We made a great team and accomplished a lot for the 150th Anniversary, despite very limited financial support from the Department. A lot of good things took place, but it could have been much bigger and better."

Mike's next personal project was to write a book, along with co-author Rodi Lee, on vintage post cards from California's state parks. He and Rodi have collected over 10,000 state park postcards, covering almost every

California Parks Training Conference - March 3-6, 2014 - Yosemite NP

state park. He says most are vintage cards from the mid-20th century – a great era for postcards and travel by automobile. Mike has created the entire layout for this book, and had to scan about nearly 1,000 images to be featured in the book.

"One of my goals was to have at least one postcard for each state park, but cards did not exist for all 280 units. A lot of the relatively new parks simply do not have postcards – visitors now send digital photos instead. To keep true to the goal of having only postcards and not just photographs, I had to start my own postcard business! I needed to create postcards, as an example, for Admiral William Standley State Recreation Area and Zmudowski State Beach. These two parks are significant, because the postcards are listed alphabetically by park name, and these are the first and the last parks on that list. The search for these postcards and the information I found on them, front and back, added greatly to my knowledge of the Department, as well as its incredibly diverse array of park units.

"Looking back at my life and my career, I have been incredibly fortunate. Soon after college, I married my high school sweetheart – the ever-cheerful Patricia 'Patsy' Dolan. While I was finalizing the requirements for my college degree, Patsy was finishing nursing school at Oakland Highland Hospital. She began her career as a registered nurse, and later worked as a public health nurse with Merced and Placer Counties. Patsy volunteered as a Red Cross and emergency medical technician instructor for many years, and also served as a volunteer firefighter and emergency medical squad member for the Rock Creek Fire Department in Placer County.

"I was also very lucky at State Parks. Working the swing shift allowed me to spend a lot of time on things that were ranger-related or parks-related, but definitely needed to be worked on 'off the clock.' For example, I was looking through some old documents when I first found about the role that Galen Clark had played in the history of park rangers. I was astounded to find out that nobody had written more than four pages about the history and contribution of state park rangers in California. It was important to the Department and to the ranger profession to ensure that Clark's historical role as a 'ranger' was documented accurately, but I was careful to do this work during my personal time.

"I think part of my motivation and my strength was the ability to recognize gaps in

With Patsy Dolan Lynch.

the body of knowledge, gaps in recorded history, and errors in the history of State Parks. Then I had all these other interests – the union work, SPPOAC, CSPRA, IPA, IRF, anniversaries, badges, pins, patches, hats, and decals. Being a patrol ranger made it possible for me to pursue these interests. In my mind, these efforts are all directed to improving the Department of Parks and Recreation – sometimes against its will. I believe that having a strong union that promotes the interests and benefits of park rangers helps the Department attract better individuals. I would say that a good half or more of what I have achieved for the Department has not been accomplished during my work time. If I had been focused on promoting or transferring throughout the state, I doubt if I would have had the same impact on the park, the department, or the ranger profession.

"I was at the same park for over 35 years. I am sure there are those who must have felt I was too set in my ways to function well at another park unit. Looking back, however, I know that my time at Auburn provided me with tremendous opportunities that I might not have had at other units. In addition to my passion for the park, being fairly close (but not too close) to Sacramento gave me the ability to become involved politically and legislatively. I could also work more easily with the union and other organizations in Sacramento and, of course, the Department.

"There are so many niches and so much diversity in the Department. You do not have to go far to find rangers who are happy and satisfied and who have made an incredible positive difference. Janet and Dave Carle are a good example. Mono Lake was not only a fit for their interests in biology, volunteer management, and interpretation, but the politics of the lake allowed them to play a role in a larger landscape, including a groundbreaking court case. They also broke new ground in their job-sharing approach. If they had decided they could not job-share the ranger job at Mono Lake, or if the Department had denied them that opportunity, the lake, and the Department, would have been a much poorer place.

Mike Lynch, Superintendent of Auburn State Recreation Area. His decades of effort resulted in appropriate vehicles, equipment, and protective gear.

"I firmly believe that you need to do things that satisfy you – that you feel good about accomplishing. You have to ask yourself what your interests are, what do you consider important, what are you enthusiastic about? Most of what you do is necessary to fulfill your obligations at work. Of course, doing that well is extremely important. But everyone gets choices on what they focus on, both on and off the job. My advice is to think of things that will enrich you and others and 'your' park, and then go do those things."

Books by Michael G. Lynch

Author or Co-Author

Rangers of California's State Parks, 1996

Insignia of the California Resources Agency – Fish and Game, Parks, and Forestry, with Douglas T. Messer and Steven D. Huntington, 2004

Auburn Images, 2004

American River Canyon Hikes, 2005

California States Park K-9 Program – Since 1969, with James Burke, 2009

California State Park Rangers – Images of America, 2009

American River Canyon – Images of America, with Rodi Lee, 2012

Bowman, Placer County California, 2017

California State Parks in Vintage Postcard – A to Z, with Rodi Lee (due out in 2018)

Editor or Co-Editor

Mt. Quarries Railroad, 2012

The Foundations of Placer County Horticulture, Revised, Reprinted 2013

Dry Diggins on the North Fork, Revised Edition, 2015

California State Park – 150th Anniversary – Staff Photo Album, 2016

Me and the Mother Tree, by Harriett "Petey" Weaver, 2016

My State Park Career, by Chuck Mehlert, 2017

PAULA PETERSON

Reluctant Groundbreaker

What is it about Paula Peterson and job interviews? At one of her first experiences with State Parks, one of the interviewers slammed a big chain on the table that separated them, got in her face, started yelling at her, and kept referring to her as a "little girl."

During another interview, a few years later, she publicly agreed, on the spot, to marry one of the other candidates, in order to get the job! Fortunately, for her and for the Parks Department, the rest of her 31+ year career was not nearly as dramatic. She went on to become an extraordinary ranger, supervisor, chief ranger, and superintendent, as well as an inspiring example for hundreds of other rangers – women, as well as men.

Paula, who became the first woman to be hired into the full-time, permanent, state park ranger classification in the California Department of Parks and Recreation, had taken the state civil service examination for state park ranger trainee in 1970. She had not worked as a seasonal aide for the Parks Department, nor did she really know that much about what a ranger did. And she most certainly was not aware that, not only were there no full-time women rangers in the Department at that time, there were many male rangers and managers who were convinced that women were incapable of doing the job of a state park ranger. A couple of those who felt that way wound up on that early interview panel.

She recalls, "I grew up in Sonoma County and graduated from Sonoma Valley High School. It was a rural upbringing, and most of our family vacations would be car trips to go camping. We often camped in Yosemite National Park, while visiting a family friend who was an engineer for the National Park Service. I never told myself, 'I have to be a ranger someday.' Thinking back, my parents never told me there were jobs for boys and jobs for girls – I just never thought about it.

"In my neighborhood, the kids closest to my age were all boys. When I would come home upset about something, my dad would tell me, 'If you can't get along with someone, just get along without them.' Much later, right after I started working for the State Parks Department, there were lots of male rangers – and more than a few 'park wives' – who did not want to get along with me. I just followed Dad's advice with them.

"I went to Chico State College from the fall of 1967 through the spring of 1971. Halfway through my junior year, my counselor told me I really needed to think about declaring a major if I wanted to graduate. We sat down to look at my transcript, and it looked like the best path would be to major in recreation administration. In addition to a few academic classes and the work experiences I already had in lifeguarding and recreation leadership, I still needed another paid internship between my junior and senior college years. I fantasized that, after graduation, I could become an activities director on a cruise ship – I could get paid for leading recreation programs while traveling the world!

"One day in the spring of 1970, in one of my classes at Chico State, it was so hot that the instructor suggested we go down to the local creek, sit in the shade, and stick our feet in the water while we continued our class discussion. We got into a talk about what each of us would do for work experience that summer, and I admitted I did not have a job lined up. One of the students, Jess, asked me if I could swim, and I answered, 'Sure, I have done some lifeguarding – why do you ask?'

"Jess told me he was a high diver in a water show in Wildwood, New Jersey. He said he was getting married, and his bride was to be hired as an 'Aqua Maid' – a synchronized swimmer – in the revue. The show's producers had authorized him to hire a second 'Aqua Maid,' and those producers offered to pay our gas to drive from California to the Jersey shore.

"Luckily for me, my roommate happened to be teaching synchronized swimming at our college, and she was able to give me a few basics. After further consideration and research, I signed on to work for the Aqua Circus – a mere 3,000 miles away. When school let out between my junior and senior college years, four of us crammed into Jess' Mustang and drove across the country, camping all along the way to save funds.

"It turns out there were six of us 'Aqua Maids,' but only two actually got in the water to swim. The other four of us were on surfboards we launched from the side of the pool, and we would perform synchronized movements in

Wildwood Water Circus. *All photos and images courtesy of Paula Peterson.*

tandem with the 'Aqua Maids' in the water. It was actually a very professional, hour-long family show that included comedy, performance diving, and the synchronized swimmers.

"In one segment of the show, 'Lucky' West would cover himself in a suit of some sort, climb 60 feet up the tower, drape a towel soaked in high octane gasoline from his shoulders and ankles, light the towel on fire, and make a 'suicidal' dive into the swimming pool. It sounds absolutely insane – however, it was quite spectacular." (History does not inform us of the fate of his predecessor – "Unlucky" West.)

"The finale of each show would always be one of the high divers performing a dive from 100 feet up the tower and diving into eight feet of water. The whole 'commercial recreation' experience was very educational for me on many levels."

After that wet summer of 1970, Paula returned to California to complete her senior year of college. "As my senior year progressed and I had limited job prospects, my stepmother encouraged me to go to Sacramento and see what state civil service jobs might look interesting. I remember talking to someone at the State Personnel Board – they showed me a list of jobs, and state park ranger and fish and game warden looked interesting. I signed up to be notified and take exams for those positions. I eventually took the written test for ranger trainee, but then I did not really think any more about it for a while."

After graduation, Paula took a job working for the city of South Lake Tahoe's school recreation department. One day she received a telegram from the State Personnel Board, informing her that she had been scheduled for a job interview for state park ranger at Folsom Lake State Recreation Area – a couple of hours west and "down the hill." She remembers being really interested in the job, although it had never been a life-long dream of hers.

Paula arrived at Folsom Lake Headquarters, having been told to expect to spend the entire day undergoing an orientation and an interview. Looking back, she recalls that it was a bizarre experience. Indeed, she believes that few parks people have ever had a more unusual interview. At that time, she was told that the Department was going to hire four park ranger trainees for the Folsom Lake location. There were four candidates for those openings – "Pretty good odds," she recalls thinking.

She and the three young men – Curt Kraft, John Kolb, and George Gray (all of whom went on to have long and successful State Parks careers) – were sitting in a conference room, when a State Parks representative came in to give them their orientation talk. He spent until the lunch break describing the job of state park ranger to the candidates. He went over the typical duties, the philosophy of what it means to be a ranger, and what seemed like an extraordinary amount of time about the importance of the ranger uniform. She kept liking the sound of the job more and more.

Paula recalls that during this orientation, particularly the discussion of the uniform, the State Parks rep kept looking over at her and repeating, "I just don't know what we are going to do about a uniform for you." And when he was discussing the job duties of a ranger, occasionally he would look at her and say something like, "Of course, we would not expect YOU to do that part of the job." Paula remembers that at this point she started to realize that there were probably not many, if any, women rangers at State Parks.

Paula says that the afternoon was spent in meetings with the interview panel. Each of the four candidates went in for their interview, one at a time, with Paula going last. "When it was finally my turn, I went through the doors to the room the candidates were being interviewed in. Because I was so nervous, that room seemed gigantic to me – on the scale of a school gym – and the interview panel was seated what seemed like a couple of miles across the room. I recall feeling extremely self-conscious. I 'clickety-clacked' across the gym floor in my heels to the table, where three men were seated.

"They directed me to sit in an armless chair. These guys had obviously not read the memo on how to make job candidates comfortable and relaxed, so that they could concentrate on the interview topics. I am by nature a shy person, and my nervousness was making my pulse rate increase and my blood pressure rise.

"We had gone through the first few questions, when I noticed one of the men bend down and pick something up from under the table off the floor. All of a sudden, he whips this long, thick chain around and slams it on the table. He gets his red face about 12 inches from mine and yells, 'Now what are you going to do, little girl, when the Hell's Angels are in your park and they are threatening you?'

"I was completely flummoxed, and I just sat there, completely quiet. Here I was – 22 years old with little knowledge of what a ranger job really entailed – and I just was stunned beyond belief. After a few moments, one of the panel members said, 'Please remind us why it is you want to be a ranger and why you think you could possibly be one.'

"After a long silence, while fighting back tears, I finally replied, 'Gentlemen, maybe you are right. Instead of becoming a ranger, perhaps I should just marry a ranger!' Well, you could feel the tension fly out of the room. The change of the mood was palpable – they were so relieved that I had come to my senses about actually becoming a state park ranger. In their minds, they had helped me realize that women could best be of value by being a good wife to a 'real ranger.' I stood up and left, thinking, 'Well, that was that. Whatever that was, it is over, and I can go back to my job at South Lake Tahoe.'

"What I did not realize at the time was that candidates were allowed three job waivers – that is, if you turn down three employment offers, you are then automatically removed from the civil service list. So these guys had successfully intimidated me, and when I walked out, that was counted as a job waiver!

"Soon afterwards, I received another telegram about an interview in San Francisco, although the job opening was in San Luis Obispo. This time the interview was not as stressful. There was only one interviewer, and he was very nice and very professional. Again, however, I could tell that he really did not think that women belonged in the 'ranger fraternity,' and he selected another candidate.

"As I think back, it is clear that there were some high-level managers trying to ensure that no women were ever hired into these ranger jobs. It would have been much more acceptable for them politically had they been able to say, 'Well, she waived three job offers,' rather than admit they had turned me down in every instance."

Paula continues, "Despite the attempts to discourage me and the lack of success I was having in interviews, every time one of the managers described the ranger job, I thought it sounded pretty cool. I also recognized that I needed to take the process a lot more seriously if I were to be successful. My curiosity and my spirit were up, and I began to do research. Also, I found some park rangers who were willing to take me on patrol with them – I could see first-hand what they actually did, how they handled a variety of situations, and I could pick their brains on many park-related issues.

"I began to believe that I finally knew enough about 'rangering' to be successful at the job. In my naiveté, however, I still didn't know that I was about to become the first full-time woman ranger in the Department.

"My enhanced confidence level came at just the right time. I also had the great good fortune to be interviewed for a job vacancy at the Santa Cruz Mountains District. That good fortune came in the person of local superintendent Curt Mitchell, who led the interview.

"Curt hired me to be a ranger trainee in his district, and his demeanor during the whole interview had been that having a woman ranger on his staff would really be no big deal. I will never forget how he left things at the end of the interview. He said, 'I will never ask more of you than I ask of the men rangers, nor will I ask less. Can you live with that?'

"That statement was music to my ears, and I almost shouted back, 'YES!' Based on the research I had done, along with the discussions I had had during interviews and ride-alongs, I knew that I was capable of being a good ranger."

At the time, ranger trainees would be hired to work at "intake areas" – one of six districts through the state that became the "on-the-job" training sites. Trainees would spend 9-12 months at their intake area, and that local job experience would be mixed together with more formal training at the Department's training center in Pacific Grove – Asilomar. Santa Cruz Mountains was one of those districts so designated.

Each intake area hired three or four trainees, and together, these 20 rookies would form a training class. At the time, the Department was in a hiring mode, and two or three classes of 20 trainees were being hired every year.

Paula's first uniform.

Although in March of 1972 there was supposed to be a new class of 20 people to begin work, there were initially only 19 trainees listed on the roster in training group "E." Looking back, Paula now understands that there was this internal struggle going on in the Department over whether a woman – her, in this case – should be hired to become a ranger, thereby breaking the gender barrier. Paula now knows that the director at that time, William Penn Mott, Jr., was really pushing hard to get women into the ranger series. Mott had a progressive ally in the field in Curt Mitchell, and Paula was selected to fill out the last slot in group "E." She believes that it was this power struggle that caused the delay in her hiring – she reported to duty five days later than the rest of her group.

According to the book, *Prophet of the Parks*, by Mary Ellen Butler, "When Mott discovered that women had never been allowed to take exams to become state park rangers, he reclassified the job – to grumbling from many old-timers. In 1972, after completing a ranger training class with 19 men, Paula Peterson became California's first full-time, female, state park ranger."

Paula later learned that Director Mott really had to battle the State Personnel Board in order to open the ranger series to women – despite recent changes in federal and state law. The personnel board controlled the exam process, and they were loath to take the words "Male Only" out of the exam announcement and the job specifications.

After a short period of orientation at Big Basin Redwoods State Park – her actual work location – Paula drove to Asilomar for her first round of formal training. Because of the delay in her hire date, the group "E" roster still did not include her name.

"I remember checking in at Asilomar and walking around the conference grounds. I was supposed to report for training in my new job as a state park ranger trainee, and I had never been to the training center before. I was happy to see a couple of young men in ranger uniforms, and they turned out to be fellow ranger trainees Miles Standish and Matt Sugarman.

"I walked up and asked them if they knew where the ranger training was being held. One of them innocently asked me, 'Oh, is your husband in the training program?' When I told them no, that it was I who was reporting for training duty, their shock was obvious. Matt exclaimed, 'No one told us there would be a girl in our ranger training program!' He was not being mean or sexist – he was genuinely surprised by this revelation and perhaps a little irked that no one had told them."

That encounter took place in March of 1972, early in the career of Ranger Paula Peterson – the first full-time, badged, and permanent female park ranger ever to work for the California Department of Parks and Recreation. Civil service rules had also been updated to ensure that women were paid the same salary as men.

A woman named Harriet "Petey" Weaver worked for the Department from 1929 to 1950, and had many of the duties of a ranger – she was a seasonal employee at Big Basin, Richardson Grove, Pfeiffer Big Sur, and Seacliff State Beach. Her job title was Nature Guide and Recreation Leader, but since Weaver gave a lot of nature hikes and campfire programs, many park visitors considered her a ranger. Indeed, in those days, many

Harriet E. "Petey" Weaver, circa 1947.

of her duties were exactly the same as those of the park rangers.

In the late '60s and early '70s, the Department hired several women as State Park Rangers (Permanent Intermittent). These women (notably Paula Pennington and Holly White – who were working as rangers as early as 1968) performed the duties of state park rangers, and that was their job title, but they were not trained as peace officers. Further, the permanent intermittent classification provided permanent civil service status for these women, but they did not work year-round.

Although most refer to Paula Peterson as the first woman park ranger in California's State Park System, she knows that others might argue with that appellation. Paula, typically, has no ego in this argument. "There are some who believe, and will always maintain, that Petey Weaver was the first female ranger in California State Parks. Others might say that Paula Pennington or Holly White was first. Of course, both of those women went on to become peace officers when they were selected for full-time ranger positions in the late '70s. Frankly, I don't care whether I am regarded as the first.

"I never really spent my energy quibbling about this. It is kind of like Anza–Borrego Desert State Park. As soon as you say it is the biggest state park in the continental United States, people in New York start arguing that Adirondack State Park has more acreage within its boundary. What is the big deal? Anza–Borrego is a magnificent park – whether it is the largest or the hundredth largest, who cares?

"In the National Park Service, there were many women working in field jobs, and they predated the career of Petey Weaver at California State Parks. I have a photograph of Herma Albertson Baggley in a ranger uniform, complete with National Park Service badge, in 1929.

"Claire Marie Hodges worked in the role of a park ranger in Yosemite National Park as far back as 1918. She was appointed to a seasonal job there during World War I, and some refer to Claire as the first woman ranger ever in the country. Claire wore a ranger badge, Stetson, and was issued a sidearm. There were also several women in the late 1800s and early 1900s in national parks who carried out some of the duties that we think of as ranger assignments.

"Then there was Ruth Ashton Nelson – she had been trying forever to become a ranger at Rocky Mountain National Park. Ruth was frustrated at her lack of success, and she finally said, 'I guess the best way for a

Herma Albertson Baggley in National Park Service ranger uniform, 1929.

woman to get into the National Park Service would be to marry a park ranger.' I did not know of that quotation when I said something similar at my Folsom Lake interview. That cracked me up. But the truth was that, for a long time, if a woman were married to a park ranger, the National Park Service would often hire her to do essential jobs so that she could help her husband with his duties.

"Then World War II changed the thinking of the State Parks Department on some of its hiring practices, at least temporarily. At Point Lobos State Reserve, for example, a park ranger and his wife were living in state housing in the park. When he was sent off to war, the Department hired his wife to carry out the essential duties of the ranger at that park. You could argue that she was the first woman park ranger.

"When that war ended, the state went back to hiring only men – many people now think that was so returning veterans would have as many opportunities as possible to find meaningful work. In any case, I choose to honor the fact that we – all of these women – played a role in advancing the ability of females to serve the public as park rangers.

Claire Marie Hodges, Yosemite National Park, 1918.

Paula meets Petey Weaver.

"I finally met Petey Weaver some years after I was hired. There was a state park ranger association conference, and Petey attended, having been chosen as an 'Honorary Ranger' in 1971. I was really looking forward to meeting her and talking with her. To my surprise, though, we did not click at all. I don't know if she felt I was taking something away from her, like her place in history, or what, but she was exceptionally cold towards me.

"It was too bad, because I had a lot of questions I wanted to ask her and stories I hoped we would share. For example, I wanted to know if she was paid the same as men doing similar work. Also, I had heard that, at one point, she took a civil service exam at State Parks and came out number one on that list. I really wanted to learn what that position was. She also wrote a number of books of her experiences in State Parks, and I wanted her to fill in a few details for me.

"There were 'eras' of the Department. For example, when Petey Weaver was working, it was a totally different park system. There was more of a 'seasonality' in those years. People would leave home in the beginning of the summer, stay at the park for months, and go back home at the end of summer. They would have their favorite campsite at their favorite park, and they would go back and camp there year after year. So they knew the staff very well. There weren't a lot of rules, and it was just a different time. Meanwhile, the Department did not need as many year-round employees back then.

"If somebody wants to argue that Petey was the first woman ranger, that takes nothing away from the satisfaction I feel about my career. I was in the right place at the right time to unwittingly open a door others followed through. I feel I contributed a lot to the Department and to the people of California, and in return I received a lifetime of good memories, a boatload of great friends, and a very satisfied feeling about my life and my career.

"Oddly enough, for one who has been recognized as a 'groundbreaker,' that was a role I never specifically sought. I am not, and never was, an overt feminist or a women's libber. There was the feeling, however, that if I did not do well that first year or two as a park ranger, it might send the wrong message to the Department and its managers about the capability and suitability of women to be rangers – I did not want to set back the progress that was being made. Further, I did not want to let down Curt Mitchell or Bill Mott. They had placed a lot of confidence in me, and they made incredible efforts to ensure that women could serve as park rangers in California State Parks.

"Back to my first arrival at Asilomar, though, those two guys – Matt Sugarman and Miles Standish – along with others in group 'E' seemed to accept me as one of them. They were supportive of me being a ranger, but I did not receive that same level of support and acceptance from all the trainees in my group It was kind of interesting how that worked out in the long run, however. The men who embraced my position as a woman ranger all made a career out of State Parks. Those who resented me personally or despised the notion of women rangers in general – well, many of them left the Department in short order. I don't know what that means exactly, but to me it was very telling. I think it said a lot more about who THEY were than about me.

"Of course, the Department was learning, in many ways, how to deal with women rangers, and I was the first one through the gate on many of those issues. At Asilomar, the 19 men were housed together, while I was given a single room in a totally different section of the conference grounds. I was hundreds of yards from anyone or anything, including the training room or the cafeteria. It soon worked out that a couple of the men would come by on their way to breakfast to walk with me to the dining hall. I never felt it was a protective thing – they sincerely wanted to make me feel as welcome as possible and make sure I knew that I was accepted in the group.

"Probably the best advantage to being a woman, however, was this. All day at Asilomar, I was in a classroom for eight hours drinking tea or coffee to stay awake. Every hour there was a short break, and there were two restrooms – one for the 19 men and one for the women, er, woman in the group."

After a week or two of formal training at Asilomar, Paula returned to Big Basin to work and get more experience and on-the-job training. In addition to her fellow group "E" trainees – Don Hoyle, Lloyd Lemprecht, and Glen McGowan – there were new rangers from other groups, as well. All of them inspired Paula throughout her career. But she loved her team of four rookies – they really looked out for each other.

Paula recalls, "They were always saying to others, 'She's with us!' That made me feel good, but I really knew that I had been accepted into their fraternity when they began to feel comfortable playing tricks on me. They were not mean, hazing tricks – just fun stuff.

"For example, Glen McGowan, among the four trainees in our group at the Santa Cruz Mountains, kept a state vehicle at his state residence. I have no idea why that was the case. Maybe it was because he had seasonal experience with State Parks. Or maybe it was because he just grabbed the keys one day and never changed the drill. In the morning, he would go around to the state houses of the other three ranger trainees, pick us up, and we would all ride to work together.

"It was a pickup truck, and there was room for two people beside Glen in the cab of the truck. The fourth ranger 'got' to ride in the truck bed! And Glen got to set the order of pickup. If it were sunny and nice, he would pick me up first or second, and I would get to ride in the cab. But if it were raining, I would invariably be his last stop, and I would have to ride in the rain in the bed of the truck. They all thought that was hilarious, of course. 'It was totally a coincidence,' Glen maintains to this day. 'Every time it rained, it just happened to be Paula's turn.'"

It was during this training year that Paula attracted the attention of the media. "I did not like being the center of attention – I still don't. That first year, I had to work with the media a lot. Even though I disliked these distractions, I understood that it was my role and part of my job. I submitted to newspaper interviews, and I was assigned interviews with various television stations to present the 'face' of the Department. I traveled to the service clubs that requested a presentation by the 'girl ranger.' Again, even though I did not like doing this, I had to make sure that I was successful in this role. Further, I did not want to give the naysayers in the Department any ammunition. I refused to let them say about me, 'Oh that Paula – we provide her with these great opportunities, and all she does is complain.'"

Some of those headlines seem, in retrospect, hilarious.

> *The Santa Cruz Sentinel* – "First Girl Ranger at Big Basin"
>
> *The San Jose Mercury News* – "The Ranger is a Lady," complete with a photograph of her in a Stetson several sizes too big
>
> *The Sonoma Index-Tribune* – "The State's Lone Ranger (female) from Sonoma"
>
> *The Monterey Peninsula Herald* – "Paula's Pretty, and a Park Ranger"

The Oakland Tribune ran a beauty – "Perils of Paula, the Park Ranger"

The Contra Costa Times – "You wouldn't call her Smokey the Bear in pigtails, but then how does one address a female forest ranger?"

30 Thurs., April 6, 1972 San Jose Mercury 4★

The Ranger Is A Lady

By BOB LIGON
Staff Writer

BIG BASIN — California's first lady ranger is on the job at Big Basin Redwoods State Park.

She is pretty Paula Peterson, 23, who's neither a Women's Lib nor one of those "I - d r e a m e d - a l l - m y - life - of - this" advocates.

"It just sort of happened," said Miss Peterson, a graduate of Chico State College with a bachelor's degree in recreation administration.

"And I'm glad it did because I like the out-of-doors and people."

"It all happened like this: After graduation she set out to find a job in her field. Looking over a list of state job openings, she spied "park ranger trainee."

She met the job "specs," applied, took the written and oral exams, placed 53rd out of the hundred applicants, and then sat back and waited.

Forty trainees were to be called under te state Parks and Recreation Department's ranger-trainee program.

TOO LOOSE—Paula Peterson, 23, California's first lady ranger, has run up against only one problem so far, getting a Stetson hat that fits. She said she intends to wear them just like the men, "square and even." She's training at Big Basin Redwoods State Park.

nance and repairs, and nature study and interpretation.

To the contrary, she says, she recently got quarters all session at Asilomar, whe the young men there had

Almost inevitably, some of these articles sparked a negative reaction. One state park ranger wrote a letter to the Monterey Peninsula Herald, expressing his displeasure at the idea of women rangers. "This California state park ranger totally dislikes the thought of allowing the fair sex into the ranger fraternity. This young lady will never be treated as an equal. There is plenty of room in the Department for women and many jobs that they can perform, but there is no room in the ranger fraternity for women, nor should there be."

Paula, as she did for the next 31+ years of public service, maintained her demeanor of being capable, competent, intelligent, and pleasant. It was these traits that enabled her to succeed in her new job and earn her (at times grudgingly) the respect of her colleagues and supervisors. She still maintains, "I learned that people were going to take shots at me. I knew that most of those complaints were not about me personally – they were about changes in the Department, and a lot of people do not react well to change. I did not seek the attention, but it found me nevertheless. I just kept working as hard as I could and never asked for special treatment.

"Curt Mitchell was true to his word – while I was a trainee at Big Basin, I was never treated differently than the male rangers. Maintenance Worker Bill Beat, who later himself became a ranger trainee, provided me with a wealth of information on the maintenance program. Don Button gave me lessons on how to clean a park restroom. Most all of the staff at Santa Cruz Mountains gave me support and encouragement – indeed, just as they did to my fellow trainees.

"At Asilomar, I unwittingly and unintentionally continued to put the Department in awkward positions. One of the requirements for all trainees was to swim 100 yards. That turned out to be the easy part. There was an outdoor pool at Asilomar, where the swim test was scheduled.

"The awkward thing for the training center staff was what to do with me, regarding this swim test. Apparently, they must have agonized about putting me out at the pool in a two-piece swimsuit with 19 guys. The staff came to me the day before the test and said, 'Hey we noticed that you have experience as a lifeguard. We would like you to serve as the lifeguard for the swim test. You don't need to do the test because of your certification, and we definitely need a lifeguard.' So I stood there, fully clothed, the entire time that my colleagues were swimming. Heaven forbid someone would actually need lifeguard services!

"Then there was the issue of having to qualify with a firearm. It would be one thing to pass me on the swim test, especially since I had been employed previously as a pool lifeguard. But to pass me on the firearms qualifications course without rigorous testing – that would have had legal implications that could not be ignored.

"Again, I was able to make their lives at the training center a little easier. In college, I had a long-term boyfriend just about the whole time I was at Chico State. He was a hunter, and he introduced me to the hunting experience. It was not just about guns and ammunition – it was also about the different species of waterfowl, marsh ecology, hunting techniques, safety, and ethics. We were often out hunting ducks at dawn – he really knew how to woo a girl!

"I give him credit for teaching me that it was the whole experience – the Zen of hunting, if you will. I was introduced to guns and gun safety the proper way – how to walk with a shotgun, how to clean and maintain your weapons, and especially, how to handle guns safely in every situation.

"When we learned about firearms and shooting in the academy, it was not as big a deal for me as some had feared. I was actually pretty comfortable with guns. I did not have much experience with handguns, but I valued the training. It really helped that the firearms instructors wanted me to be successful, as well.

"That training period of nine months at the Santa Cruz Mountains District really flew by, and the time was approaching when we would be transferred out to our first permanent assignments. Don Hoyle, one of my fellow trainees at Big Basin, was given an early 'heads-up' that he would be assigned to Mt. Diablo State Park, and it looked like I was headed to the beach parks of Santa Cruz County (the Pajaro Coast District). One evening Don and I were discussing these upcoming assignments, and, for a variety of reasons, Don wanted to work in Santa Cruz, while I thought Mt. Diablo would be a more attractive first assignment for me.

"Don and I went to Curt Mitchell and asked him if there was any chance we could swap assignments. After we laid out our reasons, Curt said he did not see why not. He called Tony Trigeiro, the superintendent at Pajaro Coast, and Tony was delighted, of course. He would get Don and would not have to deal with 'the girl ranger.'

"Next, Curt called the superintendent at Mt. Diablo, who immediately started hemming and hawing. 'Well, I just don't know about that,' he told Curt. 'It is pretty rough up here, lots of problems you know, so you'd better have her come up and check it out to see if she really thinks she could handle this place.' Naturally I was a good soldier and went up to check things out, and it looked fine to me – I loved the park, and it was also closer to my family in the Napa Valley. Again, Curt paved the way. He said, 'Both of these rangers are capable and passed the academy. The Department has said they are both qualified to take on any assignment, so let's accommodate their desires and make these two people happy.'

"Miles Standish of group 'E' was also assigned to Mt. Diablo, and it was probably the first time Mt. Diablo had ever had rangers of the 'new generation' work there. A lot of World War II veterans and other men and women from that era made up the staff at that time – not just at Mt. Diablo, but throughout the Department. They had been in the park service for 25-30 years and they kind of resented the new generation of rangers. We all had college degrees, we were young, and we were part of the generation that thought it could change the world. Again, Miles and I worked hard at being rangers – we just focused on doing our jobs, while fitting in with the rest of the staff there. It all worked out fine.

"With all the big issues and obstacles involved with being a female ranger in those days, it is kind of funny that one of the most difficult things to deal with became the ranger uniform for women. I would often think back to my interview at Folsom Lake, when one of the interviewers had said, 'I just don't know what we are going to do about a uniform for you.' Indeed, it took the Department a while to figure this one out.

Group E trainees at Asilomar. Notice anything unusual here?

"If you look at a photograph of my ranger trainee class, you see 19 men all dressed identically – complete with the ranger Stetson. And there I am – wearing a Girl Scout green blazer with a Departmental patch on the left pocket, a little cotton skirt, nylons, heels, and no Stetson.

"Culottes were soon authorized to replace the skirt. I could purchase the ranger uniform material from the men's uniform company. A sewing pattern was authorized, and then I had to have my sister sew the culottes for me. It is hard to imagine these days a female officer being required to wear a skirt or culottes on a law enforcement field assignment. Eventually, women rangers were authorized to purchase men's uniform slacks. I remember that, although I purchased the smallest size men's slacks available, the belt loops were squeezed together around my waist. Nurses' shoes at the time were all white, and I had to dye them a color called 'marine cordovan.' Man, were they ugly!"

A few months later, in November of 1972, a photograph of her class graduation from the law enforcement academy in Modesto, California, shows Paula wearing a Stetson, a khaki uniform shirt, a standard state park badge, and uniform green pants. The Department had come a long way in a few short months. Again, Paula credits Curt Mitchell for coming up with a simple and elegant solution. "There was this meeting of the Department's managers trying to decide upon a uniform for women rangers, when Curt asked, 'Um, why don't we just ask her what she thinks?'"

Paula says, "One of the really crazy things in those days – and this was for men and women rangers – was the issue of firearms. If you were assigned a weapon – and you had to be working at a 'high enforcement park' in order to even be assigned a sidearm – you needed to carry the gun in a bowling bag and lock that bag in the trunk of your patrol vehicle. I am not making this up! Can you imagine? Let's say you make a felony vehicle stop, for instance, and you tell the criminal, 'Wait one second, please. I need to get my revolver out of my bowling bag, which is locked in the trunk of my beat-up old sedan – yes, that one parked behind you with a yellow revolving light on top.' Good grief!

"On a personal level, I began to date one of the guys in my class – Harry Morse. Harry had been assigned to Folsom Lake while I was at Big Basin. There were a few single guys in my academy, including Harry. Getting into a relationship was not something I was focused on, despite the comment I made at that first interview.

Maybe I was just too busy, or concentrating on my work, or dealing with all the media attention.

"But all the time and stress you go through at the academy – especially the law enforcement training – eventually there is a bonding effect to all that. Well, Harry and I 'bonded' all right.

"When I was assigned to Mt. Diablo, Harry wound up at Lake Oroville State Recreation Area, and we continued to see one another. It took a couple of hours to drive from one park to the other, so we put in a lot of miles for a while. We kept our relationship guarded. With all the issues the Department had to face with a woman ranger, we did not yet want to raise the issue of two rangers in a relationship."

Right about the time Paula and Harry were trying to figure out what to do about their relationship, the Department decided to create the mobile "Park Experience." This idea was to have a truck-trailer set up and designed for "taking the parks to the people." Recognizing that not every schoolchild has the opportunity to visit a state park, the Department's plan was to take an interpretive trailer around the state. There, park staff would make presentations to the students about the natural and cultural history of the region and the state.

The original idea was to have a driver deliver the exhibit trailer to a particular state park and leave it there for several weeks. Local rangers would be "borrowed" to staff the trailer, and schools would be expected to get their students to the park to be inspired by the "Park Experience."

State Parks writer Joe Engbeck and interpreter Harry Batlin made the case to hire two rangers to staff the trailer and have them drive it around the state to the schools. One of the

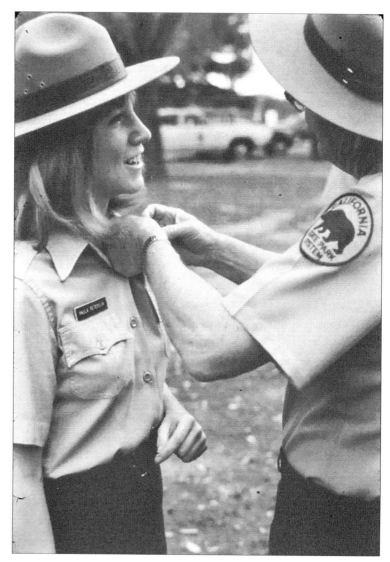

Paula becomes the Parks Department's first woman peace officer.

Presenting interpretive programs as part of the "Park Experience" exhibit trailer.

downsides was that both rangers would be required to get truck-driver licenses, but this approach would facilitate the notion of reaching out to as many "underserved" schools as possible.

They also wanted the project to be an invested assignment – something that provided real value to the local parks and schools – not just extra work. Taking the trailer to the schools would make it much easier for the students to take advantage of this opportunity. It would be a 10-month assignment for the two rangers, since this would correspond to the school year. Also, the pair of rangers would be able to work at parks that could use the extra help during those two summer months when school was not in session.

As Paula recalls, "Harry began to push the idea that he and I should put in for this assignment. We both found the idea intriguing, especially since we could finally get to spend more time together. This was a new program for State Parks, so the whole process of finding out what worked well and what did not work at all – well, that would pretty much be left up to those rangers to figure out. We did not even know if anyone else applied when we went to the interview. Again – I was going to be a reluctant groundbreaker.

"Prior to our interviews, Harry had asked me to marry him. This had nothing to do with the interpretive trailer assignment – we had arrived at that stage in our relationship. I had agreed to marry him, but we were determined to keep our relationship quiet – at least for a while. We agreed to wait and see how things unfolded before it became public. Harry and I feared we would both lose our jobs if managers got wind of our romance, and we most certainly did not want to lose our jobs over the fact that we were choosing to marry.

"We were at the interview, this time with Bill Haussler and Bud Heacox – two of the managers in the Department's interpretive services division. The interview started off well, but then at some point Bill and Bud started hemming and hawing. They eventually admitted they had envisioned two male rangers staffing the trailer – they had never really considered having a 'boy ranger and a girl ranger' working together for this assignment. They said, 'A boy and a girl on the road together – that just might be problematic.'

"I asked them, 'What are you really trying to say? Are you suggesting that we would have to be married to share this assignment – that unless we got married you would be unwilling to let us go on the road together to do this job?' They looked pretty embarrassed, but they admitted, 'Well, yeah.'

"I looked at Harry and he looked at me, and in one of the least romantic marriage proposals of all time, he popped the question! 'Well, do you want to get married?' I looked at Bill and Bud and said, 'Really – this would be a requirement of the job – to get married?' And they both nodded, 'Yes.' They figured Harry was bluffing. I turned back to Harry, and I said, 'Well, if only for the benefit of the Department, yes, let's do it!' I wish now I had taken a photo of the look on the faces of Bud and Bill!

"So we actually did get married and did get the assignment. We were even able to deduct our wedding expenses from our income taxes – hey, it was a job requirement! Seriously. It wasn't a big wedding – maybe 20 friends along with our family members. So it was not really that expensive, but we still had expenses that we were able to write off.

"We really enjoyed our assignments with the park interpretive trailer and it gave us a great opportunity to see the state. The 10 months went by quickly, and as the end of that experience drew nearer, we started wondering how the department would transition us back to regular park jobs. We also imagined that there were a lot of discussions being held regarding how the Department would handle a married couple.

"We got proactive and gave the Department a list of possibilities – parks that were relatively close to each other, where we could live together and have a reasonable commute to separate work assignments. Of course, these happened to be parks that we thought we would enjoy working at. This was before rangers became unionized – at that time, making assignments was totally in the hands of the personnel section in Sacramento. They did what they thought was best for the Department, but those decisions did not always match up with the goals and desires of the rangers.

"When Harry and I got married, we knew that we had to do things right. We would be setting the example for other rangers who might want to marry each other, but more importantly, we wanted to set an example for the Department – we wanted to show that it could work, and did work, to have rangers get married and still be successful as individuals. That included a pact not to complain about how we were being treated by the Department.

"Well, maybe someone up there in the personnel section remembered that I had once finagled my way out of working at Pajaro Coast (the beaches of Santa Cruz), because that was where I was assigned after our assignment at the interpretive trailer came to an end. Harry was assigned to the nearby Henry Cowell Redwoods State Park (in the Santa Cruz Mountains), so at least we could live together and have easy commutes to work. It was a reasonable solution on the part of the Department, but these were not our dream jobs. However, we did not complain – we just dug into our new assignments and tried to become the best rangers possible.

"We started these new assignments right at the beginning of the summer – the busy season. I could see right away why I had been assigned there. That coastal district had so many ranger vacancies, and the existing staff was exhausted. I was initially assigned to provide relief for rangers who, for a very long time, had not been permitted to take time off – either for overtime or vacations – because there had been no one available to fill in behind them.

"There was one funny incident at Asilomar not long after Harry Morse and I married. I arrived at Asilomar to attend a training course and discovered I had a roommate – last name also Morse. An assumption had been made that Ken Morse, another ranger, was my husband. We all got a pretty good laugh about that – and adjustments were made immediately!

"Harry liked the work at Henry Cowell, but he was drawn to another profession – he really wanted to teach at the college level. He did get hired at Chico State University as an instructor in their recreation administration department. He wanted to teach courses on park management and operations, because he felt strongly that many recreation departments really did not offer enough courses to prepare students for a career in parks. He believed they were usually geared mostly to city parks or active recreation programs – as had been my experience. He applied to the State Parks Department for a leave of absence, but his application was denied.

"Meanwhile, I applied for an educational leave of absence so that I could go back to school at Chico State. I did get my leave request approved, and I received my master's degree in recreation administration that year. At the conclusion of the leave of absence, I was assigned to the nearby Oroville State Recreation Area.

"Harry resigned from his ranger position and taught at Chico State only a couple of years, and then eventually reinstated at the Department's interpretive services section in Sacramento. We wound up buying a house in Sacramento, but I never lived in it. Harry and I had just drifted apart. In the meantime, I had been offered the opportunity to apply for a tremendous job at the training center at Asilomar.

"Like a lot of my fellow rangers, when I started out in the Department, I was content to strive to be the quintessential field ranger. I enjoyed the variety of work, I got to work outdoors, and I was able to work with the public. After a while, though, I began thinking that there just has to be more – I was not sure I wanted to work in campgrounds, picnic areas, and boat launch ramps the rest of my career.

"Part of the appeal for me for the position at the training center was that I believed I had something to contribute. For a number of years, the FBI had conducted training for the Department's peace officers in the disciplines of firearms and 'defensive tactics.' DTs (as it was known) were used by peace officers to make physical arrests, gain compliance from individuals, and defend themselves, if necessary. The FBI had notified the Department that, due to budget cuts, it would no longer be able to provide that training in firearms or DTs – training that the Department believed was essential in order for its rangers and lifeguards to maintain a high level of competency in their law enforcement work."

Several leaders in the Department – notably Ron McCall and training center manager Mary Wright – argued long and hard that State Parks needed to develop an "in-house" training program for DTs. Ron made a good point – "We don't shoot many people, but we sure make a lot of arrests. Our field people often use handcuffs, and we want to get them to the point where they do not have to think twice about how to put handcuffs on an arrestee safely and effectively."

Paula chose to interview for that job, and some of the questions focused on her small stature and how that would affect her ability to conduct the DT training. She had a ready response – she was unable to change her physical stature, but the whole idea of Defensive Tactics training is to give the field rangers and lifeguards the right tools. These tactics would be reinforced over and over to the point where they became second nature.

She made the point that you do not need to be a big man to make an arrest. On the contrary, it would be very effective during the training to demonstrate how a petite female ranger could effect compliance with large and strong suspects using the skills and techniques they were learning in class.

The training center already had hired a consultant – Stan Kephart – to help develop the Department-run program at Asilomar. In addition to setting up the training, one of Stan's goals was to get Paula operating at a high level. Stan mentored Paula to the point where she was very capable at teaching the defensive tactics to the students. There is a lot of "hands-on" instruction in this class, and she quickly became the Department's lead instructor for DT field coaches.

Along with defensive tactics, Paula was assigned to coordinate the Department's training in firearms. This was a different situation, vis-à-vis the level of expertise available in State Parks. When state park peace officers began being issued revolvers in the early 1970s, the Department recognized that it was crossing a major threshold. Rangers and lifeguards are regarded differently when they are carrying a gun, and liability and many other significant factors come into play.

Although the Department did not have a lot of defensive tactics instructors in the '70s, it did have a cadre of firearms experts available. In defensive tactics, a number of rangers had attained a level of expertise in martial arts, but there was no consistency among them, and few of the martial arts skills readily translated to proficiency in arrest control techniques.

In the early days of Paula's role in supervising the firearms training program, some members of the Department's "shooting competition team" approached her. Although Paula was comfortable with firearms, she never thought

Conducting peace officer training at Asilomar.

of herself as an expert. A few of these rangers – Ken Wilbur, Steve Michel, Bob Todd, and Craig Burke – told Paula they thought that they – rather than she – really should be presenting the firearms classes.

Paula, in typical fashion, had no ego in her training role. To their surprise and delight, she told them, "That's great. That is exactly how I see it, too. How about if I do all the work behind the scenes – the record keeping, syllabus updates and distribution, and all the paperwork, and you guys do the training in the classroom and at the range?" Everyone was happy with that outcome, including the students in the training classes – they knew they were getting a high level of training in a critical skill.

The defensive tactics training was a tougher sell. There were a lot of complaints in the beginning – the rangers and lifeguards in the field thought the training took too much time, and the martial arts aficionados kept carping that the Department was using the wrong system.

The training center staff came up with a terrific strategy – recruit and enlist top-notch rangers and lifeguards to be the "field instructors" for the program. Paula and Stan would start by getting these well-respected lifeguards and rangers prepared as instructors and coaches – not only to reinforce the training in the field, but to assist with leading classes at Asilomar.

As Paula recalls, "We picked people who would be role models and who had the ability to be well-regarded instructors. I really think a big reason for the program's success was the high quality of the first several groups of instructors. They all continued to instruct throughout their careers and became very supportive managers for the program."

One challenging moment for the success of the defensive tactics program occurred during one of those early training sessions at Asilomar. One of the students was from a previous generation of rangers – let's call him "Jack." He was not of the "Mott generation," and Jack had a reputation for using intimidation, along with his physical size and strength, to handle situations in the field.

At the beginning of the class, on Monday morning, Paula gave the usual first hour orientation to the group that covered the objectives of the class, the expected results for the week of training, the standards of behavior, and – most importantly – financial support for the coffee fund. After she had finished her introduction, the tall, rangy, and muscular Ranger Jack stood up and told Paula, "I'm here to see what YOU could POSSIBLY teach ME about ANY aspect of defensive tactics." Paula thanked him for his input, while Jack looked around at the other students with a satisfied look on his face and sat down.

At the break, Stan Kephart took Paula aside and told her what he wanted her to do. "Your mission, your one job this whole training, is to work closely with Jack. You will do it pleasantly, and you will be helpful – nothing more." It turned out to be sound advice. Although Jack was a big, tough guy, he was neither graceful nor coordinated. He had always relied on his size, strength, and intimidation to take care of sketchy situations.

It was obvious right away that Jack was struggling with the new techniques being taught. Stan made Paula work with Jack on these moves, which obviated the need to be physically powerful. A small woman like Paula, using the proper methods in the correct way, could effect the arrest and control of someone much larger and stronger.

Paula recalls, "So I would go up to Jack during the practical training and offer to help and show him the nuances of a particular move, and he would start to finally get it. 'Oh, that really does work!' he would exclaim.

"But here was my secret weapon – while helping Jack, I would demonstrate a 'pain compliance' move. Let's say I would put him in a 'wristlock' – solely to help him, of course! As you might guess, this simple technique is very painful for the bad guy. While he was in this wristlock, I would order Jack to stand on his tiptoes, or I would have him raise his other hand, things like that. If he did not comply, I would make the wristlock more painful. If he did comply…well, you get the picture.

"The point was, here I am – a petite woman – and I am successfully getting Jack to cooperate with me. I would often catch the other students grinning while they took a break to watch me work with Jack.

"At the end of the training, Jack apologized for his early comments and thanked me for teaching him some valuable techniques. Stan had the insight to have me use 'honey instead of vinegar,' and that approach worked like a charm."

Paula spent a total of five years at the training center, which by then had been renamed the William Penn Mott Jr. Training Center – or the Mott Training Center. Bill Mott was a true park visionary – in addition

Paula retires as the Chief Ranger of the Monterey District, 2003.

to his insistence that women be allowed to become state park rangers, he also was the moving force behind the establishment of the training center at Asilomar and the Department's major emphasis on training. As an example of the high regard in which Mott was held, after his tenure as California's State Parks director, President Ronald Reagan named him the director of the National Park Service.

As Paula's assignment at Asilomar came to a close, she moved to the nearby Monterey District to work as a supervising ranger at the state parks in that area. At that point, she began to feel relieved that her days of being a pioneer in the Department were winding down, as well. Women were now being hired as park rangers and many of those women had started to advance to supervisory and management positions. By their hard work, intelligence, judgment, and grace, they had set a magnificent example for all rangers, regardless of gender.

In 1984, when she promoted to the superintendent position of the Napa District (which included Bothe–Napa Valley State Park, Robert Louis Stevenson State Park, and Bale Grist Mill State Historic Park), the local newspaper – the St. Helena Star – ran an article on her new assignment. Rather than focus on her gender, the newspaper welcomed her home as a native daughter. This was an indication of how far the

Department – and, indeed, society as a whole – had come in 12 years. Being a woman in a position of leadership was not the story any more.

She later took a transfer back to the Monterey District as its chief ranger and spent about 18 years in that assignment until she decided to retire in 2003. In those 31+ years, she had become the first woman ranger, the first ranger to marry another ranger (actually, she and Harry Morse tied for that honor), and the first Departmental defensive tactics instructor and training coordinator. She and Harry were also the first rangers to work in the Park Experience exhibit trailer.

Paula believes that she was very lucky to have found this wonderful career. She also thinks that she was fortunate not to be selected to work at Folsom Lake or San Luis Obispo – her first two interview opportunities – back in 1972. "I really don't think I would have experienced the variety of aspects of the ranger position or such a supportive network of co-workers. At Santa Cruz Mountains, however, superintendent Curt Mitchell created and maintained the environment for me to succeed. With Director Mott leading the way, I was the right person at the right time in the right place."

She also is quick to credit the support and mentoring of hundreds of colleagues and supervisors in her 31+ years at State Parks. "My colleagues in group 'E,' the staff at all of my assignments, the 'network' of the first few waves of women rangers, those people I am not even aware of who were supportive of me in important personnel meetings – I really would not have been as successful without them. I would be remiss, however, if I did not call out the splendid mentoring of my last four district superintendents – Mary Wright, Bill Fait, Denzil Verardo, and Lynn Rhodes. When I was approaching the end of my career, I started to convince myself that I pretty much had the job under control. But then Mary and Lynn would keep challenging me to do better and keep improving – right to the end. I thank them for their love and friendship.

"I am really proud of the job I did as the chief ranger of the Monterey District during the nearly 20 years I served there. I hope the staff felt that I listened to and supported them, and I believe that the district's programs and operations continued to improve during my tenure."

For these last 20 years or so of her career, she was happy not to be a groundbreaker any more. She was Paula Peterson – Chief Ranger. She preferred wearing that hat, and, unlike several previous iterations of uniform items, it fit her extremely well.

For more information —

Butler, Mary Ellen. *Prophet of the Parks -- The Story of William Penn Mott, Jr.*
National Recreation and Park Association, 1999.

BILL DEITCHMAN

The Rafting Ranger

On a warm summer day in 1986, Bill Deitchman nervously sat in his 14-foot inflatable raft in a calm river pool at the top of Ruck-A-Chucky Rapid – a churning, roaring, boulder-strewn, and steep cataract along the Middle Fork of the American River in Auburn State Recreation Area. Another local nickname for this mess of whitewater is the Ruck-A-Chucky complex, since it is composed of waterfalls, rapids, and massive boulders with less-than-comforting monikers, such as Chunder Falls, Push Rock, Ruck-A-Chucky Falls, Coffin Rapid, and Cleavage Rapid. Gee, "Coffin Rapid" – makes you want to jump in a raft and give it a go, right? And I am not sure I even want to know how "Cleavage Rapid" got its name.

Classified as a Class VI rapid, Ruck-A-Chucky had never before been run by any boater, as far as anyone reputable knew. For boaters familiar with this complex, Ruck-A-Chucky was considered unrunnable, and any attempt to run it was deemed, well, suicidal.

A guide trying to survive Ruck-A-Chucky complex. *Courtesy of Bill Deitchman.*

According to international whitewater rapid rating systems, Class VI whitewater means, "The difficulties of Class V carried to the extreme. Almost impossible and very dangerous. For experts only. Involves risk of life. Class VI rapids are not commercially raftable." California State Parks has a shorter, but just as clear, definition for Class VI whitewater – "Unrunnable."

Often, Class VI rapids are nearly vertical waterfalls, and kayakers like to joke, "You don't really 'run' a Class VI rapid – you just try to survive it." The skill involved lies in setting up your raft in the correct spot on the river and at the right alignment (in the case of Ruck-A-Chucky, pointed directly downstream). Once the river craft gets up enough speed, the boater stows his oars or paddle, just hangs on to an inside grab rope, and hopes that he lives to tell the tale.

Bill chuckles, "After over 30 years of running this stretch of the American River, I still really don't know what 'Ruck-A-Chucky' means or how this rapid came to be called that. I have also seen maps that call it 'Rocky Chuck' or 'Rock-Chuck.'"

At the time of this first descent, Bill was not yet the river ranger for the American River that runs through Auburn State Recreation Area – he had been running rivers as a commercial river guide for several years prior to joining State Parks. Still, he was determined to pioneer a run through Ruck-A-Chucky.

For over a year, he had sought the help of other guides to run the rapid with him in a raft. Finally, another river guide – Jeff Ames – agreed to go with him over the falls. Bill had also enlisted the assistance of 12 fellow guides, who were equipped with "throw bags," spinal backboards, medical equipment, and other safety gear.

They stood ready to assist these first-descenters from both sides of the river, as well as from the mid-channel rocks below the falls. In addition to these friends and co-workers – they were standing on boulders with the various safety gear items – a few other fellow guides had carried their kayaks down to eddies, and set up there as safety boats. Eddies are small stretches of water that run counter to the main current. Usually, they are either just upstream of a river boulder or on the sides of the river. They form calm refuges in otherwise turbulent whitewater – in this case, they were good spots for the safety boats to wait during the raft's descent. If they were needed – due to a flip or a boater getting ejected from the boat – these safety kayakers could easily enter the main current and help either Bill or Jeff get to a safe haven.

This would be a very dangerous rapid to run in a boat. Running it without a boat? Well, remember the description above of a Class VI rapid – Involves risk of life! So if someone got ejected and started "swimming" the rapid instead of rafting it, he would at least have some helpers.

If a raft gets wedged between rocks or "wrapped" on a boulder, the guide typically would be on his own to work his boat out of the predicament. The typical remedy is called "high-siding" – the boater shifts his weight to the downstream end of the raft. This maneuver lifts the upstream end of the boat a tad – usually just enough for the river to push enough water under the upstream end of the boat to float the raft off the boulder. If high-siding didn't work, then the guides observing from the boulders with throw bags would try to get a rope to the rafters and help pull them out of trouble.

Bill recalls what led up to that run, "I had been commercially guiding the Middle Fork for two years. Many outfitters would 'line' their rafts through the waterfall, using ropes to guide their unoccupied boat all the way to the bottom of the rapid. That was a huge, time-consuming hassle for us guides. This technique also presented tremendous exposure to those guides working the lines on the precipices of the canyon walls above the churning waters and rocky sieves. Fortunately, the company that I was working for opted to try something new – 'ghost boating' the rafts over the falls.

"'Ghost boating' is another name for sending a raft through a rapid with no humans aboard. Think of throwing a piece of driftwood into the river above the rapid – it just goes where the river wants to take it. So, while I watched over 100 rafts being ghost-boated over the falls, I noticed that only one raft flipped while making the journey, and that was because it had taken on a lot of water ABOVE the falls. These observations told me that the hydraulics of that rapid did not naturally conspire to pitch a rafter into the river or flip the rafts.

"At that time, many of the commercial boats were hauling gear for wilderness camping trips. Back then, a Coleman lantern was standard equipment, and each lantern had a couple of mantles attached – these provided the mechanism for providing light, and they were VERY delicate. I inspected a lot of the gear that had gone through the rapid, and well over 50% of the mantles were intact after going over the falls. I became convinced that the journey down Ruck-A-Chucky was gentler than it appeared.

A raft gets wrapped on a boulder in Ruck-A-Chucky. *Courtesy of Bill Deitchman.*

"I think I was the only commercial guide at that time who believed that this monster rapid could actually be successfully run by a rafter. I became somewhat obsessed with running it, to the point where I was not sleeping well at night – and probably would not – until I had run Ruck-A-Chucky. It was just one of those things – I knew it could be done, and done safely. Now it was time to prove it."

A lot of the motivation for Bill was that he had the opportunity to run a huge "unrunnable" rapid successfully and safely – one that everyone else thought was a suicide mission. He had done his homework on the ghost-boats, and he gave himself a 95% chance for success. Besides, how many people ever have the opportunity to pioneer a river run in California – a true first descent?

"So, Jeff and I were sitting at the top of the falls in our raft, looked at each other and simultaneously nodded, then signaled the other safety crew members that we were on our way. We knew that the guides in the pools and eddies below were now on high alert."

Bill and Jeff sat on the outer tube of the mid-section of the raft while they paddled. Bill was the lead guide and called out signals to Jeff so that they could coordinate their paddle strokes and keep the raft on the correct course. Their raft began to pick up speed as it headed to the first three-foot shallow drop upstream of the falls.

They were sure to keep on the left side of the river – if the raft went too far to the right, there was the danger of entering a steep, slotted drop called "Coffin Rapid." All of the water in this slot squeezes down into an underground passageway – it is obvious how this rapid got its name.

The course of the raft stayed true, while Bill and Jeff continued to paddle towards the top lip of the falls. At this lip, there is an enormous submerged rock that creates a "hump" in the water – this hump almost crosses the entire entrance to the top of the falls, so there is really no good way to avoid it. Here the canyon narrows to about 18 feet wide. Typically, as canyon walls come closer together, rivers move more quickly and more violently.

Bill and Jeff aimed for the center of the submerged rock. Despite this weird hump of water, Bill believed that going over the mid-point would line up the boat for the cleanest possible run over the falls. The two guides maintained their coordinated and clean paddle strokes, and they nailed their target perfectly at the top of the falls. Their boat slid forward and began to tip over the lip of the falls, when Bill called out "DROP!" He and Jeff dropped to a sitting position in the bottom of the raft – side by side – with their legs stretched out in front of them so that their bodies could brace between the rear and front seats of the raft.

This maneuver served to lower their center of gravity, which helped stabilize the boat as much as much as possible. This also protected their bodies from impacts with boulders, since the inflatable tubes shielded them. They simultaneously pulled in their paddles and held on tightly to the 'grab lines' they had rigged around and through the middle compartment of the raft.

All of this happened in a couple of seconds as their raft began its drop over the 30-foot high Ruck-A-Chucky Falls. As they rushed down the steep slope of the turbulent cataract, a wall of water hit them in the face and just about filled the raft. Almost as soon as their run began, however, the raft hit the bottom of the falls – still upright – and Bill and Jeff still remained in the raft. The rescue crew gave out shouts of approval and congratulations for the first successful descent – ever – over the falls.

However, Bill and Jeff could not relax quite yet. At the bottom of the falls is a slalom course of boulders they still needed to maneuver through. If they were not careful, it was still possible to wrap or flip the raft. And if one or both of them wound up getting ejected, they knew there were spots in the rapid where swimmers would likely get stuck underwater. They finally made it to a calm pool, though, and were able to celebrate along with the safety crew.

Bill adds, "Once we ran it, we really did not advertise that fact for a couple of years. Even though there were other guides helping out on that first run, I think everybody just kind of kept quiet about it. However, my fellow river guides told me that, when they mentioned our run to guides from other companies, no one could believe that this 'unrunnable' rapid had actually been rafted successfully. These rumors eventually piqued other boaters' interest in trying it, but it was probably another two years before anyone ran it again.

"Later, about 11 years after the first descent of Ruck-A-Chucky Falls, when I became the state park river ranger at Auburn SRA, no one was really rafting the falls – either on private or commercial trips. I chose not to run the rapid during our regular river patrols, because I did not want to encourage other, less experienced boaters to attempt it.

"However, over time, it became more common for commercial guides and private boaters to run it. By the early 2000s, it was starting to become pretty common for river guides to do Ruck-A-Chucky during commercial trips.

"One day, I was rafting a State Parks manager down the Middle Fork, and I asked him what he thought about us rangers running it during our patrols. It turns out he was very supportive of the notion, and taking our rafts over the falls became a regular part of our American River patrol.

"If people asked me if they should try it, I would tell them it is possible, but you had better know what you are doing and bring your 'A' game to the river that day. Before you attempt it, go back and read the description of Class VI water – just because it has been run successfully by others does not mean that you do not have to take this stretch of the river very seriously."

In a typical season, not every descent through Ruck-A-Chucky goes smoothly – boaters occasionally get wedged, wrapped, or are capsized. Bill suspects that the visitors perched above the falls at various points along the portage trail might get a little too much enjoyment out of seeing the professionals in trouble. The guides must do this route solo – all visitors are required to walk around the rapids.

Bill chuckles and asks, "Do you know the most dangerous part of the entire raft trip from Oxbow to Greenwood? It is the people walking around the rapids or getting into or out of a raft – the rocks are very slippery there. Lots of these folks are frightened to death of the river and the possibility of 'swimming' a major rapid, but then they twist an ankle after slipping on a wet rock on the shore."

At the bottom of this rapid, visitors re-board their rafts. Downstream of the falls, there are still significant rapids on the way to the popular take-out at Greenwood Crossing. Boaters still have to navigate rapids such as Cleavage, Parallel Parking, 101st Airborne, Pop Quiz, and Final Exam. However, Ruck-A-Chucky is definitely the toughest cataract on the river.

Although the boating concessionaires compete for customers, the river guides put all (okay, most) rivalry aside at Ruck-A-Chucky. They take turns being the rescue boats at the halfway eddy and at the bottom pool. Their focus at that point is to help their fellow guides survive the ride without injury.

For about 18 years, Bill Deitchman was the only ranger in the State Parks Department assigned to rafting whitewater. Along with the ranger/pilot at Anza–Borrego, the wilderness ranger at Mt. San Jacinto, and a few others in iconic ranger assignments, Bill is still amazed and appreciative that he got to do this during his career with State Parks.

Since the Department got involved in managing the stretch of the American River that goes through Auburn SRA, there have been five consecutive lead river rangers. When Bill arrived to work

Bill Deitchman on the oars of the state park raft.

at Auburn's whitewater program, there were three rangers (including him) assigned to work on the river. Later, due to budget and staffing cutbacks at State Parks, there was only one whitewater ranger for almost two decades – Bill – and he has since transferred to Marshall Gold Discovery State Historic Park. As of 2018, his rafting position at Auburn SRA had not been re-filled.

The river can get crowded on summer weekends. *Courtesy of Bill Deitchman.*

Bill worries that this may pose problems in the future. "When I started here at Auburn, I had the advantage of being able to learn from the two other rangers assigned to running this river. I was an experienced rafter, and I knew a lot about the nuances and dangers of the all three forks of the American River in this area. I had also worked as a seasonal planner on the Interim River Management Plan (IRMP) for the park, and I had experience in its Whitewater Recreation Office (WRO).

"This background – as a boater, commercial outfitter, and seasonal park employee – all here in Auburn SRA, really gave me a wonderful starting point for being the lead ranger in Auburn's whitewater program. I also had the advantage of learning from kind, patient, and experienced mentors.

"They taught me the natural and cultural history of the area, as well as the ins and outs of the river management program. They helped me learn which concessionaires posed problems, so that I could deal with them appropriately. Now that I have left Auburn SRA, who will train the new ranger? Will there even be a new ranger? Where will the corporate memory be stored?"

The job of the river ranger is not all fun, though. Managing the river program presents its own set of "Class IV and V rapids." Prior to his becoming the lead for the whitewater program in 1997, the last river management plan update had been approved in 1992 – this was the IRMP. This document, along with its previous iterations, was very helpful in providing Bill and his team with guidance in helping to set the parameters for guiding their management decisions.

Typically, there are between 25 and 30 river concessionaires in the park every season, and, in addition to having fun, they all want to make a profit for their company. Bill knew the owners of all the boating companies, but it was harder to keep track of the skill level and river knowledge of all the guides they employed. Bill definitely had to grow into this aspect of the job, but he quickly became as good at sizing up guides as he was at "reading the water," and he soon had earned the respect of the local commercial boating community.

On a beautiful day in June of 2015, Bill agrees to take me on a run from the put-in at Oxbow to Greenwood, a popular take-out spot. I arrive at the park's boatshed at 7:20 a.m., and Bill and his crew of seasonal park aides are already there, getting everything ready for the day.

In theory, Bill and his staff worked four 10-hour shifts per week. I knew they were already working by seven in the morning, and we don't get back to the boathouse until after five that afternoon. The whole crew still has a lot of work to do – cleaning and repairing gear and getting everything ready for the following morning. Bill laughs when I mention that these warm summer days are more than 10 hours long. "My whole crew has a great attitude – their philosophy is to do whatever it takes to get the job done."

On the one-hour drive to the put-in spot, Bill pulls over a couple of times to point out the lay of the land. This stretch of the American River is rugged country – the canyon walls are steep, the canyons are heavily wooded, and there are few signs of civilization, such as roads or houses. Although it is not legally classified as state wilderness, it has much of that same wild character. There are only a couple of primitive roads that run down to the river. Boaters, fishing enthusiasts, campers, hikers, gold panners, and picnickers just wanting to cool off in the river on a hot summer afternoon – they all use these dirt roads and trails to access the river.

Bill and the author prepare for a run of the Middle Fork.

We finally arrive at the put-in at Oxbow, and the park aides have driven a separate truck to the river. Bill and a highly skilled park aide named Josh Verseman will be running the river this day with me as a passenger. Eric and Angie help carry the raft to the put-in, top off the tubes with air, snugly stow the equipment and supplies, and otherwise get the boat rigged for the river.

I am happy to get an early start, and Bill discusses the reasons for getting to the put-in early. A dam above this stretch of the Middle Fork controls the amount of flows into the river – the releases take place in the morning and only last a couple of hours. Every boater wants to raft the higher water, since this means the whole river will flow faster. Nobody wants the extra work of rowing a raft full of passengers down a slow river. The put-in parking is very busy, since all the commercial guides want to hit the high water releases. Bill adds that, on this stretch of the river, most of the rapids are more fun at higher water.

Rigging the park raft for a patrol run.

Even though I am an experienced rafter and kayaker, I make sure that Bill knows that there is quite a bit of dust on my boating résumé. "No problem," Bill laughs. "I don't take anybody on the river without a safety talk and a rowing shakedown." Bill's raft is set up as a hybrid – an "oar-paddle combo." He is on a set of oars in the center of the raft and provides most of the power and steering, while Josh and I are in the front of the raft using paddles for quick turns and bursts of speed.

Bill wants to ensure I understand the common rowing commands – forward, back, left, right, stop, and rest – as well as how to execute them. The additional lesson is how to get Josh and me to paddle as a team. Bill has to "trim" the raft as well – with three boaters of different weights and paddling skills, he wants to make us an effective boating team. There are some serious rapids on the Middle

Fork, and we will need to be at maximum efficiency as a rowing and paddling team. Bill is smiling when he adds, "The worst thing for a river ranger to do is capsize in a rapid with dozens of commercial river guides and customers watching – no flipping today, guys!"

We are finally ready to show the river who is boss, when Bill adds, "One thing I am sure you remember from your kayaking days, Dave, is that the river is the boss. If we start thinking we are in control, we are in danger. Every time we go through a big rapid, I thank the river for allowing me to pass through safely that day. The river has a lot of surprises, and our job is to be ready for the unexpected, as well as the expected. I have run this stretch of the river about a thousand times, and no two runs are the same."

At the put-in, just before the dam release point, the river is narrow and fast. There will be no gentle warm-ups for us! Very soon after we leave shore, I am about to ask Bill when we will hit our first rapid when I get a face full of river wave crashing over the bow of the raft, less than a minute into our river trip. The adrenaline of running a rapid, combined with very cold water in my face, definitely gets my attention. Bill announces with no apparent concern for my sputtering shock, "That was Alarm Clock – also known as Good Morning Rapid – Class III."

After traveling through several Class II and III rapids, we approach the pool above the top of Last Chance Rapid – also known as High Anxiety Rapid. Last Chance happens to be just above the famous Class V rapid known as Tunnel Chute. It is important that rafters get through Last Chance safely – and set up their alignment quickly – since the end of this rapid leads quickly into the entrance to the Chute. Bill guides us into a small eddy – a calm river spot safely above Last Chance – to review our plan of action.

Bill and Josh prepare the raft for running Last Chance and Tunnel Chute. River gear bags are moved from the rear compartment of the raft and stored in its midsection. The oars are taken off the pins and strapped down diagonally across the length of the raft. Bill will guide these next two rapids from the rear of the raft with a guide paddle.

Bill then reviews the drill for Josh and me. "First, we have to run Last Chance, which can be pretty tricky. I will need strong, solid, and consistent paddle strokes when I call for them. Brace yourselves after we make the turn through the rapid, since there is a really good-sized hole at the bottom that we will hit. If you fall out of the raft, it is very important to swim as hard as you can to river right and try to get out of the water above Tunnel Chute.

"If you fail to get off the river in time, prepare quickly for swimming down the Chute. Hold your breath, ball up, tuck your head, and don't panic – you will get held underwater for about 12 seconds, and it will seem like forever. Hopefully, once you pop up to the surface at the bottom of the Chute, there is a good recovery pool – we will regroup there."

Let's review – Last Chance, High Anxiety, prepare to swim the bottom of a rapid, don't panic, and "hopefully" pop to the surface. What could possibly go wrong? I am almost convinced I will survive this adventure when Bill mentions laconically, "The worst injury I have ever seen on this river was a guide

What could possibly go wrong?

who fell partially out of her boat in Tunnel Chute Rapid and hit her head on the wall of the Chute – she survived, but wound up with a fractured skull." Now I feel so much better, and I start practicing my death grip on the raft's interior grab lines.

Bill continues, "However, since I don't expect any of us to be swimming, we will need to prepare for setting up to run Tunnel Chute immediately after we exit Last Chance Rapid. Follow my paddle commands, and you and Josh will get us set up in the proper alignment for the Chute. Just above the hole at the top of the rapid, I will shout 'Ready – Drop!' and you guys grab your paddles and get to the bottom of the raft. I want the lowest center of gravity possible for the big hole, and I want you inside the raft, since we may slam against the sides of the chute as we go down."

Finally, something I am good at – providing a low center of gravity! By this point, I was wondering what effect every named rapid on the river was supposed to produce. If Alarm Clock has the goal of waking you up, what then is the aim of Last Chance and Anxiety Rapid? If there were a rapid with the moniker "Sudden Death" or "Fatal Falls," I might just have to walk around that one. I was not yet even aware of "Coffin Rapid," and our day has just begun!

In the pool above Last Chance, Bill, Josh, and I go through a couple of dry runs of synchronized paddling and the "Ready – Drop" drill. Once Bill is confident that we are working together as a team, we proceed down the river. First, we paddle into and make the sharp left turn through Last Chance Rapid. All goes smoothly, and then we approach the entrance of the 25-foot wide, 200-foot long man-made gold mining bedrock excavation known as Tunnel Chute. Here, we follow exactly Bill's commands that get us set up properly at the top of the rapid.

When we are rushing towards the first hole, Bill calls out "Ready – Drop!" and Josh and I drop onto the floor of the raft. We grab each other's back, and we're racing down the Chute. The raft jostles, turns, and bucks, and then, in a final attempt to throw us out of the raft, the river swallows us into the last monstrous hole before it spits our raft out almost vertically with violent force.

This gigantic hole at the bottom of Tunnel Chute Rapid is soon followed by a ride through the long, dark tunnel. Tunnel Chute adds to the variety of whitewater experiences on this fork of the river. Thankfully, there is a calm river pool at the end of the tunnel, and just about every boat takes a breather there.

Bill is trained as an EMT – Emergency Medical Technician – and he has had to treat dozens of incidents, both minor and major, along the river. With about two-dozen concessionaires guiding hundreds of passengers on a hot summer weekend day, things can get very busy on the river.

"There has been only one real yahoo when it comes to emergency response on this stretch of the river," Bill recalls. "A passenger went into atrial fibrillation – a racing and irregular heartbeat – that can be very frightening for the victim. His guide flagged me down from his raft, and we got the victim calmed down as we pulled over to a large river beach.

"I was already on our satellite phone – the only reliable communications device along the river – as soon as I knew what we had medically, and I had picked a wide and hard-packed beach. I was thinking ahead – we would surely need a helicopter extraction for the victim. I got hold of dispatch, and they sent the California Highway Patrol's rescue helicopter immediately. The helo and the medics got the guy to the hospital, and everything turned out fine for him.

Boaters can relax after the tunnel.

"Funny thing, though – the bozo was not this victim – it was his brother. The brother kept whining, 'Why wasn't there a road down to the river where my brother had his episode? Why did you pick that spot to pull over to the riverbank, knowing there was no road access there? Why did it take the helicopter 40 minutes to arrive?' Just on and on and on.

"I tried to explain that, um, a helicopter is a lot faster than a raft, so it made sense to get his brother stabilized and cooled down in the shade near a good landing zone for the chopper. I also reminded him of the waiver he and his brother had each signed for the outfitter that mentioned that they were entering a rugged area with scant facilities and dangerous conditions.

"He just did not want to listen to logic. At times like those, you realize that the brother was really worried, and he wanted to rant at somebody. That day, I got to be that somebody – the designated 'rantee.' In those situations, you do not try to win the argument or defend your position – you go into a mode of making sure the complainant sees that you are truly listening and that you understand his concerns. You want him to know that you will do your best to improve the situation for future victims. If you ever hear back from these people later, it is almost always to apologize for 'losing it' during a stressful incident. I see these incidents as an opportunity to gain support for our program and understanding for the conditions we work under."

Josh, Bill, and I continue our run down the river, and it is obvious that Bill loves the river and his job. He spends time discussing the history of the region – especially the river, the canyons, and the proposed Auburn dam. One phrase that is often used to describe people like Bill is, "He is a walking encyclopedia." Well, Bill is actually a rowing encyclopedia!

Being in the heart of California's gold country, the region that now makes up the state recreation area saw many attempts and a variety of methods designed to extract gold from the river, the tributary streams, and its banks. Bill chuckles as he points out one remote house and large section of land that had allegedly changed ownership, during the Gold Rush period, in a poker game. Bill adds that, as the story goes, there was an epic amount of alcohol involved.

The politics of Auburn State Recreation Area, particularly vis-à-vis the proposed Auburn dam, are very interesting. Many of these topics are discussed in this book in the earlier chapter on Mike Lynch. An additional issue to consider in this chapter, of course, is the impact that the creation of a recreational lake would have on the whitewater boating activity of the Middle and North Forks of the American River. It is easy to summarize the impact – the lake created behind the dam would eliminate that very popular activity by flooding the entire 50-mile stretch of the river and canyon within Auburn SRA.

One of the sweet spots on the river is the scenic Kanaka Falls rapid. Usually rated as Class IV, Kanaka is a short and thrilling rapid, and can be Class V at high water. One of its main assets is the large boulders on the shore that sit close to and above the river – these are great places to take photographs of the passengers in various stages of delight, thrill, terror, or even going airborne while they are getting ejected from the raft. We are one of the first rafts to run Kanaka this day, so after our run through this rapid, we set up our raft in the eddy at the bottom for a while to make sure the commercial boats make it through safely. Today, all the

Kanaka Falls

passengers seem particularly determined to remain in their raft, so we eventually push out of the eddy and continue our river journey.

Farther downstream, we pass through some popular fishing holes and fly-fishing riffles. Bill checks fishing licenses for all – another way that he is protecting the park and its resources. Today, everyone has their license in their possession, and is in compliance with all provisions of the Fish and Wildlife Code.

At lunch, we pull into an eddy on river left in some shade – it is not a "secret spot," but it only fits one raft, so we have it to ourselves. It is a beautiful day on the river, and Bill takes this opportunity to talk philosophically, as well as shine some light on his life outside of State Parks.

Bill has a B.S. from Stanford in biology – he is one smart guy. During his freshman year, he happened to pick up an issue of Sunset magazine that had an article on whitewater rafting. Coincidentally, Bill had a neighbor in Boulder City, where Bill's family was then living, who had spent some time guiding raft trips on the Colorado River through the Grand Canyon, and he would regale Bill with tales of the life of a river guide. The combination of the article and his neighbor's stories piqued Bill's interest and spurred him to try to land a summer job in this field.

As he recalls, Bill wrote to all 20 outfitters referenced in the article, asking them about the possibility of seasonal work, but about half never responded to his query. Of the companies that did respond, only two offered the possibility of work that actually included pay. Bill needed to make some money, so finally he signed on with a company named "Wet and Wild," but first he had to complete training at their whitewater school.

After the training, Bill wound up working as a guide on several trips in 1976, including the South Fork of the American River, the Rogue River, the Kern River, and the very popular Stanislaus River. The whitewater portions of the Stanislaus have been flooded by the construction of the New Mellones Dam and its associated reservoir. It is not difficult, while on the river at Auburn SRA, to look up at the canyon walls and visualize the same fate for the North and Middle Forks of the American River.

Subsequent to this river guiding experience, Bill picked up some time lifeguarding for the National Park Service at Lake Mead National Recreation Area. After the summer following his freshman year at Stanford, he decided to transfer to the University of Nevada, Las Vegas (UNLV), to save on costs. During his two-year stay at UNLV, he continued to take courses related to his pre-med major. Bill kept his lifeguard job at Lake Mead, and his supervisor there offered Bill the opportunity to get his certificate as an emergency medical technician.

He did complete this training, and during his junior year in college got a job in a hospital emergency room as an orthopedic cast specialist. This later led to a job as an assistant to an orthopedic surgeon. Bill also spent some time working in a law office, handling and doing research on tort cases. Looking back now, Bill considers all these experiences invaluable in his ranger assignments.

It was during this stint in college in Las Vegas that Bill also met his lovely wife, Dianne. They were both pre-med, and it was probably fitting that they met in a "chemistry" class. They eventually got married in 1981, and they have had three children and four grandchildren in the subsequent 36+ years. Bill's wife is a school principal, and they have had a wonderful time being parents and grandparents.

Bill continued to work at a variety of jobs, and finally went back to Stanford to complete his degree in biology. Before graduation, however, Bill realized that he really had no desire to work in medicine or law – at least not directly. He decided that he wanted to work in the environmental field in some capacity, so Bill started investigating the possibility of working for the State of California. He finally connected with the California Department of Parks and Recreation.

While he was still finishing up some coursework at Stanford University, Bill was hired as a student assistant to work on the river management plan for Auburn State Recreation Area. Bill believes that his experience as a commercial river guide helped him get the job, since he also knew the local geography and the political issues of the area. In addition, he had worked for the National Park Service at Lake Mead, so he had some background in working in a large park with a major recreation program.

While Bill was working on the IRMP, Ranger Rich Silver was selected to be the whitewater ranger at Auburn State Recreation Area. Although Rich eventually became an excellent rafting ranger, at the time he was hired, he simply did not have much experience guiding a raft.

Bill's work on the river management plan put him in touch with the managers of the Parks Department's river program, and they knew that Bill had been an instructor at commercial whitewater schools. They asked Bill if he would be willing to teach Rich how to row and guide. Bill realized that, for the first time, he was actually going to be paid by the state to row whitewater rivers.

After the plan was completed in 1992, Bill was hired at Auburn SRA to work out of the Whitewater Recreation Office (WRO). Bill recalls that Rich was an inspirational and fun supervisor, and Rich encouraged him to think seriously about becoming a park ranger.

Bill followed through on Rich's recommendation, and eventually graduated from the State Parks ranger training academy in 1995. After an initial two-year assignment to Red Rock Canyon State Park, he was able to transfer back to Auburn in 1997. After having managed the WRO for about seven years, Ranger Rich Silver transferred out of Auburn shortly after Bill's arrival. Bill was soon assigned the job of managing Auburn's WRO, and worked there for the next 18 years. He finally transferred to Marshall Gold Discovery State Historic Park in late 2015. Although the South Fork of the American River goes directly through that park, Marshall Gold does not have a whitewater program, and Bill admits that he very seldom gets on the river any more, other than private family trips.

One of his main concerns, not surprisingly, is what the future will hold for the Parks Department, Auburn State Recreation Area, and the park's river program. "Naturally, when you put nearly 20 years into managing and improving a program, you want to see the quality of that program continue well into the future. The Department needs to decide what level of service it wants to provide to the park visitors.

"When we had three river rangers, there was a ranger on duty on the river almost every day that there were park visitors on the river. We handled lots of medical emergencies, and the visitors and concessionaires knew that we would be keeping an eye on the park. Later, however, when the program had been reduced to only one ranger, I rafted the river only about two days per week – and that was in the busy season.

"What other options are there? If there are no rangers on the river, someone has to manage the river program from the office. Instead of a river ranger, you have a seasonal aide or an administrative person writing up contracts and issuing permits. But then you are allowing the park to go back to the days when lots of visitors had guns down there and treated the place like the Wild West.

"We really need a ranger presence on the river – the numbers of visitors down there and the types of activities that people engage in call for some serious oversight. I am not talking only about boaters. There are several dirt roads that lead down to the river, and those river beaches simply are not patrolled as often as they should be any more. If people start to get the idea that they can do whatever they want down there, look out!"

We finally all agree that it is too nice a day to spend much time worrying about "what-ifs," so Bill, Josh, and I pull out of the eddy and continue down this beautiful river. Bill laughs when he shows me the park's two-story outhouse near a beach on river right. "I hate to see structures in this wild area, but the usage is just so heavy down here. Before we built these composting toilets, it was a real nightmare." We pull over to the beach and head to the toilets ourselves. Bill grabs my shoulder and chortles, "Dave, you are our special guest today – Josh and I are going to let you have the first floor level of the outhouse! We'll be right above you."

Eventually we arrive at the pool just above "Ruck-A-Chucky." There are a dozen or so rafts waiting their turn. Due to the difficulty of the run, the need to off-load all passengers, and the need to stage safety boats, it is still time-consuming to traverse this rapid. I am impressed that Bill does not "pull rank" and insist on going ahead of those guides who have been waiting patiently at the top. After telling Josh to take a turn at running Ruck-A-Chucky today, Bill and I disembark – we watch from the boulders above the cataract as Josh "aces" the Class VI rapid.

"One of things I get the most satisfaction from," Bill mentions, "is the ability to mentor the young park aides. Josh is an excellent example of a young man who wants to build a career in State Parks, so this is not just a job for him. He wants to learn from me – he is always asking why I handled a situation a certain way. Sometimes I will let people off easy in a law enforcement contact, and sometimes I come down hard on them.

Two-story outhouse on the river.

"Josh is great – he is not criticizing my decisions or my actions – he just wants to understand my thought process and learn from me. I really hope he gets to live his dream. Of course, I tell him often not every State Parks job is quite as cool as this one!"

We meet up with Josh at the lower pool after his successful run through the "Ruck," hop back in the raft, and blast through the few remaining rapids. Soon afterwards we reach the Greenwood access take-out point. We load the boat on the pickup and trailer that the park aides have shuttled over for us, and we start heading back to the park headquarters.

On the steep drive up the dirt road leading back to civilization, Bill recalls one felony – grand theft – involving river users. He was able to solve the crime, but there were a lot of moving parts to the case. "For a couple of years before I returned to Auburn as a river ranger, there had been a series of thefts – a small group of thieves was hitting the river campers pretty hard.

"Commercial outfitters at that time were allowed to have their camping gear brought down into the river canyon at Ford's Bar by a fellow the whitewater companies would hire. He would drive a large pickup down the dirt roads and drop camping gear at the designated campsites. Sometimes, there were

Josh Verseman takes the oars.

so many campers that he had to make more than one trip down to the river.

"This meant that the camping gear would sit unattended for a couple of hours before the rafters arrived. The park staff started getting reports that equipment, food, and clothing would be missing from the piles of gear. There were even reports of possessions being stolen in the middle of the night – from occupied campsites!

"After I returned to work in the park in 1997, the thefts continued. The staff tried staking out the campsites during the most vulnerable time periods, to no avail. One day, however, one of the commercial river trips arrived at their campsite at Ford's Bar, and their guide noticed that the gear had been rifled through. Just then, two equestrians arrived – they had ridden down the Western States Trail to the river and needed to water their horses.

"The river guide asked them if they had seen anyone on the trail. They answered that they had passed three adult males hiking up the trail, and those guys were carrying a bunch of loose camping gear. The guide was furious, and he quickly formed a posse of river clients. They went running up the trail in the direction the equestrians had come from.

"Eventually, the guide and his posse saw the thieves up ahead and began yelling at the three men. The suspects looked back, dropped the gear, and began running up the trail. The river guide was not able to catch up to them, but he thought that he recognized one of the suspects and was able to come up with his name. That turned out to be the break we needed to solve this series of crimes.

"With this information, I enlisted the help of a detective at the Placer County Sheriff's Office, and we were eventually able to obtain three search warrants – one for the residence of each suspect. Other local agencies agreed to help, and we did an early morning search of the three properties. We ultimately recovered a lot of the stolen gear, and the ringleader went to jail for several years. His accomplices received lesser sentences, and this put an end to that crime ring. I was told that, at that time, it was one of the largest theft cases that State Parks had ever solved!"

Bill estimates that he spent about 500 hours per year on the river as a ranger. When you figure that he did that job for nearly 20 years, and then you add in all his private and commercial runs on the American River through Auburn SRA – Bill knew this river very well. It is hard to imagine this stretch of the river without Bill's guiding touch.

The main whitewater season lasts only from late spring to early fall. As the temperature of the air and the water drop, so does commercial and private boater activity. It is not just the Middle Fork, either. The North Fork of the American River through Auburn SRA and the South Fork through Marshall Gold Discovery State Historic Park also required Bill's attention while he was assigned there.

"The (normally) dam-controlled flows on the Middle Fork make it the more heavily used commercial river of the two forks in Auburn," Bill adds. "It has more rapids, and there are rapids rated at every level of difficulty – up through Class VI. It is also a 15-mile run normally – that appeals to guides and customers alike. The North Fork is a shorter run – often only four miles, but it has several challenging Class IV and V rapids. It is truly a remarkably beautiful stretch of river, and it is particularly popular with private boaters."

There are no hydroelectric dams upstream on the North Fork, so the boating season is dependent on spring run-off – that makes its season much shorter (and in some years non-existent). Part of the challenge for the outfitters is finding guides who have the experience and skill to take on a Class V rapid without dumping all the customers overboard. Every prospective guide says they can do it. But again, the river is in charge, and the company owners are taking on a lot of responsibility and liability.

Bill continues, "Guides and private boaters value their time on the river. Naturally, they would all rather be paddling or pulling and pushing on oars than setting up or taking down their equipment. Dave – you have rowed the Colorado River through Grand Canyon National Park – so you probably know why those guides like that trip so much. Of course it is a beautiful setting and an amazing and challenging river. But the bonus for the guides is that they set up their rigs on day one, and then they launch a 15-day trip. They don't have to get off the river and break all their equipment down for another two weeks!"

There is also the option of camping on the Middle Fork. Some of the outfitters offer an overnight river trip that includes one night of sleeping out – the preferred campground for both commercial and private boat trips is at Ford's Bar – about 10 river miles below the Oxbow put-in. There are other campsites along the river, and many non-commercial boaters also like to camp at the Ruck-A-Chucky campground. This is located at the Greenwood river access area at mile 15, downstream from Ruck-A-Chucky Falls. Of course, offering a camping experience means the guides have to bring a lot more gear for sleeping, cooking, and entertaining the guests.

Bill is quick to add, "The other 1,500 or so hours that I put in during the year were very important. In fact, I found that if I spent my energy and time on the right things in the 'off-season,' the result was that my 500 actual river hours became even more enjoyable, effective, and efficient."

His primary duty, when not rowing, was working in the Whitewater Recreation Office – administering all the activities associated with boating the American River for both commercial outfitters and private boaters. Bill also was available to fill in on land patrol due to staff shortages or because of emergencies.

The level of expertise, integrity, and cooperation with the park staff varies greatly among the two-dozen concessionaires. Bill learned that developing strong relationships with the concessionaires allowed him to be more successful in maintaining a safe and enjoyable river experience for all.

The park staff conducted many public meetings during the preparation of the river management plan for Auburn SRA. This document is the guidepost for staff, concessionaires, and guides on the river. It is effective at outlining river protocols, defining the parameters of commercial operations, and setting standards for outfitters and private boaters.

In order to ensure that policies remained relevant and up to date, Bill also continued to use an outfitters' advisory committee (OAC), composed of eight of those concessionaires. This committee was formed in the '80s, during the development of the draft river management plan. The OAC has worked with State Parks in dealing with various issues, problems, and concerns that would crop up over the years. Part of the job of those eight individuals was to represent – and communicate with – the remaining concessionaires to ensure that any changes were understood by – and acceptable to – all of them. Bill found that working with these outfitters in a cooperative manner helped to develop a positive and respectful relationship between State Parks and the whitewater outfitter industry.

The park has a concessions contract with each river outfitter. This contract spells out the terms of the company's ability to operate guided trips in the park. The park also limits the number of boats and passengers that can be on commercial trips each day. Normally, this works well. Bill was also responsible for inspecting their gear and operations.

Bill chuckles, "When the owner of a company applied for a contract the first time, I always got the same reaction. I handed them our 40-page contract, along with all the additional appendices and addenda. A typical outfitter just wants to be on the river, living the dream, and making a living at the same time. They would usually look at the pile of papers I gave them as though it were radioactive.

"Part of my job was to calm them down – the contracts are really not that bad, and I could help walk them through it. Most of it is common sense – requirements to carry enough personal flotation devices, a first aid kit, a flashlight, and to recycle whenever possible. But I really got a kick out of watching their body language when we first got started. If I believed that they had a sense of humor, I might even hand them a copy of the rather thick river management plan and tell them that one of the contract requirements is that they pass a test on that plan. I was building relationships, and using humor can be a terrific 'connectivity' tool, if used correctly. Some of the potential concessionaires even smiled at that point."

Bill is an affable ranger, and he tried to have a good relationship with all the concessionaires and their guides. Occasionally, though, a concessionaire would try to cheat the system. Let's say Bob's River Trips was not successful in pulling a permit for a certain Sunday. Then that day approaches, and it looks as though it will be a splendid day for a trip down the Middle Fork of the American River. On Saturday, a group of six adults comes into Bob's office and asks about booking a trip the next day. Bob tells them, "Sure, but we'll have to do it under the table. You will need to pay in cash, we will all go in one raft, and if anyone asks, you are my 'friends' out for a private trip and not for a commercial journey."

After 18 years, Bill was pretty much on to all the tricks and knew which outfitters were trying to scam the system. "Remember, I was a guide on the American River before I was its river ranger. This was not my first rodeo. If caught, Bob would have to pay a fine of up to $1,200, and his company could be suspended from operating in the state park for a while."

Bill was always trying to improve the program. The Middle Fork run is extremely popular. It is a good length for day customers and provides an excellent combination of excitement, fun, beauty, difficulty, and risk. Bill saw this as an opportunity to reach a segment of California's population and inspire them – not only about the resources of Auburn SRA – but also the fun of whitewater boating.

To this end, Ranger Rich Silver, an office technician named Theresa Reed, and Bill organized a river interpretive program they named "The Many Voices of the River." Bill assembled a number of experts to teach about archeology, the gold rush and other local history, natural history, geology, and the politics of the river and the region. Bill even recruited J.S. Holliday, who wrote the definitive book on the gold rush period – *The World Rushed In* – to teach a class.

They began by offering this educational program to company owners and river guides. "We would teach them interpretive skills – how to relate the natural and cultural history of the river canyon to the experiences of their customers – as well as the etiquette of the river. We were able to offer a whole week of training to the guides – two days on the North Fork and three days on the Middle Fork. Rich, Theresa, and I rounded up about 20 presenters for this five-day interpretive program.

"Here is the great thing – I loved interpreting the local natural and cultural history to all those people I came in contact with. But with this program, we created a whole class of ambassadors for the park. The guides could provide an appreciation for the river to an amazing number of people – far beyond what the rest of the staff and I could possibly hope to accomplish.

"It was a popular and valuable program, so we soon expanded it to include teachers. By training local educators, we could reach a much larger audience with the 'park message.' We worked with a university so that teachers could earn continuing education credits by completing our course. Unfortunately, this initiative eventually ran out of gas at some point, due to time constraints and decreased staffing levels."

Bill is quick to credit the river rangers who preceded him, the office staff, and the seasonal aides that worked out of the Whitewater Recreation Office. "I got to stand on their shoulders and build upon something that was already really well-established when I arrived. It was an excellent program – one the Department can be proud of. State Parks really had no blueprint for running whitewater river recreation. I think the staff at the WRO did a terrific job of building and sustaining this program.

"I want to emphasize a point. One reason I was so successful in dealing with the outfitters on the American River was that I used to be one of them. As a commercial guide, I had experience leading rafting trips on all three forks of the American River. That provided me with the ability to assess more accurately the concerns of the outfitters and prioritize the importance and urgency of each of their issues. Also, when I was on the river, I could usually tell the good guides from the scammers.

"I also believe that my background in the medical and legal fields was very helpful. I was an EMT, so I had experience working in the emergency room. I had been a park lifeguard, and I had worked side by side with an orthopedic surgeon. Those experiences were key to improving my skills for dealing with medical emergencies in the field. It was rare that I had to deal with a first responder issue that I did not feel prepared to handle. Remember that guy who was upset about my handling of his brother's river emergency? From my time in the ER, I knew how people often react during life-threatening crises. I was there, as it actually turned out, to help both brothers.

"The work with the attorney who dealt with dozens of tort cases was also very valuable. Commercial rafting can be a risky business, and managing the contracts of roughly 25 to 30 outfitters carries a lot of liability with it. Seeing how a good attorney approached a variety of situations gave me a good feel for how the legal profession deals with these often very complicated issues.

"Although it is not mandatory for a river ranger to have any of these backgrounds, I firmly believe that my experience as a rafter, river guide, whitewater instructor, EMT, lifeguard, medical assistant, and legal assistant really prepared me well. You have to earn the respect of the outfitters in order to be successful, and I tried to build and maintain that respect over the course of many years of careful river program management.

"Rivers are great teachers, and they can be stern and unforgiving masters. I want to thank the American River for allowing me to pass safely through about a thousand times. I would like to think that I have given back a little in helping to protect this river and its amazing bounty – in perpetuity."

For more information —

Holliday, J. S., *The World Rushed In.* University of Oklahoma Press. 1981.

JON MUENCH

Renaissance Ranger and Ace Pilot

It is hard to know which amazing story to start with for this chapter on Jon Muench.

There is the tale of Jon, a troubled youth who, after his parents divorced when he was 9 years old, acted out his anger and guilt by turning to a life of rebellion, trouble, and crime on the streets of Detroit. Jon was, to be blunt, a juvenile delinquent. However, through a long and sometimes tortuous path, he reconfigured his life and his values through force of will and mental discipline as he went on to become a legendary state park ranger/pilot who set the gold standard for that unique and remarkable job.

Then there is Jon at the age of 18 who, upon high school graduation, enlisted in the U.S. Air Force and volunteered for duty in Vietnam. After spending his teen years in Southern California, diving deeply into both the surfing and the hippie cultures of the '60s, Jon was thrown as a boy into the geopolitical maelstrom of war in Southeast Asia. It is hard to imagine a more wrenching life change, and Jon recalls that it was one of the most important and formative experiences of his life. He had to grow up, become a man, and straighten out – and fast.

Jon now chuckles that he had been told that the Air Force was the best – meaning safest – branch of the military for enlisted men and women, and that was why he chose it. "In the Navy, Army, and Marines, the generals and admirals are in the rear, and the grunts are taken to the front and thrown into combat. To the contrary, in the Air Force, the officers fly aircraft into battle, and my mates and I worked in the air traffic control tower, many miles from the conflict."

Another formative experience occurred during his first job after graduating college with a degree in journalism. He became a security guard at a women's dormitory at a local college – "a dream job," he laughs. The dream became a nightmare when three huge football players tried to rape one of the dorm residents, and Jon stepped in to try to prevent the rape. He did stop the assault, but at the cost of being hospitalized himself for serious injuries. This caused him to question his own ability, and this self-doubt led to his becoming totally immersed in karate. He eventually earned a third-degree black belt in karate – a martial art that he credits with giving him the mental discipline to survive many challenging, even life-and-death, situations.

Then when Jon decided he wanted to apply for the position of ranger/pilot at Anza–Borrego Desert State Park, he had a small hurdle to overcome – he had been a licensed pilot for a grand total of two days. He had no official hours – zero, nada, nil, the null set – as the pilot-in-command of an aircraft. The other applicant was a state peace officer with, ahem, over 20,000 hours as pilot-in-command of single engine fixed-wing aircraft. Of course, Jon got the job.

As a ranger at Anza–Borrego Desert State Park and living in the small village of Borrego Springs, Jon decided to try his hand in local live theater. He was soon cast in the role of Tevye, the patriarchal dairyman in "Fiddler on the Roof," – set in rural Imperial Russia in 1905. Many of those fortunate enough to have seen Jon play Tevye remarked that his portrayal of that iconic character was as inspiring as it was professional.

There is another fascinating part to the Tevye story. As a rural dairyman in Russia over 100 years ago, Tevye got his water from a well, picked his potatoes and beets from his farm, relied on horses for heavy work, and lived in a house without plumbing. After retirement

Tradition! Jon as Tevye in "Fiddler on the Roof."

Working Alla's family farm in Ukraine. *All photos courtesy of Jon Muench.*

from the State Parks Department, Jon joined the Peace Corps and was sent to Ukraine. These days, when he and his Ukrainian-born wife Alla return to visit her family, they stay on the farm where she was raised – picking beets and potatoes, driving a horse and buggy into the local village, getting water from the well, and using the outhouse. Tradition!

Then there is the time that a man robbed the community bank in Borrego Springs. In the rural desert, there are not many hiding places or secret escape routes. Jon was on duty, but not flying, that day, so he was able to respond when deputy sheriffs and highway patrolmen tried to apprehend the robber about five miles south of town. The felon came out of his vehicle shooting at the peace officers, and they returned fire from fairly close range. But no one could find the target. Jon drove up, parked at 50 meters from the shoot-out, and calmly put two lethal rounds into the bank robber's chest. Of the four peace officers involved and roughly 40 rounds fired, Jon's were the only two bullets that found their target.

Years later, in retirement, Jon was still acting when he was asked to play a criminal in some training films that would be shown to peace officers. The short movies presented scenarios of "Shoot/Don't Shoot." In other words, the trainee would watch the film while wearing his unloaded firearm, and would be required to make a split-second decision on whether and when to use lethal force on the bad guy in the film. Based on his assessment of current training protocols, Jon now questions the possible implications of that instruction vis-à-vis the uproar over police officer-involved shootings.

And later, as an experienced pilot, Jon had gained a reputation from his fellow rangers for being willing to help in almost every given situation. This desire to contribute led him into more and more dangerous situations, but he was loath to turn down the opportunity to lend help from the air and thereby let down his colleagues and park visitors. Finally, this courage got him into a deadly situation where, because of extremely high winds, he had to take off from the local airport without a good plan on where he would eventually land the aircraft. On this search for a victim in a life-and-death situation, Jon clearly risked his own life and safety.

This is a book about park rangers and the incredible work they accomplished, so, let's start with that story…

His aircraft, a Christen Husky, was well suited to the rigors of the desert. A single

On patrol at Anza–Borrego Desert State Park.

engine, fabric, tail dragging, tandem-seating (front and back single seats, rather than side-by-side) airplane, it was designed to fly at slow speed and low to the ground. Along with a powerful, 180-horsepower engine, this configuration provided the patrol aircraft and its pilot the ability to perform law enforcement patrol, search and rescue, communications relay between dispatch and the rangers on the ground, and surveillance of criminal operations.

When park visitors were observed with heat illness, the pilot was even able to drop a plastic one-gallon bottle of water suspended from a very small parachute out of the aircraft window as a life-saving measure. The plane was equipped with a public-address system, as well as an antenna for tracking radio-collared wildlife, and it had also proven useful as a firefighting spotter plane. The 180-hp engine that powered the light aircraft enabled the pilot to fly in conditions and terrain that would prevent other aircraft from being successful. The pilot had confidence he could overcome most of the conditions the desert presented – severe up and downdrafts, turbulence, strong winds, wind shear, icing, heat and cold, and the steep canyon walls of the park's patrol area.

As Jon's familiarity with and confidence in the Christen Husky increased over his 11-year assignment as the park's ranger/pilot, he also recognized that these two factors were also growing into the largest threats to his personal safety. Normally, Jon would decide every day he was on duty whether it was a good day to fly. Based on many factors, he was careful about not flying unnecessarily in conditions that might exceed the capabilities of the aircraft or the pilot.

However, when emergencies arose, it was a different story. Whether the situation was people who went missing on hot summer days, victims who were injured in the park's backcountry, or backup for a law enforcement incident, Jon would have to consider other factors when deciding whether to fly. The environmental conditions affecting flight would have to be balanced against the ability of rangers on the ground to handle the situation successfully and the chances for success if Jon were to use the aircraft to help with the emergency. Jon occasionally had to risk his own life in order to save those of park visitors and to help his ranger colleagues in difficult situations. Jon would usually respond, "Hey, that's my job!" when asked if he had made the right decision.

Jon recognized that the rangers on the ground came to rely on the aircraft as an incredibly valuable tool, and his personal goal of not letting his colleagues down was becoming a concern. He feared that he would eventually fly in a situation in which the most important law that all pilots must obey – the law of gravity – would win, and the outcome would not be a good one. For Jon, he feared that it was just a matter of time until he ran afoul of that law.

On Saturday afternoon, May 24, 2003, an ugly situation arose. It was a hot and very windy day when a couple of park visitors – 16-year old Brett and his friend Adam, along with Brett's two dogs – hiked to the Calcite Mine area of Anza–Borrego Desert State Park. The Calcite Mine region is very beautiful and geologically interesting – there are deeply incised canyons that offer amazing opportunities for wilderness hiking. The park rules do not require hikers to stay on designated trails – although dogs are not allowed on those trails – and the two boys decided to explore the wilderness landscape that lies beyond the abandoned mine.

At one point, Brett took a small leap from one boulder to another, slipped, and injured his left leg – he was now unable to walk out. It was about 105 degrees at this point. The boys were out of water, and Brett began having an asthma attack. Adam was faced with a difficult decision. He did not want to leave Brett, but he feared that if they both stayed in the wilderness, there would be little chance of survival for either of them.

Adam left the dogs with Brett and walked out in the heat and the wind to seek help. Adam did reach Highway S-22, where a passing car, driven by a park volunteer, stopped to offer assistance. The docent was able to notify park rangers of the situation, but given his heat-induced disorientation and unfamiliarity with the park, Adam was unable to provide Rangers Paul Remeika and Jennifer Rodriguez with Brett's location.

The rangers tried to find the victim, but they recall that it was the proverbial search for a needle in a haystack. They drove and hiked to likely sites, but the high winds and blowing dust thwarted their attempts to locate Brett by yelling to him. Frustrated, they finally requested via radio that the park aircraft be dispatched to aid in the search, and Jon was summoned to assist.

When Jon reached the Borrego Springs airport, where the aircraft was based, he received word from the local flight office that the winds were steady from the northwest at 60 knots, with gusts to 80 knots. Jon realized immediately that, should he take off under those conditions, and should those wind conditions persist, he would not be able to land at the Borrego Springs airport after the search. The angle and strength of the crosswinds were well beyond the capability of the Christen Husky. The airplane would, without question, flip during landing. He would have to find a landing spot elsewhere – probably somewhere without airport facilities or a paved runway – and he would still have to cope with the incredibly strong winds. Jon knew that the victim with the injured leg was in a life-and-death situation, so he decided to take off and begin the search, fully aware that he was risking his own life with that decision.

He understood that finding a landing zone would be difficult, but first he had to face a very tricky takeoff. Although the aircraft is powerful for its size and weight, that lightness also makes it very susceptible to the strong and variable winds. The local runway is aligned east and west, and the winds were from the northwest – a "quartering wind." That is, these gusty winds were hitting the aircraft at about a 45-degree angle from the front and right side at 60 knots.

Once he was ready for takeoff, Jon applied full power, full rudder, and had to fight the "stick" for aircraft control. He also had to tilt the right aileron into the wind while speeding down the runway. Jon recalls that it was a rare, one-wheeled takeoff, due to the wind and the extreme control measures he had to employ. The right wing was, at times, less than two feet from striking the runway. Immediately upon becoming airborne, the wind shot the plane sideways, but Jon was able to gain altitude, gather a modicum of control over the plane, and head to the Calcite Mine region.

Finding Brett from the air was the easy part of the mission, and Jon was able to direct Rangers Rodriguez and Remeika to the victim's location. They called for more assistance, and were able to carry him out on a Stokes litter through the rugged terrain to their patrol vehicle. Brett was eventually transported to the hospital and made a full recovery.

For Jon, however, the real trouble was just beginning. He was airborne in extreme winds, without a good option for a safe landing. He decided his best chance was to try to land at Ocotillo Wells airport, about 15 miles south of Calcite Mine. This airport is unusual, since it is located on a dry, flat, desert lakebed, and its surface is dry mud and gravel. There are two designated runways, but both are unpaved, and they would pose the same dilemma as the runway at Borrego Springs – any landing on a designated runway would exceed the aircraft's crosswind capability, and the plane would likely flip.

Jon knew that his only option would be to land directly into the wind and avoid the use of the runways – he would have to land on loose sand and gravel. Again, Jon's experience in and knowledge of the aircraft provided him with the only possible solution to get on the ground safely – he would perform a "helicopter" landing – that is, he would basically need to hover the aircraft over the ground and let it settle to earth. This is an incredibly difficult and dangerous maneuver, but it was the only option Jon had.

The landing speed of the Christen Husky is 52 knots – this is relative to the wind, not the ground. And, given the gusty and unpredictable nature of the 60 knot headwinds, Jon would need to have a cushion of airspeed over 52 knots so that the plane would not suddenly stall a couple of hundred feet off the ground and rather dramatically fall to earth.

The airport does have a wind sock, so Jon was able to determine the wind direction, line up the aircraft directly into the headwind, center the aircraft over the middle of the landing zone, and decrease power. The plane, indeed, began to settle to earth. Jon says all was going well – "I was hovering over the lake bed, maintaining airspeed, and the aircraft was slowly dropping in altitude. About 20 feet off the ground, however, the wind began picking up the sand and gravel to the extent I could no longer see anything outside the cockpit – I was flying blind. It is probable that the aircraft was actually moving backwards relative to the ground in these last few seconds of flight!"

Jon's judgment and skill paid off when the aircraft finally touched down safely. Again, Jon's troubles were not over, since now he had a very light airplane on the ground, while the winds certainly had not abated. He jammed on the parking brake, called dispatch for assistance, jumped out of the aircraft, and grabbed the nose of the airplane to prevent it from tipping over or rolling away.

Rangers Jeri Zemon and Bob Theriault drove Jon's patrol vehicle to the scene along with one of their own, brought Jon some supplies, and were able to secure the plane to Jon's truck. Jon spent the night at the scene and slept in the truck. By the next morning, the winds had died down, and he was able to fly the airplane back to its base at the Borrego Springs airport.

Besides search and rescue, the aircraft has a variety of other uses. One day Jon was slowly approaching his chosen quarry in the state park. The element of surprise is essential to a successful encounter with prey – every hunter knows this. Staying very low to the ground, Jon also kept the wind in his face so that any noise he made would not reach his targets. As invisible and quiet as possible, he came over a small rise, and there they stood – a small herd of deer poachers! Yes, the hunters had become the hunted.

The real surprise for the poachers was that Jon, a state park peace officer, was in an airplane. The Husky was so versatile it was almost as though it had been designed for ranger work at Anza–Borrego. It is not an easy task to patrol 500 miles of dirt roads and the almost 640,000 acres (over 460,000 acres of which are rugged wilderness) that make up Anza–Borrego Desert State Park. The park also is replete with mountain ranges and steep escarpments, and soars from just above sea level to 6,700' in elevation.

Although this aircraft could land and take off on short runways of a variety of surfaces, Jon did not land to arrest these poachers. His typical approach would be to call in park rangers on regular vehicle patrol to write the citations for illegal hunting. The ground rangers would also have the option of confiscating weapons and any illegally taken game. He would usually stay around, in the air, to ensure the other rangers would be able to make contact with the poachers. The Husky was equipped with a public-address (PA) feature, so Jon could give the poachers instructions until the patrol rangers arrived.

Jon would "turn about a point" in the aircraft while giving instructions to those on the ground. To do this, the pilot finds a visual reference point on the ground, and puts the plane in a turn that keeps that point in the center of the turn. The plane would be in a continuous banked turn, and this maneuver permitted Jon to keep the poachers under observation, as well. Since seating is tandem, the pilot can make a banked turn in either direction without compromising ground surveillance.

Of course, this technique worked only if the rangers on the ground were a reasonably short distance away. In a park like Anza–Borrego, which is nearly 1,000 square miles in size, that was not always the case. Sometimes Jon had to direct the poachers to wait for the rangers while he kept them under watch from a greater distance.

Jon adds, "Keeping hunters under watch, no matter how you do it, inherently entails risk. Think about it. Here are skilled marksmen, with high-powered rifles, and they start to get bored with having to wait for another ranger to arrive and write them citations. They know there is nothing I can do except monitor their activities from on high. They are very unhappy, and at some point, you just know they are going to start joking among themselves about their options. You just have to hope they are actually joking."

One of those options – one that Jon nor any other state park pilot actually ever encountered – would be to use deadly force on the airborne pilot. For that reason, Jon's regular seat cushion in the plane was his bulletproof vest. He adds, "I doubt if anyone would intentionally fire their weapon at the park plane, but you never know who is out shooting and drinking in the desert, and you don't want to take the chance of an odd, stray bullet becoming a real pain in the ass!"

More than once, Jon had to land in a desert wash to help the rangers on the ground. He would get out of the plane, wearing his service weapon, and help write citations to the violators. In addition to the immediate assistance he provided to the other park rangers, Jon is convinced that the stories of a ranger landing an airplane in the open desert and writing a violator a citation may have made it onto social media.

One of Jon's philosophies in being a successful, and living, pilot was to head off bad outcomes in the plane.

He ensured that the plane was well-maintained, that he repeatedly practiced difficult maneuvers in marginal conditions, that he carried survival equipment and rations for himself as well as for visitors, and that he had a mental plan in place for almost every possible situation. Sitting on his flak jacket for up to seven hours per day was just one of his techniques for ensuring he walked away from the plane safely every afternoon. As it turned out, Jon was a perfect match as the park ranger/pilot for Anza–Borrego, and his plane was a great fit for the tasks required of it. However, when Jon first applied for this job, his suitability for the ranger/pilot job was not immediately evident to those sitting on his interview panel.

The first Christen Husky was purchased by the park in 1986. Since the park had justified this acquisition primarily on the basis of efficiency for patrol, law enforcement, and search and rescue, the state "bean counters" required that the park reduce its ranger force as a condition of approval. The park accepted this condition, but the next hurdle was the extremely slow process of hiring a ranger/pilot to fly the aircraft. This was the first pilot position ever in State Parks, so the position description had to be written, justified, and approved before the vacancy could be advertised and filled.

One of the problems with a department owning a piece of equipment is that state "control" agencies monitor its usage. If the control agency, in its infinite wisdom, becomes convinced that a piece of equipment, like an aircraft, is not being used often enough, it can remove that equipment from its assigned park. The park was concerned that, if the initial delivery of the aircraft occurred a lot sooner than the pilot arrived, the plane would be "repossessed."

Finally, Gene Hammock was hired as the first park ranger/pilot at Anza–Borrego. Jon credits Gene with establishing the excellent and often complicated protocols for the use of the plane at the park. As Jon says, "Gene was an outstanding aviator, loved flying, and saved many lives as the park pilot. He always downplayed the serious nature of the job, but he was extremely careful. The plane was maintained very well, and Gene was intent on ensuring the sustainability of the ranger/pilot program. I flew with him in unbelievable conditions, but he never flew into situations he did not think he and the plane could handle. He set the bar high for all of us who followed him."

When Gene retired, the park advertised the position vacancy statewide, not just inside the Parks Department. Park managers were not aware of any current park rangers who would be interested in the job. Like a lot of ranger opportunities, it is a terrific job, but it has its drawbacks. Borrego Springs is a remote, small, desert town. Supermarkets, sporting events, hospitals, movie theaters, and even graveyards (rather surprising for a retirement village) – they are all a long way from Borrego Springs. If the ranger has a spouse, there is a dearth of "professional" work available for that partner. So, it is important, and difficult, to find the right person who understands, accepts, welcomes, and even thrives in those conditions.

Advertising the position statewide meant that state employees in other departments in state government could apply for the position. Parks was hoping that a pilot in Cal Fire, California Highway Patrol (CHP), or other state agency might be attracted to this unique job.

The park managers were pleasantly surprised when they were informed that there were two candidates. Jon applied, as did an experienced pilot who was then flying for the California Highway Patrol. The managers reviewed the two applications and saw that the CHP pilot had over 20,000 hours of experience in light, single-engine, fixed-wing aircraft. They also noticed that, as pilot-in-command of any aircraft, Jon had, um, zero hours.

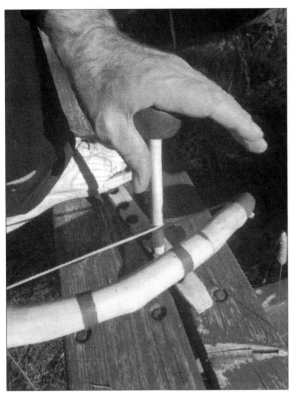

Jon loved to give interpretive programs on Native American toolmaking.

So, they interviewed both candidates and, of course, selected Jon Muench. Their reasoning was this – after a year or two, the CHP pilot would be a terrific pilot, but would never be a park ranger. He would probably hang around the airport with other pilots and not really mingle with the other rangers or, more importantly, the park visitors. Jon, on the other hand, would in time become a very good pilot, and he was already renowned as an excellent park ranger. The managers were willing to let Jon take the time to grow his abilities as a pilot, and they knew he already had a tremendous set of ranger skills. There was huge upside potential with Jon Muench. He received his pilot's license, and was able to spend time with Gene Hammock learning the ins and outs of the park and the aircraft that was to become his "partner."

So, what was the path that Jon took that led him to land, in his words, "the most incredible job in the world?" As with many great rangers, it was not obvious in their youth or even early adulthood that they would flourish as a park ranger – it was truly a long and winding road.

While Jon was growing up near Detroit, his grandparents owned a cabin in the woods of upper Michigan, and Jon remembers spending a lot of summers and vacations there. "There was so much open space and open water that we did not need designated parks around to have fun. The cabin had a lantern for light and an outhouse, and I would spend hours reading Hemingway stories. He really inspired me to be a writer, and for a while, I thought writing might be my profession of choice. Back then, nothing really inspired me to become a park ranger – I had never met one or even heard of one."

His mother moved Jon and his siblings to Southern California in the '60s, just in time for the surfing scene and the hippie era. He took that opportunity to specialize in surfing and rebelling. He does, however, remember thinking that when he grew up, maybe he would either become a cop or an airplane pilot, rather than a writer.

"When I graduated from high school, college was not an option – my family had no money. So, I joined the

Air Force and became an air traffic controller. I volunteered for duty in Vietnam – at that time it just seemed like something I should do. Remember, I was still a teenager. I was a young man with a lot of problems, so naturally I wanted to go to Vietnam.

"I was there for a year, and then was sent to Germany to serve for two years. As the war was winding down, the Air Force was more supportive of those of us who wanted an early out in order to attend college. I got out a year early, took advantage of the GI Bill, and enrolled in Heidelberg University, in southern Germany. Heidelberg was a private institution, and quite expensive. I could afford only two years there. I took some time to travel in Europe and Israel, and supported myself by 'busking' on sidewalks and in plazas with my guitar – singing songs by Bob Dylan, Gordon Lightfoot, and Cat Stevens. I would wait for tour buses on the corners of the streets near Heidelberg, and made $100 a day – that was my beer money for a week.

"Finally, after five years in Germany, I returned to the U.S. to finish up college. I was accepted at Long Beach State University, and graduated with a major in journalism and a minor in German in 1975. At the time, I still thought I might become a writer. Like a lot of college graduates, I had trouble finding work in my field, and I needed to support myself. I had a series of odd jobs, including working as a security guard in a women's dormitory that housed 800 women at Long Beach State. Here I was – single and in my 20s – it probably sounds like a dream job.

"One time, though, I responded to a situation where several guys were trying to rape one of the women in the dorm. These three guys were football players – large and in shape – and I pretty much got the crap beat out of me. I was hospitalized, and I am probably lucky they did not kill me. But it became a defining moment for me, since I realized how ill-prepared I was for those situations. I decided right then to get in better shape, stop smoking, and build some defensive skills. I turned to the martial art of karate.

"Most people can catch on to the physical moves of karate. But even more important is to learn the mental discipline that karate requires. You have to train your mind to understand that your potential is realized only through mental focus. If you truly believe in your own capabilities, they will be enhanced. Americans are considered weak-minded, according to my sensei (martial arts instructor). Your training gives you confidence that you can physically do more than you think you can do. For three straight days, we had six hours of training per day. Talk about exhaustion – mental and physical.

"But these experiences, although I did not know it at the time, were preparing me for the incredibly strenuous things I would have to do as a park ranger – like doing CPR without assistance for 45 minutes straight, and the physical toll and stress of flying in the desert for long periods of time under marginal conditions.

"At one point in my karate training, we students were required to establish and maintain the 'horse stance.' Now that is not too difficult, except that we were required to maintain the stance for 90 minutes! My muscles were soon screaming for relief, but my mind was convinced I could hold the correct position. I firmly believe that martial arts training prepared me well for the rigors of flying a plane in Anza–Borrego – a plane that was only marginally more comfortable than the horse stance.

Jon greatly values his martial arts training.

"My pathway did not fit the mold of how to become a park ranger. I got in totally by chance. Unlike many of my fellow rangers, I never was a seasonal park aide, nor did I have a college major that was even remotely relevant to ranger work. By pure luck, one of my friends – he was my roommate in Germany – called one day and told me he had seen a flyer posted on campus that was encouraging people to become state park rangers. I already knew by then that journalism would never pay me well enough to live on.

"I had no idea what rangers did, and I recall asking my friend if he believed we would spend our time rearranging picnic tables and helping people figure out how to roast a marshmallow! We both took the exam, but during the interview it became clear that carrying a firearm was a requirement of the job. That was enough to get my friend to withdraw from the testing process. I wasn't crazy about wearing a gun either, but I was intrigued enough about being a park ranger that I continued on through the hiring stages.

"I became a state park technician in 1976 at Carpinteria State Beach, in Santa Barbara County. I was lucky to have three great mentors there – Mark Jorgensen, Rick Sermon, and Matt Sugarman. Mark was the best law enforcement ranger I ever worked with – he was good because he was confident and smart, while he knew his 'stuff' so well. At the same time, he was so good with the park visitors – he empathized well with them. Rick was absolutely dedicated to the interpretation and resource management programs, while Matt insisted that rangers be good at everything. These guys set excellent examples, and I personally benefited from their leadership.

"After my training year, I was promoted to state park ranger and transferred down the coast to Malibu State Beach, where I was fortunate to reside in a state house overlooking the Pacific Ocean. Here I was – this poorly paid park ranger – living among the millionaires of Malibu.

"As a ranger there, I had a very hectic, stressful job, but I loved it. You can become addicted to the stress and the ways you develop to deal with it. Beaches in Southern California attract a lot of people, and they can be very hectic. The combination of young people, alcohol, drugs, vehicles, parties, and the beach can be overwhelming. You almost get addicted to the pace and the excitement. You go from a vehicle accident scene to breaking up a fight to calming down a mob to making a drug arrest – sometimes in just a few hours.

There is a theory among rangers and lifeguards that salt air affects the brains of those visitors who live some distance from the coast and makes them lose all reason when they get to the beach. It sure seemed like being at the beach could bring out the 'crazy' in people.

"I was married at the time, and I would be pumped up when I got home. Or some days, the rangers and lifeguards would get together after work to have a few beers and come down from the stress of the day. In both cases, I would get home to my wife, Yoko, who had spent the entire day with two little kids by herself. And living in Malibu, she did not naturally make a lot of friends – there were not many local Japanese women her age who had two young children and little money. I thought it was a great job, and we lived in a beautiful house overlooking the ocean – in my mind, everything was going well. But my wife hated the situation, and she eventually divorced me and took our kids back to Japan with her.

"I have to say that the State Parks 'family' was very understanding of my state of affairs. I was not the first, or the last, ranger to fall victim to this situation. Park spouses often live in beautiful places – state parks are where everybody else goes on vacation – but they may not always have the professional stimulation or network of friends that help provide a happy, satisfying life. In addition, a lot of rangers move around the state a lot, especially at the beginning of their careers, so the spouses have to start over – again and again – with friends, new communities, menial jobs, and isolation.

"On my own now, I really threw my energy into all aspects of the job. I became a lead defensive tactics instructor. I started really spending more time in interpretation – giving nature walks, tide pool talks, and campfire programs. Native American culture, tool making, archeology, and astronomy became my new passions – hobbies I had as a kid I could now weave into my job. Ranger John Mott taught me how to make fire with a pump drill, and I would demonstrate that in my interpretive programs – the kids loved it! I even received an award from the Parks Department for my interpretive work.

"The local park managers were great about helping me deal with the divorce and the loss of my kids. While being understanding about the devastation this caused me personally, they also encouraged me to relocate and start over at a new park. So I moved up the coast, where I worked at Pismo State Beach and Montana de Oro State Park as a supervising ranger.

Jon became one of the Department's first Defensive Tactics instructors.

"I was there a couple of years when I heard that Gene Hammock, the ranger/pilot at Anza–Borrego Desert State Park, was about to retire. I had learned to fly gliders in Germany, and I had always had an interest in becoming a pilot. This was a golden opportunity to make flying part of my ranger job.

"I took a bunch of vacation days, and put all my time and energy into getting my pilot's license. It took about six weeks of intensive ground school and flying lessons, and I received my license two days before my interview for the job. My flight examiner passed me – in part, I believe, because he knew I had a pilot job lined up – but he admonished me to come out the next few days and 'work on my landings.'"

Although Jon had finished up the training necessary to become a licensed pilot before he arrived at his new assignment, he and his managers knew that, like a motor vehicle driver's license, it is really after you get your license that you learn to fly or drive. And flying the mountains and ridges of Anza–Borrego is not to be taken lightly.

Once at the park, he signed up for a course in "Mountain Flying Safety," taught by a local flying instructor named Cliff Caldwell. Ol' Cliffy was a terrific teacher, and ensured that he taught Jon how to fly the Husky in a variety of challenging conditions. Jon later wrote a manual on flying in various weather-related conditions – he wanted to pass his knowledge on to successive pilots. He wanted them to benefit from his knowledge and experience, just as he had learned at the hands of Gene Hammock and Cliff Caldwell.

Instructor Cliff was a large man though, and this caused some problems. The Christen Husky is a "tandem" airplane, meaning that the second (co-pilot's) seat is directly behind the pilot's seat. The Husky is not built for, let us say, comfort. It is a bare-bones airplane with the capacity to operate in extreme conditions. So amenities not necessary for performance and safety are not in this airplane – they would add weight and, correspondingly, detract from peak aircraft performance. Given the number of weather-related problems extant in Anza–Borrego, the pilot really appreciates the ability of this airplane to be maneuverable, safe, and utilitarian.

Cliff had to squeeze into the rear seat so that Jon could get experience flying from the pilot's front seat. The extra weight of a passenger also meant that Jon could not fill up on aviation fuel – this additional load would affect the plane's stall speed in a turn. But the real problem arose when Cliff was suddenly NOT in the plane.

Cliff and Jon would practice and practice landings and takeoffs together. When the instructor believed that Jon was ready to try these "touch and goes" solo, he pried himself out of the cockpit. Unfortunately, he failed to mention to Jon that removing 250 pounds from the rear seat would dramatically alter the performance of the aircraft during landing. Jon failed to account for this difference, applied too much brake during his first solo landing, and the plane pitched forward onto its rotating propeller. Jon walked away unharmed but embarrassed, and the propeller was soon repaired. History does not provide us with the reaction of those supervisors who were on Jon's interview panel, upon learning of this mishap.

It is testimony to the rugged flying conditions of the park that all three long-term pilots experienced an accident in this aircraft. The good news is that none of them sustained a flying-related injury – this reflects well on their training, experience, aviating skill, and judgment.

All pilots love to "hangar-fly" – this is the opportunity pilots take advantage of to tell anyone who will listen their harrowing tales of heroism and examples of using their unique skills to protect parks from crime and disease. As Jon tells the story, "Once I was called to Ocotillo Wells State Vehicular Recreation Area, a legal off-roading park adjacent to Anza–Borrego, to assist the local rangers locate and apprehend a guy who had just stolen a motorcycle. The ground rangers just could not catch him.

"I eventually spotted the stolen cycle and called in my position. I flew in behind him slowly and just off the ground, then used my siren and public-address system to advise him to turn off the bike and stay put. The rider looked up, gave me a few interesting hand gestures, and continued to flee in an attempt to escape across the open desert. He knew I could always keep him in my line of sight, but he could continue to evade the rangers in their patrol vehicles.

"Fortunately, it was early in the day and I had full fuel tanks – enough for seven hours of flight! All I had to do was to circle over him, keep him in sight, and wait until he ran out of gas. At that point, I could guide in the field rangers to make the arrest. This went on for over two hours. Each time he got close to a ranger on the ground, he would turn around and race off in the opposite direction. He kept waving at me for some reason. Finally, I was about 500 feet above the ground when Ranger John Ruddley noticed a low-flying Navy jet headed for me. 'Um, Air Patrol One, you have an F-18 off your right wing!'

"Just as Ruddley said this, I looked up and spotted the aircraft coming straight toward my plane at precisely the same altitude. The Navy pilot must have seen my aircraft simultaneously, because he put his jet in a shallow dive, streaking over the sand below me at about 100 feet above the deck, and then zoomed off toward Split Mountain. He unwittingly flew right over the motorcyclist I had been chasing. Without realizing it, the Navy pilot had joined in the pursuit of a felon. The rider, probably thinking we had called in the military to assist in the chase, parked and turned off his stolen motorcycle and raised his arms in surrender. You never know when low-flying military jets will come in handy!"

Jon adds, "Well, I think Gene Hammock had the best hangar-flying story ever for Anza–Borrego. In the summer, pilots play a key role in visitor safety, due to the extreme seasonal heat. The pilot is always on the lookout for broken-down vehicles, since this situation can be life threatening. Sure enough, Gene was flying Split Mountain one summer day and saw a Jeep with the hood up and no one around. He flew down the canyon a ways and noticed three pairs of human tracks hiking north. He soon located the three distressed hikers – two women and one man – who should have stayed with their vehicle. Gene got on the public address system and asked if everything was okay. They all waved, and Gene realized he had not asked the right question – he had no way of knowing whether their wave meant everything was okay or not. So he circled around, and this time told them that if they needed assistance to wave an article of clothing over their heads. He reported that both women stripped off their tops and began waving them wildly. Gene also reported that one of the women was wearing a bra.

"Unfortunately, Split Mountain is a very rugged area, and Gene could not land and provide the necessary life-

saving measures personally, so he called for field rangers to respond as soon as possible. As fate would have it, the three stranded visitors were on vacation from Austria, and the ranger who was first on the scene, Manfred Knaak, spoke fluent German. The visitors, in their subsequent thank-you letter to park staff, expressed amazement that the pilot somehow figured out that he needed to call in a German-speaking ranger!"

Like a ranger with a canine unit or a patrol horse, the pilot comes to appreciate the myriad ways that the aircraft can be used to assist in managing a potentially dangerous situation. Jon explains it best, "The plane is a tool at your disposal in a law enforcement encounter, and once you learn its capabilities and its effect on the public, it can help you defuse incidents. Think of it as you would a peace officer's baton, dog, or horse. Normally, you would begin with a non-aggressive stance and quiet demeanor. But, if necessary, you would brandish the baton in a more threatening manner – like a rattlesnake poised for a strike.

"Same thing with the plane – usually you are pretty aloof when you're aloft. You are coolly and calmly observing from a distance while circling the scene. If needed, however, you come in low and fast with siren blaring and giving orders on the PA. It is amazing the effect that approach can have on the situation. Many times, rangers have told me of the change in attitude once the aircraft arrived. It is almost as though the cavalry has come charging in, and the psychological effect on the situation can be rapid and dramatic.

"One time I was flying over about 30 undocumented immigrants in a Borrego Springs citrus field, who were fist-fighting border patrol agents, park rangers, and sheriff's deputies. On that occasion, I flew in low enough to use the PA and siren to restore order, while I simultaneously relayed to the officers on the grounds the miscreants' locations each time they tried to flee the scene. We captured all of them."

The capacity for search and rescue was initially one of the primary justifications for the purchase of the aircraft. The park is so large, rugged, and roadless that the meager ranger staff cannot always be expected to be successful in finding and rescuing persons lost or in trouble.

As Jon tells one successful story – one that he is particularly proud of, "We got a report that three teenagers had been camping in the Diablo Canyon area, but were overdue in coming home. The boys had left a detailed itinerary with their parents, which provided a good starting point, but the parents were still very worried. A brief aerial search of the area proved futile, so I flew to an area about five miles from the boys' planned campsite – a region that is notorious for stuck vehicles. Sure enough, I spotted their vehicle mired in soft sand, but the boys were nowhere to be seen. I called the situation into dispatch, and then noticed footprints heading east from their Jeep. I could make out the word 'HELP' scrawled in the sand and kept heading east. I finally came upon the three lost boys, who understandably were wildly celebrating their rescue – after all, it was 110 degrees! They were out of water, completely dehydrated, and probably would not have survived much longer."

The plane also is a great tool in the resource management efforts of the park. Radio telemetry equipment was installed on the plane's wings with a link to equipment inside the cockpit. The pilot can pick up signals from radio-collared sheep, mountain lions, and deer, and thereby provide updates on the location and range of these important mammals.

Jon has also conducted surveys for eagle nests, elephant trees, palm groves, and even the massive numbers of dead fish at the Salton Sea.

On the cultural side, the aircraft can provide an aerial platform that provides perspective to discover and map Native American trails, villages, historical routes, and other features. For example, a large geoglyph (a large ground figure made from emplacing rocks or removing rocks) of a two-headed snake was first observed from an aircraft – it was just too large to be recognized by someone on the ground.

For interpretation, the park created a "Sky Trail" for pilots – it provides an aerial guide to some key features of the park. Also, Jon and photographer/videographer Chris Pyle taped a camera on the wing of the plane and took many hours of aerial photos. Chris edited those photos into a stunning visual program that is sold in the park's visitor center.

The plane and pilot were also responsible for providing extraordinary and vital visual evidence that, without question, prevented the absolute desecration of the park's beautiful Coyote Canyon. In the summer of 2002, a wildfire was ignited east of the small community of Julian – just west of the park. It quickly spread to the north, and was threatening to make a huge run northeast through large swaths of wilderness before reaching communities in Riverside County. There were very few places, in the opinion of the fire officials, to stop the fire's spread towards civilization.

The Pines Fire's incident command team decided that, in order to stop its spread to the north and east, a huge firebreak would need to be created in Coyote Canyon. The plan was to send in three large bulldozers to remove flammable material. That would have meant turning a beautiful riparian ecosystem – one that is extremely rare and important in the desert – into bare earth and rubble.

Now Coyote Canyon's importance to the park and to the village of Borrego Springs cannot be overstated. Riparian plants and animals add greatly to the local biodiversity, since there are so few streams in the park with reliable water. It is rich in birds, as well as the rare and beautiful desert bighorn sheep. It was a favorite spot of the local Cahuilla tribe for similar reasons. It is rich in history – Juan Bautista de Anza used the canyon for both of his 18th century treks through the region. And the creek provides a majority of the recharge for the underground aquifer that provides water to the community.

The park's superintendent, who had been trained in wildland fire and was a certified prescribed burn boss, was not unfamiliar with how the fire would likely behave. He was mortified by the prospect of the destruction of Coyote Canyon – the threat of firefighting was more severe, in his opinion, than the threat of fire. He also learned that the 'dozers had already been dispatched to Coyote Canyon by truck transport.

The superintendent approached the Cal Fire incident commander (IC) and offered this theory – that the fire approaching Coyote Canyon would be moving against the wind, going downhill, and traversing progressively thinner accumulations of fuel as it went from chaparral to desert plant communities at lower elevations. In short, the fire would never reach Coyote Canyon, and the creation of a huge firebreak was totally unnecessary.

The incident commander asked a couple of his top managers how much time they thought it would take the fire to progress from its current location to Coyote Canyon. They told him about six hours. The IC then told the park superintendent, "You have three hours to convince me." He added, "You had better hurry, because the 'dozers are on their way to Coyote Canyon on the back of low-boy transports, and we have no cell phone or radio contact with them!"

The park superintendent reached Jon Muench, who contacted L.Louise Jee, the park's geographic information systems (GIS) specialist. L.Louise grabbed a camera and her laptop computer, which had the GIS loaded on it. Together they took off and flew over the likely path the fire would take on its way down the hill to Coyote Canyon. They would take oblique photographs of the landscape, showing the ground cover, while L.Louise would simultaneously plot the photo locations on the GIS. The GIS would also provide data on the ground cover in the area, which, in this case, translated to fuel. This combination of maps, photographs, and data of the local biotic community were then used to display the ground cover and slope at these various locations.

Jon and L.Louise hustled back to the park office, where she loaded all the information on a file transfer protocol (FTP) site. L.Louise informed the fire agency staff of her progress, and they were able to access the site and match the maps and GIS layers to the photos. According to the park's spies, the IC's response, upon seeing the evidence, was, "Hell, there's no way that stuff is going to burn!"

Meanwhile, the park superintendent was driving at breakneck speed down the mountainside towards Coyote Canyon. He caught up to the 'dozers as they were being off-loaded from their lowboy transports, and let them know they should stand down. Coyote Canyon was saved from destruction, while the utility of the aircraft had expanded into new and unexpected territory.

After all this amazing productivity and the daily stress of flying, some rangers might be tempted to have some downtime. Jon just laughs. "My off-duty time was so much fun. Borrego Springs is a small town, yet there always seems to be something going on. I decided to get involved in acting. The local joke is that the community of Borrego Springs is large enough to have live theater and small enough where everyone who wants to be in a play will get a part. Now if you are a middle-aged guy who is willing to sing and dance on stage, you can be a star!

"Starting with a fun supporting role in 'The Music Man,' I soon was cast as Tevye in 'Fiddler On the Roof!' That was a great experience, and I reprised that role at the nearby Pine Hills Lodge. The director of the Christian Community Theater in La Mesa scouted the Pine Hills production of 'Fiddler,' and cast me in their production as well. But one of my favorite roles was playing the plant – Audrey II – that loved to eat humans, in 'Little Shop of Horrors.'"

Jon went on to act in over 80 plays, and remains active in the theater in retirement. He also teaches advanced acting classes and writes instructional books and articles for budding actors. Jon was offered roles in a series of training films for peace officers called "Shoot/Don't Shoot." These films present a series of scenarios that an officer may encounter on the job. Given the visual information available, the trainee must decide whether to use lethal force – fire his weapon and kill the bad guy – or use other, non-lethal techniques. It may also be a false alarm – no law enforcement action is necessary. Then the training staff provides feedback on whether the trainee made the right decision.

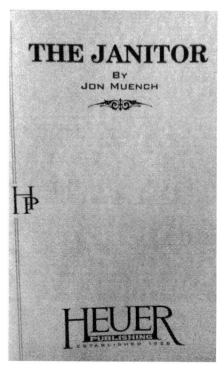

Jon's original screenplay.

As might be expected, these are often not clear-cut, black-and-white decisions. There is a lot of information that must be processed by the trainee in a very short period of time – the trainee must make a split-second decision that could affect several lives, including his or her own.

After acting in a few of the training films, Jon innocently asked the training crew if he could go through some of the other scenarios as a "trainee." They agreed, and probably figured Jon for a well-meaning, middle-aged actor who was clueless about the "real world" of law enforcement. But it was Jon who was shocked when he failed the scenarios. The trainers told him that he had not passed because he had not used lethal force when, in their opinion, he should have.

Jon had not told them about his 30-year career as a peace officer, nor of the incident where he, with absolute justification, decided to take the life of a bank robber in a gun battle. So, rather than being a naïf, he actually had more experience in these situations than any of his trainers.

Jon interjects that, although he regards his years flying at Anza–Borrego as the best of his career, there were bad days thrown in there. The day of the bank robbery in Borrego Springs was, without question, the worst. Jon was not assigned to fly that day, but he was on duty. Shortly after noon, dispatch sent word that the local bank had been robbed, and the thief had been seen driving south of the village. The local deputy sheriffs and highway patrol officers had spike-stripped the narrow highway, and that action disabled the robber's vehicle. Jon and other rangers raced to that location.

The bank robber came out of his car shooting, and the deputies and patrol officers returned fire. Jon came upon the scene, parked and fired two lethal rounds into the robber's chest. Again, Jon credits his martial arts training with enabling him to become focused and stay calm during this highly stressful encounter.

The debriefing concluded that the robber was seeking "suicide by cop" – that is, he wanted to commit suicide, but he chose to get in a gun battle with peace officers in order to die dramatically. Jon's actions were found to be totally appropriate.

Given his experience, Jon was shocked that he had failed the training scenarios. Jon told the trainers of his background and informed them that he had absolutely followed the protocols he had been trained in. He defended his decision in every scenario.

He was startled to learn that the "needle had moved" for peace officers required to make the decision to fire their service weapon. In other words, current training for peace officers gives them the "green light" in situations that, in the past, would have called for restraint. Based on Jon's training and experience, he would have needed more information in the scenarios before taking someone's life. There were steps missing – like yelling at the alleged criminal to stop before pulling the trigger. He absolutely believes that this new training is wrong, and could, in part, be one cause of the problem that police departments and communities are currently dealing with.

As with many peace officers, these incidents begin to take their toll.

After the terrorist attacks of 9/11, Jon started to think of what his life would look like after retiring from the Parks Department. He thought back to the early '60s, when John F. Kennedy was president, and the Peace Corps was created. Although it was a couple of years before Jon officially retired, the idea of volunteering for the Peace Corps continued to grow on him – it seemed a logical step to take in his life of public service.

His last couple years at Anza–Borrego, however, were some of his most fulfilling. He had nearly perfected his skills at flying

Jon mentoring Kelly McHague — the ranger who followed him as park ranger/pilot.

the Christen Husky, but at the same time, realized that statistics can catch up to even the best pilots. Eventually, it becomes more likely that you will have a serious incident in the aircraft – one that ends with an "unscheduled landing."

There were other factors that helped him make the decision to retire. A fellow Anza–Borrego ranger, Kelly McHague, was very interested in the ranger/pilot job when Jon was beginning to contemplate his departure. Jon started taking Kelly on lots of flights, and it was clear to him that she would be well-suited to the job. So, he knew that when he did retire, there would likely be a capable successor ready to step into the cockpit. Jon adds, "Every time we flew together, I tried to teach her something I had learned that was not covered in typical flight training."

He also believed that, for over a decade, he had held the most incredible and fulfilling job in the Parks Department – perhaps on the planet. The ranger/pilot gets to fly almost every day, "slip the surly bonds of earth," and patrol the incredible Anza–Borrego Desert State Park – replete with scenic and natural beauty. When he gets to work, he gets to decide what he is going to work on that day – where to go and what to do. None of his supervisors typically have a background in flying, so they rely on the pilot to be the expert in the aircraft program. He develops a close relationship with the plane – his work partner.

Jon's recognition of the excellence of his chosen profession was borne out one day at the Borrego Springs airport. At that point, Jon had decided that he should retire at the top of his game. A pilot from Los Angeles approached Jon and asked if he would be interested in giving a presentation at the Adventurers Club in L.A. Jon consented and put together a talk and slide show. After the speech, two men approached him and began telling him what a great job he had – one of the best in the world, in their opinion. After a while, they revealed that they were both NASA astronauts, and they both had been on missions to the moon.

After retiring from State Parks, Jon did enlist in the Peace Corps, and he was soon informed that he would be sent to Ukraine, although it was not his first choice of assignments. He actually wanted to go to a Muslim country. Again, however, it turned out to be a terrific experience in "the toughest job you'll ever love." He went through four months of Peace Corps training – intense immersion in the language and culture of the country to which he would be assigned. Jon recalls that he learned "how to see life from different eyes – you just can't get that as a tourist."

Jon was single when he was assigned to work in Ukraine, and he jokes that one of his fellow rangers at Anza–Borrego, Mike Stalder, started a betting pool among park staff on how long it would take Jon to marry a local Ukrainian woman. Jon recalls telling Mike, "No way!" When Jon arrived in his new country, he went to a large outdoor festival, and, in a gesture of friendship very typical of Jon, he boldly got up and recited a poem he had memorized in the Ukrainian language. This act paid off – the locals immediately accepted him.

A few weeks after arriving at his Peace Corps work assignment, Jon met his future wife, Alla, at a meeting in Kiev. She was assigned to be his coordinator at an ecological center for students, which was a holdover from the old Soviet after-school system that is still in place today. They were serving at after-school educational centers for children and young adults after Ukraine became independent. She served as a teachers' teacher

Alla shows Jon her moves – moves that eventually lit his fire.

there before Jon arrived, and they soon became friends – "Just friends," Jon adds quickly with a laugh.

For the first year of his Peace Corps service, he went on field trips with other educators and basically tried to learn the language. Alla was assigned to be his project coordinator as well as his translator and language teacher. One of the reasons Alla had been chosen to be his coordinator was that she spoke both Russian and Ukrainian. She was assigned to help him with Ukrainian, since Jon had personally chosen to speak Ukrainian rather than Russian. Thus, they spent a lot of time together, learning the language and planning programs in natural history and lessons in grant writing. They became very close friends after several months.

Jon grins and remembers the moment when everything changed. "I really fell in love with her, to my great surprise, one day when I watched her stacking hay with a pitch fork in the local garden. She had grown up on a farm and was adept at pitching hay. It was a warm and sunny afternoon, and the light on the hay dust was almost surreal with natural beauty. I began planning on how to make a pitch of my own as I realized my feelings for Alla were beginning to change dramatically. Fortunately, her feelings towards me were growing at the same time.

"The only problem I had with this situation was that there was a new local director who was a very difficult woman – she was suspicious of Americans and didn't like us being there. She was convinced I was in the CIA and called me out on it one day at a meeting. I had to contact headquarters, and the Ukrainian staff came down to reason with her. She wouldn't budge, so they decided to reassign me based on their needs and my skills.

"They knew about my martial arts background, because by that time I was already teaching 'rape prevention classes' to Peace Corps volunteers around Ukraine as part of my service. Because Alla had contacts with another school, I was reassigned to a school where I could teach English and karate instead of ecology. So everything worked out well, and Alla and I continued to see each other outside work.

"Of course, Alla eventually took me home to meet her mother. At first, her mother disliked me and trusted me even less than the local director did. Looking back, I guess I am not surprised. No mother wants to contemplate the notion of her daughter moving halfway around the world with a stranger.

Jon and his mother-in-law on the farm in Ukraine.

"Her mother eventually came to like and trust me, and after two and a half years of dating, Alla and I were married in Ukraine. When I finished my Peace Corps service, she came back to the U.S. with me. Every year we spend a month or two with her mom – working on the farm in Ukraine and being emissaries for America. My mother-in-law is a terrific person, and we get along really well now.

"There seems to be a common belief that the Peace Corps discourages romance between its volunteers and the local citizens. On the contrary, the Peace Corps believes that these relationships benefit the individuals and the program, since they help to bridge the cultural divide. The Peace Corps was very happy that Alla and I had found one another, and there were no problems there. We continue to affect the lives of people both in Ukraine and America – for the better, we hope. The best result is that both Alla and I have become better people as well."

Jon shakes his head while he marvels at his good fortune – both personal and professional. Given his rough start as a teenager, he deserves a lot of credit for his drive and his ability to mentally discipline himself. Good fortune is usually a result of hard work.

"Getting that pilot job was one of the best things that ever happened to me. Those times were the most rewarding and adventurous of my life. Not only did I have this fantastic job, but the park is also a wonderful place to put into practice all aspects of the generalist ranger – resource management, interpretation, and law enforcement. If I had any advice to offer today's rangers, it would be to become a well-rounded, generalist ranger. There is so much variety to the job, and it can be so satisfying if you keep challenging yourself to learn new skills."

DAN WINKELMAN

Win With Winkelman

One of the most memorable moments in Dan Winkelman's personal and professional life arose when he was a ranger at the beautiful and remarkable Angel Island State Park. On a typical temperate day at Angel Island, in the middle of the San Francisco Bay, Dan learned that a park visitor and his family were having trouble with their overnight reservation. When Dan stepped in to help, little did he know that he would enter into a friendship with this visitor that would culminate in Dan mounting an election campaign to become president of the United States. He would become the first park ranger in history to run for president, and he would be forever tied to his catchy campaign slogan – "Win With Winkelman."

Winkelman for President! ©*Phil Frank, 2007. Artwork courtesy of Susan Frank.*

At the time, park visitors could stay overnight on Angel Island at the East Garrison officers' quarters, or at one of ten "environmental campsites." Although the vast majority of visitors to the island stay a few hours and then return home, being able to spend the night was an incredible experience.

An overnight visitor could walk to the south side of the island and see the beautiful city of San Francisco all lit up at night. In the late afternoon and early morning, it was possible to explore the island's natural and cultural features and rarely see another soul.

Hiker on Angel Island. *Courtesy of California State Parks (Image 090-S8998).*

On a clear day, hikers could walk up to the top of Mt. Livermore, the highest point on Angel Island, and get a 360-degree, overwhelming, shockingly beautiful view of the bay and its environs. And it was possible stay inside a historical building rather than camp out. Needless to say, this opportunity was in high demand, and reservations were difficult to obtain.

Ayala Cove is the starting point for most visits to Angel Island. The ferry from Tiburon stops there several times a day and lets off its load of hikers, bicyclists, history buffs, birders, sightseers, and the usual contingent of people who don't know exactly why they are there or what they are supposed to do. This is a good spot to place information signs to help visitors have a good experience, and it is where the ranger and seasonal staff spend a lot of time giving directions, answering questions, and providing other "visitor services."

One Saturday morning, Dan was working at Ayala Cove when he overheard a group of two families talking dispiritedly about their situation. It seems that the group of four adults and two children had reserved overnight lodging in a building that – at that time – was called Quarters 11 in the Camp Reynolds area of the island. Lodging was in a restored Victorian home that had been fixed up beautifully by a retired physician who was working as a park volunteer. (In a stroke of genius designed to improve the home by roughly 9%, it is now called Quarters 12.) However, when the families arrived with their bedding, ice chest of food, and other gear, they were informed that the overnight quarters had been "double-booked" by the local cooperating association, and the other party had arrived first. This family group was told there were no other accommodations available, and they would not be able to spend the night on the island.

The ranger recalls that the parents were taking this misfortune in stride and were telling the kids, "Well, we will just have to try again another weekend." Now Dan is an affable fellow with a big heart and a dry sense of humor. He went up to the group, introduced himself, and offered to let them all stay at his park residence on the island for the night, which had plenty of room, since Dan was single. After the requisite, "Oh, we couldn't impose on you, but thank you," the group finally reconsidered and decided to take Dan up on his generous offer of a couple of spare bedrooms, and they all wound up having a marvelous time together.

When Dan is asked if that was standard procedure, he gets a twinkle in his eye and admits that he had recognized one of the men in the group – Phil Frank, a cartoonist for the San Francisco Chronicle. Dan had already gotten wind of the situation that not only was Phil on the island with his family and some friends, but they had just been displaced through no fault of their own. Phil was very popular with readers of the Chronicle, and many of his comic strips focused on state parks and national parks in California. Phil had created a whole cast of crazy rangers and animals to carry his stories forward, and he had a huge audience for his artwork in the daily "Chron."

Dan, Phil, and Susan, Phil's wife, immediately hit it off, and Phil and Susan would often travel to the island thereafter to visit Dan. To thank Dan for his initial hospitality, Phil did a drawing of Hospital Cove, another name for the area where they stayed on that first visit, and gifted it to Dan. His "Travels with Farley" cartoon strip artwork was so beloved by State Park employees and park supporters that Phil was later honored by being named an Honorary Ranger by the California State Park Rangers Association.

The first time the Franks came back to visit, Dan had already driven up to Salt Point State Park and gathered a few abalone and fresh fish. He cooked those up for dinner, which just whetted the Franks' appetite for more Angel Island visits.

Soon afterwards, Phil put on a birthday party for Susan at a rented home near the town of Bolinas, and they invited Dan. It was on this occasion, Dan recalls, that his dry and understated sense of humor led to "The Big Mistake." This was during the President Clinton/Monica Lewinsky scandal, and during the birthday party, Dan leaned in and said, "Phil, Susan, I have been thinking about running for president." Phil raised an eyebrow, "Oh yeah?" Dan said, "I hear being president of the United States is a good way to meet girls." Then Phil asked, "So, what party are you with?" Dan chuckled, "I am running on the Peace and Quiet Party ticket." Phil and Susan, a publisher and creative journalist in her own right, both had a "BOING" look that told Dan that he had struck a nerve. Indeed, the Franks recognized this "presidential run" as having great potential for the "Travels with Farley" strip.

Phil and Susan started figuring out how this would work as a feature in Phil's comic strip. Soon after, somewhat to Dan's surprise, he opened up the morning Chronicle, and there was a strip featuring a ranger out on Angel Island! The new and fictitious campaign motto, "Win With Winkelman," would forever be woven henceforth into Dan's personal and professional tapestry. The other two eventual party candidates in the fall of 2000 – George W. Bush and Al Gore – initially had little reason to be nervous. Actually, they never had any reason to be nervous about Dan's run, and undoubtedly never heard of the Peace and Quiet Party.

Dan had about as much experience being featured in comic strips as he had in national politics, so he started out sending in ideas to Phil for the strip. Phil was quick to respond, "No, No, No…I write Farley – I am the idea guy. All I want you to do, Dan, is to tell me what you are doing in the campaign."

This was not the easiest task, according to Dan, since 1) he already had a full-time job as a ranger at a busy park, and 2) he really had no idea how to run a presidential campaign – especially one that is totally fictional. Dan started sending Frank some campaign strategies and thoughts, and Phil ran the series for the next two years. Farley featured the Winkelman campaign 86 times, and that artwork is now archived in the Parks Department facilities in Sacramento and at UC Berkeley.

The "Win With Winkelman" picks up steam. ©*Phil Frank, 2007. Courtesy of Susan Frank.*

The intensity increased one day when Phil inserted in the strip the notion that Winkelman supporters could order a bumper sticker with the "Win With Winkelman" motto. Phil went to the Chronicle's marketing division and got some money to produce the bumper sticker. Phil did the artwork, naturally. The orders started pouring in, but Phil had not really thought out how he was going to fill all these orders. So he put his retired father to work stuffing envelopes. After his dad got tired of doing that – after all, they received over 5,000 orders for the Winkelman bumper stickers – Phil prevailed upon Dan to fulfill the order requests (on his own time, of course). How many presidential candidates have had to stuff their own envelopes?

Who could resist voting for the estimable Dan Winkelman? ©*Phil Frank, 2007. Courtesy of Susan Frank.*

Over the two-year run of the "campaign," Dan would occasionally not think about it for a while. But then he would be driving on the mainland, say, through Tiburon, and would spot a car with the bumper sticker. Dan wanted to pull them over, knock on the car window and say, "Hey, that's me!" He suspected that most people thought the characters in the comic strip were fictional (after all, it did feature talking bears). He wanted to let them know that Dan Winkelman was a real person, although he was not really running for president.

People would arrive on Angel Island during the campaign and say to the park aide on duty, "Hey, we read Farley, and we think it is great that Phil Frank created this fictitious ranger to run for president." And the park aide would respond, "Well, that is Dan Winkelman standing right there!"

Often, Dan would have trouble changing gears from ranger to presidential candidate and back again. After all, on a busy day, a ranger has a lot of varied tasks to carry out – activities that have a lot to do with running a state park. Then a visitor would approach him and tell him that his daughter really wanted to meet him. Well, Dan could not afford to lose votes or alienate voters, so he would take the time to engage the visitors as Candidate Winkelman.

As time went on and ideas for the campaign comic strips became more difficult for Phil to create, he started to press Dan for more ideas. Dan, of course, was enjoying the strips immensely and having fun with the notoriety, but he was careful to remember that it was the state controller writing his paychecks, not the Chronicle, so doing his ranger job was a higher priority than running a campaign – especially a fake one.

Predictably, the State Parks managers in Sacramento were a little puzzled about how to react to this campaign phenomenon. On one hand, the comic strips were very amusing and brought a ton of good public relations to the Department. However, there are state rules against running for political office while you are a state employee. Obviously, Dan did not want to quit his ranger job for this imaginary campaign.

So the solution was to have Dan meet with local State Parks management. The district superintendent for the Marin District called Dan in and started off by telling Dan that he had reviewed the Department's "Incompatible Activities Policy." He reminded Dan that, according to Departmental policy, it is not permissible to run for political office while a state employee. He looked Dan in the eye, and without smiling, said, "You are not REALLY running for political office, are you?" all the time shaking his head NO vigorously. Dan, being a quick study, said, "No, I am not really running for political office." Then the superintendent said, "Very good answer. And this is REALLY a marketing campaign to gain support and notoriety for Angel Island State Park, for the State Parks Department, and it is not REALLY a political campaign, right?" This time, he was nodding his head YES just as vigorously. Again, Dan picked up the clue and said, "Yes, this is really a wildly successful marketing campaign." The superintendent said that was great, and based on those responses, there were no further issues. The Department would support what Dan was doing, because not only was it all in fun, it was also really terrific publicity for Angel Island and the Department. So the whole grilling session lasted for two questions.

Dan recalls being surprised that the folks in Sacramento actually realized what a gold mine in marketing they were sitting on. It was an amazing and unbelievable time. Of course, this was before blogging and e-versions of newspapers became so popular. People actually read the newspaper. The Chronicle back then really had some clout through its incredible reach into millions of homes. The "Win With Winkelman" strips were a marketing boon for State Parks.

Dan soon helped to create a website for Angel Island, and also added a webcam, called Angelcam. Visitors to the website could punch up the Angelcam, which was mounted in the upstairs window of the visitor center, looking down at Ayala Cove. Picnic tables, boats that were docked, ferries coming and going, and what the weather was like – these all could be seen through the webcam. The weather was very important for boaters, since the weather conditions and fog changed rapidly and often.

After the Angelcam was up, Dan got the idea that Phil Frank could put it to use to further market the island. So Dan called Phil and informed him that planning had begun for the national presidential nominating convention of the Peace and Quiet Party! Phil was used to Dan's crazy ideas and was fairly nonplussed about this notion. Phil said, "Oh yeah?" But when Dan let Phil know that the convention would be televised, this got Phil's attention.

Phil actually put information about the Angelcam website in the "Travels with Farley" comic strip and let readers know to go to the Angel Island website to watch the national convention of the Peace and Quiet Party – it was scheduled to be televised on a Tuesday at 11 a.m. The last panel of that particular strip was a classic, Dan recalls. It showed a squirrel sitting on top of a computer monitor looking straight out of the panel at the reader and saying, "It will be SO exciting!"

On the stump. *Courtesy of Dan Winkelman.*

Dan and his campaign "volunteers" put red, white, and blue bunting on the picnic tables, and Dan climbed up on one of the tables and doffed his Stetson – just like the drawing on the bumper sticker. The frame of the Angelcam would change about every 30 seconds. Docents could be seen walking around with posters and banners, and one of Dan's friends even wandered in and out of the camera view in a Smokey Bear costume.

People who accessed the website were treated to a camera looking at Ayala Cove and a bunch of folks walking around at the "national convention." Amazingly, the website got about 17,000 hits. Of course, there was no sound attached to the webcam, so the whole convention was silent. Dan recently mused that perhaps more national presidential conventions should be held without sound.

Dan wrote an article about the convention for the Tiburon Arc, a local newspaper, and this item got the attention of the town's Rotary Club. They invited Dan over to give a campaign speech at their regular meeting. That notion also caught on, and Dan and Phil started getting invitations to other groups to give a speech. It was a short speech, and Dan can still recite it word for word, over 15 years later – "You know, I have been a bureaucrat for almost 30 years now, and one day I realized I had been saying the company line for so long that I was no longer capable of forming my own opinion. And so I went to a doctor and was diagnosed with ODD – Opinion Deficit Disorder. I figured there were a lot of other ODD sufferers out there, so we all got together and formed the Peace and Quiet Party. All those people with no opinion on any issue – they are our target demographic."

Since Angel Island is, ahem, an island, transportation on and off the island can be a little tricky. During the day, there is a ferry that runs regularly to the mainland and back. At night, however, residents of the island have to provide their own transportation. One evening, Dan was due to give a campaign speech to the North Bay Mayors Conference. He would have to get back to the island after the ferry stopped running, so he wound up taking the sailboat that he owned over to the mainland. Dan was wearing his "Class A" uniform, which is the formal uniform for rangers. He took on a little water during the journey to the mainland, so Dan showed up to give a speech with very wet pant legs. Great start!

Many years ago, there was a deadpan comedian named Pat Paulsen, who also ran a fictitious presidential campaign. Paulsen would start his stump speech with zero emotion and a very monotonous voice – "I can't tell you how excited I am to be here tonight."

Although the comedian had passed away, Dan used Paulsen's line and began his speech to the North Bay Mayors with it, followed by his very short campaign talk. The mayors, of course, were all politicians, so they got the humor. Dan thought they were going to fall on the floor laughing, and he recalls that night – wet uniform and all – as the most memorable of his campaign.

As with all great ideas, the campaign eventually had to come to an end, and along with it, that emphasis in "Travels with Farley." Phil had to figure out how to wind down the strip featuring the "Win With Winkelman" campaign. He concluded that the actual election would provide the perfect vehicle for that.

On election night in November of 2000, Phil and Susan Frank actually came out to Angel Island. Amazingly, Dan got TV reception that night, so they were able to watch the returns from the networks. Phil's strip about that evening features those who are gathered around Dan's television wearing antlers that are wrapped with tinfoil – all trying to get reception.

Susan was very political and was getting more and more upset as the results trickled in from around the country. Dan recalls that she was not a big fan of George W. Of course, this was the election where the TV news first reported that Gore had won Florida, but then gave it to Bush. There was a tremendous controversy over the vote in Florida, and eventually, the case went all the way to the U.S. Supreme Court to be decided.

When Susan realized that Al Gore probably would not win the election outright that evening, she turned to Dan and asked, "So, whom did YOU vote for?" Dan responded that, with the Electoral College system, in California it was a foregone conclusion where the electoral votes would go, and said, "I voted my conscience!" Phil immediately picked up on that peace-keeping nuance and joked, "So what you are really saying is that you voted for yourself."

Dan recalls that he was not, of course, on any real ballot. Even as a write-in candidate, you have to register as a write-in, in order for any votes for you to actually be tallied. And it had been made abundantly clear to Dan that if he actually ran for president that he would lose his park ranger job. This was a marketing gig, right? So it all went nowhere, and he never found out about any real vote tallies. He never knew if anyone really voted for him, but given the fact that it was a California election, who knows? Dan is quick to point out that he will never be remembered as a "spoiler" – the term used to refer to the roles of H. Ross Perot and Ralph Nader – Perot in 1992 and Nader in this same 2000 election.

There is not one book that captures all 86 of Phil Frank's comic strips on the Winkelman campaign. Dan has copies of all the strips in a binder. The original artwork by Phil undoubtedly has incredible value that is a true treasure, and a significant part of the tapestry that makes up the history of the State Parks System. There should be a small book published that captures all 86 episodes of the amazing "Win With Winkelman" campaign, issued under the banner of the Peace and Quiet party.

Of course, Dan's career and life were not defined by that one quixotic run for the presidency. He had a marvelous and meaningful career at State Parks, including his stay at Angel Island, and he had quite an impact on other parks and programs. This was due to his strongly held belief that public service was, indeed, a high calling.

Dan credits his mother for developing his passion for a life in parks and recreation. Ruth Winkelman was a fourth generation Californian who had a very strong tie to the land. She traced her roots in the state back to 1858, when Dan's great-great-grandparents arrived in California in a covered wagon – just a few years after California gained statehood.

Ruth grew up in logging camps all over Northern California. Her father was a teamster, and back in those days that meant driving a freight wagon drawn by six horses. She became interested in parks, to the point where she wanted to become a park ranger. However, it said right on the job announcement bulletin, "Women may not apply." So Ruth decided that her son Dan should become the family's ranger. She started taking the whole family to parks all over California, trying to ingrain into Dan a passion for parks. He had other ideas at the time, however. Since he was a whiz at algebra, he preferred to think about a career in mathematics.

As it did with many people in Dan's generation, serving in the military during the Vietnam War drastically altered his life and his plans. He recalls that his whole set of values changed. After returning from Vietnam and subsequently being honorably discharged by the U.S. Navy, he was hired by Sacramento County Parks. His main job there was to patrol, with three other rangers, the American River Parkway and specifically Ancil Hoffman Park, east of Sacramento. There he met, worked with, and learned from the estimable Effie Yeaw, who taught him how to love the natural world and interpret that world to the public by providing meaningful nature walks.

Wonderful memories and feelings would wash over him as he recalled the frequent family trips to a variety of California's myriad parks. He soon realized that maybe his mother was right – he felt a strong calling to preserve a little piece of nature in the Golden State.

While looking into how to become a state park ranger in California, Dan realized that he would have to get a bachelor's degree, since that was required at that time. He was accepted at Sacramento State University, and worked as a public pool lifeguard for Sacramento County to earn a living. With the help of the GI Bill, because of his service in Vietnam, he was able to work out a schedule where he could both work and go to school.

He was able to get his classes on Mondays, Wednesdays, and Fridays at Sac State, and work the other four days. He went through his entire college career working 32 hours per week and taking 12 units. Dan was one busy guy!

He was also a valued employee at the pools, and was soon promoted to the position of swimming pool supervisor. This role allowed Dan to become quite accomplished in aquatics. This experience and expertise would serve him well later as a ranger at Sonoma Coast State Beach.

For a while, he was torn between the thought of staying a lifeguard and the possibility of becoming a park ranger. He was promoted again, to recreation supervisor, while he graduated from Sac State in 1973 with a degree in history. Running swimming pools was fun, and Dan was in his comfort zone.

After turning 30, though, a dose of reality hit and he decided that he should get serious about becoming a state park ranger. Ironically, the State Parks Department had just lowered the entrance qualifications to 60 units of college instead of a bachelor's degree. Although he passed the ranger civil service exam, it took about five years for him to get hired on a permanent, full-time basis. In the meantime, he worked as a seasonal ranger at Sutter's Fort State Historic Park in Sacramento. Here Dan picked up three interpretive skills that would be useful throughout his career – historic baking, black powder cannon firing, and puppetry.

The best thing that happened then for Dan's career was a statewide hiring freeze. It sounds odd that a hiring freeze would be beneficial to prospective employees. However, it was actually the specter of a freeze that provided the benefit. As the rumors of a freeze became stronger, the various departments throughout state government began to hire new employees like crazy. Dan got picked up as state park ranger trainee at Fort Ross State Historic Park, and his career took off.

On his first trip to the academy for formal training, he realized that one of the negative by-products of a fast-track hiring process is that some of the new hires probably should not have been hired. With 10 years of experience, including a couple of years as a seasonal ranger with State Parks, Dan had a pretty good idea of what the job involved and how different situations should be handled. Some of the trainees appeared to have been hired off the street with little or no experience.

Today, candidates undergo thorough vetting through background checks and psychological exams. Remember, rangers are full peace officers in California. Let's just say that more than a couple of trainees did not survive their first year in state service.

Dan recalls developing a lot of great ideas at Asilomar. After all, he had good, experienced instructors, and a lot of after-hours time to spend with fellow trainees in philosophical discussions of park work. So, upon his return to Fort Ross, he presented his supervisor with a list of ways to improve the park.

At the time, the Department employed the "district concept" – that is, several parks would be grouped geographically into one administrative district. This allowed for greater efficiencies, particularly in the management and administrative functions.

The district concept also meant that management could reassign rangers to different assignments within that geographic unit – at least they could back then. After contemplating Dan's ideas for improvement for at least several seconds, his supervisor told Dan that management realized that he had spent most of his nascent career at historic units, and perhaps an experience with a little more law enforcement would be a good career move. Soon, Dan was reassigned to Sonoma Coast State Beach.

As Dan recalls, that idea sounded fine at the time. Sonoma Coast – what could be more bucolic than that, he mused. Its name implied that perhaps it was a nice little "pocket" beach, tucked away in a rocky cove. It turned out to be 14 miles of free day use, and when Dan arrived in 1982, it was anything but pastoral.

Shortly after his arrival, he pulled over a motor vehicle for a violation. Now, for most rangers, their first vehicle stop is usually for something pretty minor, such as a broken taillight, rolling through a stop sign, or for not having any gloves in their glove box. The first arrest that Dan made, however, was for a fellow firing a handgun out the window of a moving vehicle. Dan's first thought (okay, maybe second thought) was that he should get this guy off the street and into jail as soon as possible.

One of the traditions among the members of the public at the time was a celebration for the Fourth of July at Sonoma Coast beaches. In order to honor their freedoms – inscribed in the Declaration of Independence over 200 years previously – visitors would light off fireworks and aim them horizontally at other visitors. Ah, democracy!

In order to make a big showing to the crazies and begin the process of bringing this tradition to a halt, almost every ranger was assigned the night shift on July 4th. Only Dan was assigned to the day shift, and his supervisor shook his head and told Dan how lucky he was to not have to work that evening.

Just to celebrate that slow day shift, on duty by himself, Dan's first four incidents that day were a Code 3 run (lights and siren) to a case of food poisoning, an auto accident, a drowning, and then a cliff rescue. Next up was responding to an incident where a guy was physically beating up his wife, and then another Code 3 run. Thank goodness he had the easy shift that day!

On nice weekend days, every parking place was taken – remember, it was free – and there would be over a million visitors annually on those 14 miles of beach. To Dan, it seemed as though two-thirds of those would be minors drinking alcohol – always a fun situation.

One accomplishment that Dan is particularly proud of is helping to ramp up the aquatic safety effort at Sonoma Coast while he was there. Dan credits his experience in aquatics at Sacramento County parks with giving him the background to assist in developing safety programs – programs that have, to date, saved many, many lives.

This region of the coast, where it meets the Pacific Ocean, has a reputation for "sleeper waves" – those waves that come up on shore with little warning and are much larger than other waves immediately before or after. Let's say a parent is walking along the beach with their spouse and two children, and every wave for 10 minutes or more washes up to approximately the same spot. Then seemingly out of nowhere, a larger wave rolls in, and one of the kids is washed out to sea.

The typical parent's reaction would be to jump in the ocean without hesitation to attempt to rescue their child, but due to the surf and cold water, they would be in trouble immediately, and would be of no help to their child. The job of bystanders and first responders would also be made more difficult by having two people to rescue – not just one.

The State Parks Department's position at the time was based on a legal foundation – since the state's property line ends at the mean high tide line, the Department's opinion was that the responsibility to rescue those in trouble in the ocean legally lay with the Sonoma County Sheriff and the U.S. Coast Guard. Rightfully so, the local park staff felt frustrated with this, since the Sheriff and the Coast Guard were not really a good solution in terms of rapid responses. It was impossible for the Coast Guard to get to the scene reliably in a timely manner, and deputy sheriffs are typically not trained to make rough water rescues. Most well-meaning deputies, in this scenario, would likely soon become the third victim in the ocean. The Sheriff's Department did have a rescue helicopter available. However, the length of time for the Coast Guard or the Sheriff to respond, even with excellent equipment and intentions, made these response methods less than optimal.

Over several years, Dan and others, including state park lifeguards, lifeguard supervisors, and aquatic specialists throughout the state, lobbied and developed budgets to provide the Sonoma Coast with lifeguards. If lifeguards were on scene, there were several positives that would result. The guards could make contact with visitors who were unaware of the sleeper waves and warn them of the problem. And, if a victim did get sucked into the ocean, a trained professional with appropriate rescue gear would be available to perform the rescue and relieve friends or family of having to try to save their loved one in the ocean.

Eventually, state lifeguards were assigned to Sonoma Coast, and the number of drownings dropped dramatically. Dan remembers the statements in the budget request for more staff that seemed to resonate with decision-makers in Sacramento – "We can either perform rescues or we can do body recoveries. The public is now attempting rescues, and double drownings are the result. Professional lifeguards are needed to effect successful rescues."

In the meantime, though, Dan and others – notably District Interpretive Specialist Vic Maris – tried to help ease the drownings problem in other ways. Dan first wrote a comic book entitled "Floyd the Shark." Next, he rewrote the interpretive signs on the beach to be more blunt in their language warning of the local dangers. Vic and Dan produced a video called "Sleeper Waves of the North Coast" to be shown in schools, at service clubs, and to civic organizations. Dan is still proud – years later – that the result was a broadcast quality video that only cost $8,000!

Dan stayed at the Sonoma Coast for several years, and is proud of the fact that he, along with other rangers, helped to create a new cooperating association call Stewards of Slavianka – the Russian name for the nearby Russian River.

He also worked for several years at Salt Point State Park. While there, Dan became a state-certified scuba diver, and worked closely with the Sonoma County Ocean Rescue Team. At Salt Point, water incidents were typically due to divers in distress, and the opportunity to have a successful rescue was enhanced by the fact that those divers wore wetsuits. The County had purchased a helicopter called Henry 1. If there were a victim in the water, a state or county first responder would swim out and secure a rescue tube on the victim. Henry 1 would arrive and lower a cable (static line) that would then get hooked on to the victim and the rescuer. Then Henry 1 would lift both people out of the water and drop them on shore gently. Dan recalls with a slight smile, "After a while, at age 45, I stopped doing that."

Dan also played a big role in refurbishing the visitor center at Salt Point State Park. A storm had destroyed it, so Dan worked with a local contractor, volunteer divers, and other volunteers to re-create a beautiful building with a splendid view of the ocean and Gerstle Cove. Again, this was accomplished with very little capital. Dan and his team were able to reconstruct the center for a mere $14,000. Vic Maris was able to secure funding for the "biotic zones" exhibits, and the visitor center now serves thousands of visitors annually.

In 1991, Dan got the notion – a wild idea, in his words – to transfer to Angel Island State Park. He had decided by this time that he really did not want to be promoted to a "higher job." He originally had taken the job as a ranger to work in the field, and being a field ranger was still very appealing. Dan is proud of those accomplishments noted earlier, and he does not feel he could have had such a positive impact on parks and people had he not been a field ranger. Dan adds, with a wry smile, that the desire to work for supervisors – rangers a full generation younger than him – was not among his motivating factors. Still, the urge to work at new parks was there.

Angel Island State Park would allow Dan to enjoy two of his favorite pursuits – sailing and bicycling. Since it is primarily a day-use park, and access is by boat, there were plenty of times when Dan would have the roads to himself for bicycling. Dan's favorite cycling route, by far, was the fire road – a three-mile dirt road around the top of Angel Island – complete with stunning bay views.

Dan felt it would be great to be so close to San Francisco without living in the city. He would get to live on this rural, beautiful, pristine, historic, and natural island in the middle of the San Francisco Bay.

However, when it is necessary to rely on a ferry for transportation, unusual problems can arise – especially since the ferries do not run all day and night. For example, Jim and Susan Burke were neighbors of Dan's on Angel Island for several years. When they left the island to move to Cuyamaca Rancho State Park in San Diego County, it took them a while to get used to the new drill. They would be shopping in the nearby town of Lakeside, when Jim would glance at his watch and panic, thinking they would be too late to catch the last ferry to the island. Susan would then remind him that they were traveling in an automobile. They could take their time and walk the streets of beautiful downtown Lakeside, strolling along the side of the magnificent lake.

Welcome to Angel Island. *Courtesy of Dan Winkelman.*

Dan moved to Angel Island and had to adjust to island life. Almost every visitor begins their trek on Angel Island after disembarking at Ayala Cove. Many of them would look around and start thinking of how and when to get back on the ferry to the mainland. Park staff would think of how to get people to enjoy their visit more, stay longer, and gain more appreciation for the history and importance of the island. Dan and other staff started working on maps and signs – the primary methods by which visitors figure out where they are and where they can go.

Lots of visitors had suggestions for how to improve operations on Angel Island. Of course, they were viewing the operation through their paradigm of urban or suburban mainland life and often did not take into account the conditions that park staff had to deal with. For example, there was limited fresh water on the island, and precious little space for treating sewage. But people would want to have more facilities and services anyway. Park staff referred to most of the ideas for improving visitor services as "Fantasy Island."

The island had an excellent Environmental Living Program, where fourth- and fifth-graders would come out to the island and stay at Camp Reynolds. The goal was to re-create an experience that approximated life at the time of the U.S. Civil War. To make it as realistic as possible, Dan instituted a "chain of command" among the students. They were organized into squads, took an oath of allegiance, and for all intents and purposes, the students were now in the U.S. Army. If a student had a question, they had to ask the corporal in charge of the squad – they could not ask the ranger a question directly.

Dan was focused on increasing the number of students attending the program. The park sponsored a workshop for teachers, so that the students had some knowledge of what to expect before they arrived, as well as follow-up assignments once they returned home. The program became so popular that the park hired an interpretive specialist to manage the effort. Since the students were using historic buildings and historic objects, such as muskets, there was concern about damage and vandalism. Having a park staffer there all the time really helped to avoid negative impacts.

Another special event that Dan added at Camp Reynolds was called the Artillery Battle. The artillery stations were put in during the Civil War to protect "Raccoon Strait" from Confederate raiders. At the time, there were many pots of gold coming out of the mines in California, and a lot of that gold wound up at the mint in San Francisco. It was providing a lot of the funding for the North's Army of the Potomac. So the concern at that time was that raiders from the Confederacy would come into San Francisco Bay, come ashore, and take all the gold in the mint. This would have two obvious consequences – more money for the South and less money for the North.

Dan convinced the owners of two historic tall ships – the Hawaiian Chieftain and the Californian – to participate in a reenactment of what "could" have happened, although it never did. The tall ships raised Confederate flags and sailed by Camp Reynolds. On the island at the artillery stations were the 3rd Artillery and the Cal 100 with a row of cannons "firing" on the ships, to the delight of visitors and students.

Artillery battle at Raccoon Strait. *Courtesy of Dan Winkelman.*

Dan gained notoriety for his candidacy in the "Win With Winkelman" run for the presidency. However, that was all in fun. It is also imperative to recognize his many "real" accomplishments – creating interpretive programs, establishing an ocean safety program, restoring a demolished visitor center, and producing maps and signs. Dan is quick to point out that he did none of these things alone. He worked with other terrific park staff to serve the public, provide safe parks, and protect park resources and visitors.

After 10 years there, Dan left Angel Island and retired in 2001. He moved to the town of Folsom, California, where he is currently a docent at the Folsom Powerhouse. Dan has written a couple of books, and volunteers at Lake Natoma for the "Adopt a Trail" program.

When I asked Dan why he retired, he said he was tired of going to meetings. He then smiles wryly, "When I first retired, I was so thankful that I would not have to attend meetings anymore. Now I am on the board of the Save the American River Association and the board of the Sacramento County Historical Society, so I go to meetings all the time!"

Some folks, they just really cannot give up the park life.

In retirement, Dan remains involved in local protection efforts.

For more information —

Huell Howser. 1993. Angel Island State Park.
Huell talks to Dan Winkelman about Angel Island State Park.
https://blogs.chapman.edu/huell-howser-archives/1993/12/10/angel-island-californias-gold-408/

Books by Dan Winkelman —

Non-fiction:

Lake Natoma: A Ranger in Search of Walden Pond

Sacramento Pioneers of Power and Light

MARK FAULL

Poet, Guardian, Scientist

After seasonal and full-time assignments at Humboldt Redwoods State Park, Pfeiffer Big Sur State Park, and Half Moon Bay State Beach, Ranger Mark Faull decided that he needed to have a little more diversity in his career and in his life. He recalls that he and his wife Marsha rented a U-Haul trailer, loaded up their ragtag and meager assortment of furniture, and drove away from commonly foggy Half Moon Bay on an uncharacteristically "scorching" sunny May day of 73 degrees.

A Northern Californian his entire life, Mark figured he would spend two years in Southern California, gain some valuable experience, and then "scoot back home." At the time, he had a list of additional parks where he wanted to work in the northern part of the state.

Ranger Mark Faull and Marsha. *All photos courtesy of Mark Faull.*

On June 1, 1984, when Mark and Marsha arrived at their new primitive home at Red Rock Canyon State Park, in the middle of the Mojave Desert, it was a balmy 108 degrees. The heat literally took their breath away. He and Marsha quickly learned the first rule of exploring the wonders of the desert in the summer – it is best done early in the morning, or after the sun has set.

What started out as, "Oh my word – what have we done, and what were we thinking?" evolved into a long love affair with the desert in general, and especially this state park. Mark maintains that this arid region possesses biodiversity, history, geology, and paleontology that he would match up favorably with those of any other California state park.

Mark compares his awakening appreciation for the desert to that described by Edward Abbey in his classic book about the life of a ranger in arid lands, *Desert Solitaire*. Although Mark and Marsha had to overcome their initial paradigm about how stark the desert appeared, their evening explorations of the park's canyons, washes, and cliffs began to peel back their preconceived notion of a barren desert wasteland.

The desert unveiled its beauty to them as they sought to discover its moods and secrets. Mark marvels that they would go to the same place in the park, but at a different time of day or year, and it would look so different – the shadows, the colors, the biota, and the light.

One advantage to learning about the desert is that its resources are out in the open – trees, shrubs, and forest duff do not cover and obscure them. The geologic layers are visible. There is space between perennials. You don't have to look under a log in order to see herpetofauna – lizards and snakes are often out on the sand. As wind and rain erode the soil and rocks, fossils that were previously hidden come into view. Some of these fossils are seeing the light of day for the first time in thousands, perhaps millions, of years.

"At first glance, in the desert," according to Mark, "everything might look the same. But then the deeper you look, the more you find beauty in that starkness. You recognize patterns of activity, as well as hibernation and estivation.

"That first summer, fall, and winter, we felt we were getting a terrific orientation to Red Rock. I kept asking myself, 'How do these species survive out here in this land of savage heat and sparse rainfall?' And this personal quest for knowledge of the desert's systems and secrets was great fodder for nature walks and campfire programs. I figured if I was asking these questions, our park visitors were, too.

"Then the spring arrived, and it provided even more breathtaking beauty. Everything comes to life in the desert during spring. The rain drives the germination of the flora, and the animals that rely on those plants ramp up to a higher level of activity. Then the animals that prey on those small animals are energized, and the whole desert does this 'dance of nature.' This interaction is phenomenal. Again, Marsha and I would hike at different times of the day, even late at night, and the diversity of plants and animals was simply astounding!

"I remember developing a campfire program from the perspective of a creosote shrub. The story of the creosote is a story of survival and uniqueness among plant species. I would compare the longevity of the creosote to other, more famous long-lived plants – coast and giant redwoods, the Bennett juniper, bristlecone pines – but the creosote could outlive them all. We had creosote rings in the park with a radius of six meters!

"I loved interpreting the desert's natural history to our park visitors. I would explain that I had previously worked in redwood state parks, and they were really surprised when I would tell them that there is more biodiversity in the flora and fauna of the desert than in the heart of the redwood forest. I would take visitors on nature walks and would explain that I was trying to learn as much as possible about how things survive in this environment.

Mark got a lot of satisfaction from sharing his love for and knowledge of the park.

"The more we know, the better we can manage the park's resources. Then someone would ask a question I could not answer, and this would send me back to do more research. Research fuels interpretation, and interpretation fuels more research. I would get so excited when people would return to the park the next season and I could fill them in on all the new stuff I had learned about Red Rock and its resources."

For a long time, the State Parks Department considered some of its units – particularly desert parks – as "hardship" assignments. Rangers and other staff would only be required to work at these desert parks for two years, and then would be guaranteed a transfer out.

Another reason for this two-year assignment philosophy was the Department's desire to maintain a corps of "well-rounded" rangers. That is, the Department considered it advantageous for a ranger to have a mixture of experience in the redwoods, beaches, mountains, reservoirs, and historical parks. It was believed that this background would better prepare a ranger for a supervisory role, since his or her knowledge would not be limited to a single type of park. This policy of frequently moving rangers around the state has pretty much been discarded now.

Another reason for this transfer policy was that the Department did not want a ranger to get too tied to one park and take "ownership" of it. One of the themes of this book is to support the notion that it is very valuable to maintain and support staff that DOES feel ownership of their local geography. It takes a while to learn the resources, local politics, operational issues, and key representatives of other local agencies. And it takes some time to recognize the role that local staff can play in improving the overall operation and knowledge base of "their" park. It is because rangers and other staff stayed a long time at a park and, yes, fell in love with it, that the wonderful people featured in this book took a very protective stance vis-à-vis "their" park!

For example, it is doubtful that Ranger Dave Carle, had he been re-assigned after two years, would have written over a dozen books about his beloved eastern Sierra and Mono Lake. If Carlos Porrata had transferred out of Tomales Bay State Park after two years, there would not be thousands of schoolchildren who look back fondly on the Environmental Living Program experience he provided them. Mark Jorgensen knows more about Anza–Borrego Desert State than anyone in the world, past or present. Why would you not want him stationed at Anza–Borrego, conjuring up myriad ways to make it better?

It is an important concept to pass on – the notion that places and resources need people to be their advocates. Through public speaking, writing, and leading by example, Mark Faull and his colleagues inspire many others to become advocates, protectors of the state parks, more informed voters, and more likely to support the park movement –financially and politically. Bighorn sheep, the California gulls breeding at Mono Lake, the elephant seals at Año Nuevo, the artifacts at Red Rock Canyon – these resources cannot advocate for themselves or attend public meetings. Mark Faull obviously is one of those rangers fortunate enough to be given a spark, and he sees his role now as fanning that flame into action by others.

Mark believes that "two-year" policy did not work well for a lot of people, and it may have not served the Department well either. Mark discovered that, although he was very inquisitive, and explored cultural history as well as natural history of the region, it took him a long time to become really grounded and knowledgeable about the local ecology and geography. It takes time to get in tune with the richness and fullness of any given region, large or small.

Mark knew that getting kids excited about parks and conservation was important work.

It is difficult to believe that there is a park ranger – anywhere – who is so excited about his career and life as a park ranger – even more than a decade after he retired. Mark is inquisitive, eloquent, ethical, friendly, passionate, and bright – perfect attributes for a ranger.

Mark recalls that it took him a while to be

inspired about the outdoors. He grew up in Mountain View – the heart of the Silicon Valley – now the home to Google, Intuit, and other large tech companies. But in the '50s, it was an idyllic, pastoral, post-war, suburban, "Donna Reed" town (as Mark calls it), and a great neighborhood to grow up in.

Surprisingly, his was not an outdoorsy family. Although Mark's parents did love nature, they were more apt to go to Disneyland or SeaWorld than go camping in a park. However, once Mark heard the call of nature, he delighted in introducing his family to the wonders of the outdoors.

It was his freshman year in high school when Mark began to develop a stronger interest in natural places. There were a lot of primitive trails in the area, and Mark would take the opportunity to walk the sloughs of the San Francisco Bay or the trails around Stevens Creek Reservoir. He recalls reveling in the sight of great blue herons, egrets, avocets, stilts, and even startled pheasants rising just feet in front of him.

Mark began to realize that the idea of spending his career in the outdoors in a park environment really appealed to him. His school offered a test that sampled students' interests and abilities, and matched those with some possible careers. Not surprisingly, looking back, the test results matched Mark up with a career as a park ranger, forest ranger, or wildlife manager.

His first biology class at Los Altos High School ensued. Frank Smith was the father of one of Mark's good friends, and a gifted instructor of biology. Mr. Smith had the ability to convey the information about natural history in a manner that held the students spellbound. Information about biology would be woven into thematic stories that helped the students really understand the concepts being taught and hold on to the information long after the lecture.

Mr. Smith would present the material in a way that made students run to the library or the local park after class in an attempt to find out a lot more about the subject. Mark recalls that Mr. Smith did not really "lecture," and he now realizes that his teacher was really the first "interpreter" he had met. Mark credits that teacher as the inspiration for his own interpretive talks at Red Rock Canyon State Park.

Mark also began to go camping with friends in the Santa Cruz Mountains at both Big Basin and Portola State Parks. This kept feeding his desire to spend time in the outdoors, and kept reinforcing the idea of becoming a park ranger someday.

Mark was fortunate to attend Los Altos High School – a very dynamic learning environment for its era – since the school offered any student considering a career as a ranger an amazing array of specialized coursework. Beyond the standard classes such as biological sciences, physics and chemistry, Mark was able to pursue curriculum covering physiology, geology, astronomy, California history, and even a course in existentialism.

After graduating high school in 1971, Mark enrolled at Sacramento State University. The primary reason he selected Sac State was that the college had a major that emphasized research and careers in national and state parks. Although other California universities soon followed with similar majors, Sac State was the only institution that offered this major back then. Mark recalls feeling so inspired by his biology classes that he would take walks to the American River, on the fringe of campus, where he could learn more about the biotic communities of this riparian environment.

In addition, this was the time period when the environmental movement really gained momentum. The first Earth Day, in the spring of 1970, really sparked colleges and universities across the nation to begin offering courses of study that focused on the environment, the value of the natural world, the impacts of human activities, and the role of parks vis-à-vis those issues.

The college courses also gave parks some historical context. He learned about the Yosemite Grant in 1864, the formative years of National Parks, and other key events that created this uniquely American idea. Mark gained a new understanding of the rich role that parks play in our society. That knowledge not only inspired him further, but was very useful when he later worked for the Parks Department.

Although Mark's career path was clearly focused on natural parks, it was a different type of park venue that gave him his first paid experience in recreation. For four summers during college, Mark worked for the Mountain View Parks and Recreation Department's youth baseball program. Teaching and coaching youths helped him gain an understanding of how to reach and communicate with a variety of young people. For the first two years there, Mark was a recreation leader – he took on assignments as a baseball coach, umpire, and announcer at local city parks. For his last two seasons, Mark worked as an assistant supervisor, helping to oversee and guide the city's youth baseball program.

Mark credits these summer jobs with helping him overcome his initial shyness, and learn how to better communicate with the kids. He also developed skills in working as a team member with fellow staffers, supervising the work of others, and fostering strong community relations.

One connection that made Sacramento State such a nurturing place for a budding park ranger was the tie to California State Parks. When Mark attended college, the university reached out to several subject matter experts at Parks who were working at the headquarters offices in Sacramento. These instructors taught classes in interpretation, historical reconstruction, and the management of natural and cultural resources. Mark says that he and other students appreciated the "real world" basis on which these classes were taught – it was not just an "ivory tower" approach to current park topics.

Sacramento State also encouraged its parks students to take a wide variety of courses in biological sciences and geology, and Mark was able to rely on the knowledge he gained in these classes later in his career. Once he was a ranger, he looked back on these courses fondly – he believes they helped inspire him to learn everything there was to learn about his assigned park. The new knowledge he gained from that personal research then gave him the desire to publish findings and to translate that information into new and enriching interpretive programs for the public.

After college graduation, in late 1975, Mark was itching to start work for State Parks. Many people graduate from college and start asking what they should do for a career. In contrast, here was Mark, educated and interested in natural history and state parks, and intent on becoming a full-time park ranger. Unfortunately, it was not to be, at least not for a while.

One reason Mark wanted to work for the State Park System was the tremendous diversity found within the state of California. He knew that during his career he could move around as a ranger and gain experience in a whole range of fabulous parks and ecosystems. Although this notion of career variety appealed to him early on, Mark was one of those rangers who ultimately did find "his park," once he had relocated to Red Rock Canyon State Park.

Fortunately for Mark, the state offered a state park ranger trainee exam right after he graduated from college. His newly minted parks management degree, experience in recreation work, an internship with Sacramento County Parks during college, and his performance during the interview all helped him get a score in the high 90s. The difficulty Mark ran into was that the Vietnam War had only recently ended, and a whole boatload of U.S. veterans were entering the nation's workforce.

California state civil service rules, reasonably, gave veterans 10 extra points on exams to reward them for their service to their country. This meant that veterans, most of whom had scored lowered than Mark originally, now moved ahead of him on the list, once the veterans' points were added. Mark recalls that suddenly he had dropped to number 32 on the hiring list. The Department appointed only 28 ranger trainees from that list, and then promptly abolished it.

While he was obviously disappointed, Mark's philosophy was that this adversity was challenging him to do better. To be a "generalist ranger" is a complex and challenging profession, and Mark credits his, at times, arduous journey with helping to shape his spirit, sense of professionalism, and passion.

Fresh out of college, Mark had no direct experience with State Parks, so he decided to seek seasonal employment. That way, he would be able to improve his knowledge of the State Park System. By getting to know rangers at various state parks, he could learn key ranger skills from them while he picked their brains about how to do well on the ensuing ranger trainee exams.

The first step was to get hired as a park aide. During the 1970s, however, employment with California State Parks was highly sought after – competition for parks jobs was fierce. Mark started applying for seasonal jobs all over the state. In order to demonstrate his eagerness, he even drove to various parks, from the Bay Area to the Oregon border, to hand in his application in person. He thought by talking to the people doing the hiring and by showing initiative, he might improve his chances of being selected.

However, he did not get a single response to his applications. With a slight sense of panic, he then began calling around the state asking questions and trying to understand the process better – but he was getting nowhere, and was starting to get discouraged.

Finally, one day he was talking to the office manager at Humboldt Redwoods State Park – one of the parks at which he had personally submitted his application for employment as a park aide. The office manager kept telling Mark they had filled all their vacancies already, but Mark kept asking her how to crack the code on getting hired. He described his passion for parks and asked how could he improve his chances for employment.

Mark let her know that this was not just a job to him – it was a stepping-stone towards his real goal of becoming a state park ranger. All he wanted at that point was an interview. At last there was a long pause, and the office manager put Mark on hold. When she came back on the line, she told Mark, "There might be one job left." Could he come up for an interview the next day? Mark, of course, was at Humboldt Redwoods the very next day, impressed the heck out of the chief ranger, and got his first job at a state park.

Mark was single when he was hired for the summer of 1976, and he profited greatly at Humboldt Redwoods from three seasons of work and adventures. At the conclusion of his second season, he and Marsha Ann Wright, his college sweetheart, got married on a sunny autumn day, not far from her hometown of Castro Valley. They had one year working together at Humboldt Redwoods – Mark continued to work at Albee Creek campground, while Marsha was employed in the park office.

Mark's career might have taken a different trajectory had he not met numerous outstanding mentors who truly helped to shape his career path. Mark recalls that Humboldt Redwoods State Park was a perfect assignment to help him learn about the Parks Department. He had terrific supervisors in Joe Hardcastle and Dan Ash, who began to mentor Mark while they instilled in him the values it takes to be a great ranger. They also reinforced in Mark the notion to keep plugging away in the face of adversity – they believed he had what it takes to be a good ranger, and that he would eventually succeed in his quest.

There were also important resource issues on site – the destabilization and erosion caused by the historic clear-cutting of the upper Bull Creek watershed above the Rockefeller Forest, for example. This led to devastating losses of protected virgin redwoods downstream. So much erosion had occurred following this private logging that two bridges were buried intact in gravel along Cuneo Creek in the Upper Bull Creek Basin.

And then there was also visitor services work, which Mark found delightful. The Albee Creek unit had a cozy little campground of 34 campsites. Mark recalls that he got to know everyone there. He would visit every campsite – he was not content to just stay in the kiosk and sell tickets. Campers would come back every year, so he would look forward to seeing old friends. Law enforcement issues seldom arose, and it was a very pleasant way to break into parks work.

Always a hard-working self-starter, Mark broke out his college textbooks and various field guides on the local natural history, and became somewhat of a self-taught expert on the region's resources. He soon began to update the park's lists of mammals, reptiles, and birds, to distribute to the public.

During Mark's first season at Humboldt Redwoods, he worked at Albee Creek Campground three days a week, and was asked to cover the regular dispatcher's day off by working two graveyard shifts as an overnight dispatcher in the park's main office. It helps to be young to flip back and forth between day shifts and graveyard shifts every week, and Mark was determined to take full advantage of this opportunity.

Late night dispatching was an important, but usually uneventful, task. These slow periods provided Mark with both time and access to peruse the park's rich natural history files – composed of rangers' observations and formal studies on the park. Mark says that he was spellbound by the opportunity to read and assimilate all of these hidden treasures tucked away in the park archives.

Humboldt was also where Mark began to give interpretive programs – nature walks and evening campfire presentations. Although Mark was still a bit shy, having the public respond so favorably was a great step in overcoming that introversion. Although the park possessed a good library of short nature films, Mark knew that personally narrating slide programs would be a much more effective way of interacting with the park visitors at the campfire center.

Challenging himself to participate in public speaking roles, albeit on topics he was very familiar with, helped him to continue growing beyond his initial bashfulness. He began to recognize just how much these educational programs touched the lives of and improved the experience of the park's vacationing visitors. Opening and unveiling new worlds and realms of understanding for park visitors proved very intoxicating for young Mark Faull.

Unlike Mark, his new bride, Marsha, had been raised in a family that visited state and national parks all the time. She did not let Mark know this for a while, but while growing up, she had secretly thought that she wanted to marry a ranger. This prophetic vision had come to her when visiting Pfeiffer Big Sur State Park as a child. Apparently, Mark's stated goal of wanting to be a park ranger enabled him to score very highly on her interview for lifelong partners, even without veterans' points!

Although at the time they had very little money, Mark and Marsha also knew that there were a lot of things in their lives more important than wealth. They demonstrated this by asking their wedding guests to forgo giving them "normal" wedding presents. Instead, guests were encouraged to donate to the Sempervirens Fund – a nonprofit conservation group that helps to protect redwood groves throughout the Santa Cruz Mountains. Mark chuckles that a positive outcome of their marriage (one of many, he is quick to add) was the permanent protection of several acres of redwood trees. He says that this gesture held significance for them, and it was fun to do something a little different to celebrate their special day.

The couple had one season together at Humboldt and, although it was a magical time at a beautiful park, they both knew that Mark had to keep pursuing his goal of becoming a ranger. The ranger trainee test was offered again, but this time Mark got a slightly lower score – still in the 90s, however.

This scenario is really frustrating and discouraging for people trying to get hired or promoted. You take the test and get a high score. In an attempt to improve your score, you work for three years as a park aide, get all sorts of experience, get mentored by two terrific young rangers, and receive a lower score on the same exam the next time it is offered!

Then another roadblock arose – Proposition 13 – approved by the voters of California in 1978. Due to its anticipated impact on revenues to government agencies, the state implemented a hiring freeze. In the opinion of many, the State Parks Department has never been adequately funded after that time, and has been struggling to keep parks open, staffed, and maintained ever since.

After three years at Humboldt as a park aide, wrapping up in 1978, and with the avenue to becoming a state park ranger temporarily blocked, Mark began to look at this time as an opportunity to seek more, and different, experiences. To augment their income in between opportunities for seasonal employment, Mark took on a job servicing seismographs along the back roads of southern Humboldt County. This played into Mark's passion for geology — suddenly, he was privy to data being collected in support of plate tectonic theories involving the triple junction at the northern end of the San Andreas Fault.

Marsha, who had dreamed of being an educator since childhood, pursued a teaching credential at Sacramento State, and both she and Mark soon found themselves working for the Southern Humboldt Unified School District. Mark worked as an aide in a Special Education Master Plan classroom with middle school and high school students. Meanwhile, Marsha became employed, first as an aide in an elementary classroom, and then in the high school library. For Mark, working with youth proved extremely rewarding, and he was even assigned to help mentor two high school males.

In a constant effort to increase his skill set, Mark began investigating a new beneficial State Parks pathway. The Department had a job classification midway between state park ranger and seasonal park aide, and it really rolls off the tongue — State Park Ranger (Permanent Intermittent). Someone in this position has the moniker of PI ranger, and they hold a permanent civil service appointment, but work intermittently. Although it may seem awkward, it does make sense.

Think of a park that really has three busy months and nine months that are pretty low on public visitation — parks in the redwoods or the Sierra are good examples. After the summer season, kids go back to school, the weather turns cold and rainy (or snowy), and the parks are remote. Those parks really need a lot of staff in the summer, but fewer staff in winter. During spring and fall — the "shoulder" seasons — visitation may spike on weekends, but remain low during the week. Also, rather than hire and train a new seasonal crew every summer, the park would benefit from a staff that returns every summer and already knows the operation, issues, and geography.

When the Department matched that need to those people who might be interested and available, two types of candidates typically stood out — teachers, and young men and women who wanted to become rangers. Those teachers who wanted to work in the summer were a great source of PI rangers. They were educated and believed in public service. They were usually able to communicate well, and they possessed the ability to deliver nature walks and campfire programs with ease. Then there were those young people, like Mark Faull, who wanted to become full-time, permanent rangers. PI rangers have a few benefits that seasonal park aides do not receive, and they are paid much better. It was an attractive option for many.

One of the problems with the PI ranger classification is that, in many cases, these rangers were not sworn peace officers. In order for a teacher to become a peace officer, they would have to go through a law enforcement academy on their own time and expense. In California, cadets must spend several consecutive months on site in order to graduate from an approved academy. Teachers just do not have enough time to dedicate to that endeavor. Over decades, the use of PI rangers has dwindled to nearly zero. As budgets shrank, managers began to use seasonal park aides for the roles that the higher paid PI rangers used to fill.

Fortunately for Mark, he was offered a job at Big Sur as a PI ranger. Although he was reluctant to leave Albee Creek, his supervisors strongly encouraged him to move on and move up. They recognized his potential as a park ranger, and they believed he needed to gain a greater variety of park experiences. Typically, upon his arrival at Big Sur, Mark immediately set out to learn all there was to know about that region and its plethora of state parks.

The science that really sparked Mark's interest at Big Sur was geology. Although Mark had taken geology classes in high school and college, this was the first time he got to really dive into this field and learn about it at the local state parks. Seeing the very visible trace and impact of the Big Sur fault expressed within both Pfeiffer Big Sur and Andrew Molera State Parks, which includes the presence of popular and attractive waterfalls, was a newfound thrill for him.

Mark, however, was still trying desperately to become a full-time ranger, so he used his off-season at Big Sur to put himself through the law enforcement academy at the College of the Redwoods, near Eureka. Although he was one of only three park rangers in this particular class of cadets, the interaction with law enforcement cadets from all over Northern California proved extremely beneficial. Mark was proud to be elected as the cadets' liaison with the academy staff, and to receive honors at graduation in both academics and firearms proficiency.

While Mark was attending the academy, the State Parks Department was aware that he was progressing towards being a sworn officer. The Department had already conducted a background investigation on him, as it does on all potential peace officers. Once the background has been completed, it is valid for one year, and then the process would have to start over. The theory is that, perhaps, the candidate really cannot get into TOO much trouble during that year, right?

Mark was also very aware of the timing for his background, and he soon realized that the one-year cutoff was drawing very near. He started calling the law enforcement division in Sacramento and telling them he was running out of time. Just days before the one-year anniversary deadline, they called to tell Mark that when they opened his file folder – which ordinarily contains the paperwork related to his background check – there was nothing in the jacket!

There is a happy ending though – they called Mark back the next day and informed him that not only had they found the paperwork in his file, but they had approved his background as well. Once Mark came down from the ceiling, he realized, "There is always a lesson to be learned from each experience, and from that situation I learned to balance patience with assertiveness. I had to convince the staff in Sacramento to work on solving my issue without my becoming a nuisance."

He credits the rangers at Big Sur for teaching him that there are many ways to succeed at being a ranger – particularly in dealing with the public. As Mark recalls, "Ralph Fairfield had a very gentle way of pursuing and handling things. His friendly and outgoing style was very efficient and effective, especially in difficult situations. He had almost a glow about him that got difficult people to comply with his requests."

Mark also worked extremely closely with Bill Berry, for whom he had a lot of respect. Mark strove to adopt some of Bill's attributes and learn from his self-discipline. Berry was also a "dog handler" at the time, and Mark jokes, "Yeah, Bill had a glow, too – he just didn't need it very often, since he had a German Shepherd canine partner with an even more persuasive glow of his own!"

Then there was Ray Patton, whom Mark also considers a very influential mentor. Ray and Mark would patrol Andrew Molera State Park – along the Big Sur coast – often at night. The beach closed to the public at sunset, which meant that every contact at night was with someone who had violated the closure regulation. One thing that Ray taught Mark was to use the "interpretive approach" in as many law enforcement contacts as possible. That is, the start of the contact should be low-key, and the ranger should try to gain compliance – not just make an arrest or write a citation. If there were a serious crime occurring or if a riot were imminent, that is a different scenario requiring a different approach, obviously.

According to Mark, "Ray had this great ability to write a citation and, through his demeanor and approach, have the people thank him at the end of the contact. He would take the time to explain everything to them. That taught me that our job is to correct behavior and get the park visitors to conform to the park's rules and regulations – there was little value in just writing a lot of tickets and moving on.

"We should try to help our visitors understand the underlying principle behind the regulation, and we can interpret that to them. You don't need to totally alienate them about their state park experience. Ray would ask them why they came to the park – to have fun and recreate, right? If we as rangers can integrate the visitors' enjoyment with protection of the park's resources, and get their behavior to be in alignment with park norms, we have succeeded.

"You also have to realize that Molera is a remote park, and at that time, radio communications was pretty sketchy. Backup law enforcement was a long ways away, and the ability to resolve law enforcement situations quickly and satisfactorily at the scene made sense on many levels."

Around this time, State Parks created a new entry-level position for state park rangers. With the advent of the state park technician classification, the minimum educational requirements changed from a bachelor's degree (four years) to 60 units (two years) of college. Mark took the technician test, and scored 99 out of 100. His experience and persistence were paying off! Meanwhile, he was still on the existing state park ranger trainee list, but with a lower score.

In 1981 the specter of a yet another hiring freeze in state government suddenly arose. Naturally, the Department, which had numerous open positions, acted swiftly to fill as many vacancies as possible. Mark was on two lists simultaneously, and he finally received a phone call from the personnel section, asking him if he would accept an assignment as a ranger trainee at San Mateo Coast. He chuckles that his final interview consisted of one question – "Do you want this job or not?" Later, he learned about the truly hectic nature of that hiring process. Personnel staff had gone down the list, making phone calls in order of ranking on the list. If a candidate did not answer the phone, staffers in the personnel section would just call the next person on the list and offer them the job.

Mark was hired in the fall of 1981 at the San Mateo Coast District, and believes he holds the distinction of being the very last ranger trainee ever hired by State Parks before that classification was abolished. At the end of his training year, Mark stayed at San Mateo Coast, working principally out of Half Moon Bay State Beach, for his first permanent ranger assignment.

By 1984, after nearly three years spent along the San Mateo Coast, Mark and Marsha thought a new park might offer new growth and insights. They became excited when a ranger job became available at a very special and beautiful park in the Mojave Desert. Since they admittedly knew virtually nothing about desert landscapes, this seemed like a terrific new adventure for the young couple.

Once Mark and Marsha settled in and got over their initial thermal shock upon arriving at Red Rock Canyon State Park on the brink of summer, they both fell in love with their new home. Mark got more and more acquainted with the park, and gradually became an expert on the natural and cultural resources of Red Rock.

Shortly after Mark's arrival, he also began to document the movies that had been filmed in the park, and quickly came up with a list of 12 movies. There is now a list of over 150 movies (stretching back to the silent film era), in addition to another long list of television shows that have used the park for at least a portion of their shoots. Success breeds success, and as the park's popularity as a filming site grew, so did the amount of time Mark and his colleagues had to spend evaluating film permit applications and monitoring the actual film crew activities.

Filming is a big industry, especially in California. The industry can have a big economic impact, and the

It was a big move to go from the redwoods to the desert, but Mark took full advantage of the opportunity.

studios are quick to point out that other states and communities would love to have their business. So, there can be this tension between the California Film Commission, the film company, and the local state park. The stance of the State of California is that the state wants this industry to remain in California, to the extent possible. There can be quite a positive impact on local communities, as the demand for motel rooms, food, fuel, and other services can really spike during a film shoot. Sometimes the studio will offer to make a financial contribution to the park's cooperating association and to thank the park staff during the roll of credits at the end of the show. A few of those studios would, on occasion, actually follow through on some of those promises.

Some park staff film monitors see this whole activity as a nuisance. Mark, however, saw the upside instead. Featuring the park on screen was a great way to market the park to millions of people for free. One of the concerns of film monitors is the impact that filming can have on the park's resources, and that is a valid concern. As Mark's knowledge of Red Rock Canyon's natural, cultural, and paleontological resources increased, he was better able to direct the film crews' activities. Once he knew what they were trying to accomplish, he would help them find a site at the time of day that met their needs, while mitigating the impact of their activities.

Of course, some film directors can be pretty creative and quite pushy. If the movie or television show calls for a car chase, explosion, or nudity, the park's film monitor often has to draw the line and tell the director they simply cannot do that in the park and will need to find a different location.

One of the resources at Red Rock Canyon State Park – the paleontological record – is one that most rangers do not deal with in their careers. Red Rock, along with Anza-Borrego Desert State Park, is one park where this record is not only significant, but it is relatively easy to locate. Since the fossils are more apparent than they would be at more temperate sites, scientists have more success finding these resources in the desert parks.

Typically, Mark jumped into learning about paleontology early in his stay at Red Rock. He read everything he could on the subject and spent a lot of time in the field studying the geology and paleontology of the local canyons, walls, rocks, washes, and mountains. He also had the good fortune to connect with Dr. David Whistler, a paleontologist at the Los Angeles County Museum of Natural History, which includes La Brea Tar Pits. Dr. Whistler had already adopted Red Rock as one of his major research sites decades earlier, and, upon Mark's arrival, the two men readily hit it off.

In addition to learning as much as he could from Dr. Whistler, Mark also set up several collaborations with the museum. Of course, the museum is in the middle of a major metropolitan area, so it can reach a vastly greater audience than can a remote state park. The two men were able to use the museum's resources to set up field trips for the public – trips for 25-30 people, young and old, that Dr. Whistler would lead to the park. Once at the park, Faull and Whistler supervised the effort to provide the search for and excavation of fossils, with 30 extra pairs of eyes to help in locating microfossils. Mark adds, "Part of the joy for these visitors arises when they find a previously undiscovered fossil. Here you have an urban visitor who sees a bone from an animal that lived and died here up to 10 or 12 million years ago. Then at some point, they realized that they were literally the first human EVER to lay eyes on this fossil!"

One source of satisfaction for Mark is the knowledge that many people who took these paleo field trips as kids, often returned to the park as adults. These field trips developed a whole generation of park supporters. Mark says, "The park and the museum both earned revenue from these experiences. Although the primary goal was not to simply earn money, but rather to provide a high-quality experience, it can serve to model for today's park managers how educational opportunities can generate revenue as well. We would split a portion of the field trip earnings with the museum, and the park would also earn campsite rental fees."

Mark's enthusiasm in describing his 20 years at Red Rock is infectious. "I believe the park is truly a combination of art and science. I started out learning as much as possible about the science and cultural history of the park. But then I realized I should also learn as much as possible from the artists,

Mark was determined to learn all he could about the geology and paleontology of his beloved Red Rock Canyon.

photographers, and filmmakers. They see the park differently from the scientists, but their view is no less valid. Artists and photographers see the light, shadow, and the color as a beautiful means of describing the park. Almost all of them comment that the light is different in the desert. Now I know that is true."

Mark wants to affirm his tremendous regard for "park spouses" in general, and, more specifically, his wife Marsha. As he relates, "Being a ranger's spouse means being flexible – open to both change and challenge. In many cases, spouses have to put up with 'their' ranger transferring around the state in order to gain varied experience or accept promotions. Even if the couple is more stationary, the spouse may have to endure odd and often remote park housing, midnight callouts, having wildlife in the house, and living in busy public-use areas – of course, these experiences can also be fun and memorable."

One of the couple's most memorable occurrences was the time their park residence was drenched by the floodwaters of the flood of 1997 – it filled their home with nearly three feet of water, sand, and mud. As Mark facilitated portions of the extensive park cleanup, where several buildings had been washed away, he asked Marsha if she could try to wash out their mud-covered clothing. They were living temporarily in a local motel – their park residence was no longer habitable – and she decided to take their clothes to the local coin-operated car wash to rinse off all the mud before taking them to the town's laundromat.

Mark recalls, "There was Marsha, standing in the car wash bay, plunking in coins and rinsing off clothing, when the owner of the car wash just happened to show up! You can imagine his reaction to some strange lady, standing in the bay of his car wash with her six-year old son, while she was apparently trying out some new ridiculous method of doing her laundry. He was not pleased, to say the very least. But after hearing the family's plight, he joined in to help Marsha wash the family's clothing. He would not let her pay – it was his treat."

It is important to recognize that, although Mark is a terrific defender of the park's resources, he also knows that, to quote State Parks legend Jim Whitehead, "Parks are for People!" Mark loves knowing that people are outdoors enjoying the park. He even became a member, and then chair, of the local Tehachapi Tourist Commission. He recognizes the economic value of parks and believes in marketing all of their attributes. "A key to community relationships," according to Mark, "is the ability of business owners to understand that the park and its visitors provide a significant financial benefit to local communities."

During Mark's long tenure at Red Rock Canyon State Park, strong desert winds were blowing politically at the national level. Senator Alan Cranston of California, and, later, Senator Dianne Feinstein, pushed legislation – called the Desert Protection Act, or DPA – that would conserve a large swath of the state's Mojave Desert.

As a field ranger for the State Parks Department, Mark did not play a large role in the design or passage of the bill. Its authors did want to entrust the Department with more protected land – approximately 20,000 acres – that would become part of the park. Mark's role was to provide the movers and shakers behind the bill with scientific information on the park so that they could make informed decisions.

As Mark recalls, "The primary individual who deserves the credit for pushing to expand the boundary of Red Rock Canyon State Park is Jim Dodson, who was a Sierra Club member from the nearby Antelope Valley. I got to know Jim pretty well – he drafted the general boundaries for the lands that would be added to the park. This boundary, in general, conformed to the vision for Red Rock Canyon that was expressed in the 1928 Olmsted Report."

The park supervisor at the time, Vic Maris, also knew Jim Dodson, and the two of them agreed on the proposed addition of lands to the state park. They combined the information found in the Olmsted Report with field trips through the surrounding desert to create what Vic refers to as "our dream park." However,

Vic departed Red Rock Canyon just as the original bill was being formulated and introduced into Congress by Senator Cranston. Vic did return to Red Rock as a park superintendent just before the bill was signed into law in 1994, and was able to attend the celebration of its passage with Senator Feinstein, her staff, and many other supporters of the Desert Protection Act.

Mark continues, "I also met with Elden Hughes, who was the overarching architect of the entire DPA. He stopped by Red Rock on a visit, and he was interested in special attributes of our area. I conveyed to him a number of specific details about the special nature of the Last Chance Canyon addition – including how the expansion would encompass the entire documented population for the Red Rock Tarplant (*Deinandra arida*). If successful, the bill would enable California State Parks to manage for this species' conservation. I discussed with him how additional populations of a sensitive plant, the Red Rock Poppy (*Eschscholzia minutiflora twisselmannii*), would become protected as well.

"I was also able to convey to Elden Hughes the global importance of the fossil heritage located on the lands that would be conveyed to the park, data on the locally endemic snail whose type locality would be preserved via this expansion, and information on the nesting birds of prey – including golden eagles and prairie falcons – that utilized the canyon walls."

For a state park ranger at Red Rock at the time, it must have been fascinating to watch the federal legislative process proceed at glacial speed – the effort took many years. Much like Dave and Janet Carle at Mono Lake, Mark was careful not to represent that he or the State Parks Department had a position on the DPA. In fact, the bill took so long to become a law, the Department's position would have changed several times along the way. Mark, though, was definitely the local expert on all things Red Rock, and was able to provide important factual information to those who were moving the bill forward in Congress.

Ironically, the passage and implementation of the Desert Protection Act in 1994 led, in part, to Mark's eventual decision to retire after 20 years at Red Rock. Originally, Mark intended to become a park superintendent as his career progressed. His love affair with the park, though, made him unwilling to relocate, which is usually part of the promotional process at State Parks. "Every time an opening at a great park became available," Mark says, "I just kept thinking of all the wonderful things at Red Rock I would miss if we left."

Mark had passed up several promotional opportunities, but eventually secured a training assignment in place as an associate state park resource ecologist – the classification for park scientists who spend their efforts managing and protecting the natural resources and habitats of California's state parks.

The DPA had designated extraordinary new lands to be added to Red Rock Canyon State Park. Mark was excited about this action, because of the splendid resources extant on this roughly 20,000-acre addition. At first, the Department's planners were determined to afford the new property strong conservation measures. However, the off-highway vehicle lobby and off-road enthusiasts were equally adamant that these lands be widely available for their recreation. Mark was asked, as a resource ecologist, to make decisions he could not morally support. After he was placed in circumstances he felt violated ethical standards, he decided to retire, in 2004.

Self taught in archeology and history, Mark became so knowledgeable in cultural resources that he was asked to co-teach a class at Asilomar.

Like many career parks people, Mark has remained connected to actions affecting the State Parks Department. For example, he was determined to attempt to pass on his knowledge and enthusiasm to the next generation of park rangers. He considered the need for greater training in history and archeology for rangers, and joined with State Park Archeologist Michael Sampson to establish and teach a cultural resource management class to the cadets. Mark saw this as an opportunity to improve the ranger profession, enhance their appreciation for cultural resources, and foster more interpretive programming at parks. At the Mott Training Center, he and Michael co-taught 14 cadet classes over the years.

The class focused on site recognition of cultural resources. The goal was not to make cultural managers out of rangers – it was to give the rangers the tools to recognize significant resources in the field so that these sites could be protected until the professional archeologists were able to assess them. Mark recalls that they tried to make the class enjoyable, as well as educational. "We would bring in all these artifacts to demonstrate to the ranger and lifeguard cadets how to recognize cultural sites and artifacts in the field. As part of the fun, we would even spice up the demonstration tables with historic beer cans. You can date a lot of sites with beer cans – they are terrific teaching tools.

"We started out with a four-hour class, but it was successful enough that it expanded to a 12-hour class. During the breaks, all these cadets would swarm the tables, asking us tons of questions as they examined the artifacts. It was so exciting.

"Then, with the increasing emphasis on law enforcement in the ranger series, we found that the Department was hiring an entirely different type of ranger cadet. The last time Mike Sampson and I taught the class, not one student appeared to show interest in the artifacts on the table. They couldn't wait to get outside for their break. Resource management seemed to appeal less to this new breed of state park peace officer. I had thought that my background as a ranger would help me promote the idea to the cadets that a ranger is a peace officer, but a peace officer is not necessarily a ranger. In my view, being a park ranger is more challenging than being a city cop or a deputy sheriff, as well as being a noble calling. When my views no longer appeared to ring true with these younger cadets, it seemed logical for me to stop teaching the class."

Mark was asked, having been at Red Rock for 20 years, what he considered his greatest achievements there. "Over the course of many wonderful years, I had the opportunity to work on and write up many studies, projects, programs, and improvements. But what I was always the most proud of were letters of thanks I received from the public. The fact that I had touched someone's life – opened up their eyes and perhaps even inspired them – to me that was the highest pinnacle and calling I could achieve. That was the ultimate public service.

"Of course, Red Rock Canyon was an intrinsically easy theater to unveil and present to our eager and appreciative visitors. Pulling back the curtain was great fun! Seeing the eyes of a child or an adult widen with amazement as they begin to connect with nature, or start to understand our cultural history and how it resonates with us – that is truly an absolutely amazing experience. Rangers become very good storytellers, and they come to savor the audience reaction!

"In many ways, in a very abstract sense, I felt we ministered to people's souls. We helped them rejuvenate – in the truest sense of that word –and shed their life's burdens. At Red Rock, these burdens dissipate out into the broad desert expanse before you. Red Rock is truly a place where you can fully exhale.

"During interpretive programs, I was fond of talking about how a visit to our parks encompass our sense of adventure, exploration and discovery. These all become a part of us as we delve into each park wonderland. I also believe strongly in the important sense of anticipation that parks provide to our society. Just knowing, especially in the midst of a hectic or stressful day, that these places of refreshment and solitude exist, can profoundly ease our burdens.

"Even picturing these places of serene majesty, beauty, and solitude can provide comfort, uplifting our spirit. Spreading this message more fully and effectively – especially to populations that are isolated, stressed, and 'wired' – is a profound challenge for the next generation of park rangers."

Mark is keenly aware of the fact that the quiet town he grew up in, Mountain View, is now home to a vibrant, evolving, new global community. The Silicon Valley is now headquarters for Google, the self-driving cars of Waymo, YouTube, Intuit, LinkedIn, Symantec, Kahn University, 23andMe, and the SETI Institute. Knightscope is creating a new generation of patrolling security robots, skyTrans is developing mass transit pod cars, and even Facebook and Microsoft are expanding into Mountain View.

Considering the juxtaposition of Mark's commitment to the conservation of wild places – and life as a park ranger – with this high tech tsunami, can be disconcerting. However, as he describes it, "No matter how these

companies reshape our world, and no matter the advances of virtual reality – the sensual and spiritual experiences of the sights, sounds, smells and textures of the natural world cannot be truly replicated electronically. There remains an ascending need for the 'authentic.' These landscapes and our cultural sites are special places that nurture our spirit, refresh us, rejuvenate us, and heal us. They also tend to wash away most daily barriers, and thus help us achieve new perspectives and insights into our lives. In that sense they revitalize us as human beings.

"I believe that parks and natural landscapes are amazingly powerful because they represent this amazing alchemy of both science and art into a solitary experience. They engage our minds in the fascinating and beautifully complex details of our surrounding world, and they engage us with the drama of wildlife that unfolds about us. At the same time, they touch and evoke our spirit, appealing to all of our senses, as we absorb the light and color, the shades of a shadow, the smooth or furrowed textures, the height of a pinnacle, or the delicate beauty of the tiniest desert flower."

Then, what does it mean that a ranger becomes a poet, a guardian, and a scientist? This is Mark's way of explaining in shorthand what a ranger's job encompasses. Poet = the interpreter and the educator. Guardian = the enforcer of the law and guarantor of proper conduct. Scientist = the resource manager. Of course, rangers perform many other tasks, such as managing campgrounds, community outreach, providing recreational opportunities, maintenance, search and rescue, and administrative tasks. But being an amalgamated poet, guardian, and scientist – that is the core of park ranger work, in Mark's opinion.

Mark's enthusiasm, even in retirement, is still evident and refreshing.

"Working for State Parks is just heavenly when you have all this geology, biology, archeology, paleontology, and history to play with," he says. "You are living in the park, and all this stuff is your back yard. After work, you take off your uniform – then you can explore and learn even more about the park to your heart's content."

To this day, Mark remains a lifelong learner, and still has a burning desire to keep living a life of public service. He adds a touch of advice for the next generation of park rangers – "May they, too, be blessed by their experiences, and pass those blessings that flow from our parks on to as many Californians as they possibly can."

For more information –

Abbey, Edward. *Desert Solitaire.* Simon & Schuster, 1968.

Wheat, Frank. *California Desert Miracle: The Fight for Desert Parks and Wilderness.* Sunbelt Natural History Guides, 1999.

Huell Howser. 2008. Red Rock Canyon State Park. Huell talks with park staff and volunteers about the park.
https://blogs.chapman.edu/huell-howser-archives/2008/09/04/californias-golden-parks-163-red-rock-canyon-state-park/

Mark Faull has written dozens of technical papers on natural and cultural resources – particularly those of Red Rock Canyon State Park and the Mojave Desert.

He is regarded as an expert on *Deinandra arida* – Red Rock tarplant.

GREG HAYES

Writer and Poet, Loved by Everyone He Touched

First Will and Testament

by Greg Hayes

After lying abed listening

to the nocturnal voice of God

in the guise of crickets'

sequential throbbing, their insistent

message syncopated like a jazz riff,

I wake up this morning

understanding that I must

take my blues harp and climb the Mountain

again. Not because it is new or has changed,

but to offer my own notes to its diurnal song.

Protecting only my feet with stiff boots

I rise through the gauntlet of redwoods and tanoaks,

my arms and face scored by whipping branches –

the only ritual scarring I crave.

Walking on aboriginal paths

requires no thousand mile

flight across oceans: Outback is truly

just that, only steps away, and unbidden

the coded message

surges up through the earth's skin

to meet each rhythmic footfall.

Called to attention by the staccato

shriek of a pileated woodpecker,

I am filled with quiet expectations,

prepared to receive the manna

of truly ordinary things:

revisitations of lost trails

where an unseen bobcat lay in wait

until the last moment to discern whether I

was small enough to be eaten

or big enough to do the eating.

My next step revealed it to me,

tail-less body flattened in elongated flight,

ears like exclamation points,

head and hind end maneuvering through duff

like a hook-and-ladder truck

through downtown traffic.

Another familiar totem waits:

a Pacific Giant, the dinosaur of salamanders,

crouches on a slippery rock ledge

I need for support to squeeze

through the canyon walls. He does not blink.

I find another way through.

                              This morning's walkabout takes me up

                              Wildwater Creek, a penumbral canyon

                              presided over by the undercut towers

                              of second growth redwoods, the walls

                              festooned with five-fingered ferns

                              that on cue reach out as I pass

                              to thumb a ride. Bootless and naked,

                              submerged on my back

                              in one of the shallow rock pools,

                              I let the music of falling water from

                              upwelling springs fill my ears.

                              In my haste to begin

                              I forgot to bring paper and pen

                              to jot down these notes; therefore I must

                              sing them into memory:

A Greatness of Spirit

Sunlight pierces only

the upper canopy of branches,

framing the sky and marking the boundary

of a separate realm. Nothing ethereal down here,

I am clutched in an embrace

of dark wet earth. The hollowed root caverns

of two great sequoias athwart the creek create

a throne room that feels like a womb

returning home should always

feel like this: the unhurried

and unplanned steps of the aborigine

shaping the songline in the earth,

planting the night seed of the crickets' serenade

that will help hatch the cicadas in seven years

who will dig out of soil, climb tree trunks

and shed the battered, used–up husks

of their bodies, their electric chirping

and hard-won flight accompanying

my ascent to this watery grave,

this subterranean Olympus where the giant elk clover

fans my root-furrowed brow and, lacquered red

and populous as China with swarming ladybugs,

my metamorphosed and bending knee

becomes resting place or foothold

for the next pilgrim who follows.

On the harp I've carried to this place

joining the water music

an ancient blues tune of Robert Johnson's warbles forth:

You better come on

in my kitchen

it's going to be raining outdoors.

Greg Hayes – ranger, writer, poet, husband, father, friend, intellectual, teacher, mentor, and "repository of the knowledge of all things Jack London" – died of cancer July 9, 2014, at the age of 62. Greg spent the vast majority of his State Parks career as a ranger at Jack London State Historic Park (SHP), near the community of Glen Ellen in rural Sonoma County. It was his life's work.

An illustration of Greg's passion for the state park and its eponym was his schedule soon after he retired from state service in 2003 (11 years prior to his death). On a Friday, he turned in his state equipment and cleaned out his desk at his office at Jack London State Historic Park. The following Monday, he showed up to work at the park as a volunteer, put on the uniform of a docent, and immediately began to lead hikes in the park and train the other volunteers. Greg was ultra-dedicated to providing the best information possible to the public on the subject of Jack London. He simply loved to share his encyclopedic

Courtesy of Robin Fautley.

knowledge of the famous author and the park with the other volunteers – in his opinion, this was a sure-fire method of accomplishing that goal.

While he was still a ranger, Greg had been asked to join the board of the local park support organization – The Valley of the Moon Natural History Association (VMNHA). In 2004, after he had retired from state service, he became the association's board chairperson – it was in this leadership role that Greg guided the park safely and brilliantly through the most perilous period in its history.

Greg Hayes was about to graduate from the University of California, Los Angeles in the spring of 1973, with a B.A. in literature. Graduates with a degree in literature are, let us say, seldom ranked highly on the list of "most sought after" by prospective employers. Recognizing that reality was on the horizon, Greg started regularly perusing the "Jobs" bulletin board outside the university's guidance office.

One day, hidden among all the offers for fry cook, house painter, and cold sales marketer, Greg noticed a professional-looking flyer for "State Park Ranger Trainee." He thought that sounded pretty interesting and signed up to take the state civil service examination. In short order, Greg was hired and assigned to the Parks Department's Channel Coast District, headquartered in Ventura.

Like many of his fellow ranger trainees of that era, he really had no experience in seasonal park work, nor did he have a traditional academic background. Actually, there was no common major that most successful candidates possessed. The theory at the time was that the Department would give you the training you needed to be a successful park ranger. You just needed to have demonstrated that you had what it takes to earn a college degree.

During his initial nine-month assignment, Greg received formal training at Asilomar, in addition to the on-the-job, less formal training at the beaches and campgrounds of the Channel Coast. Greg was not fond of working at those beaches, because of the heavy law-enforcement emphasis that was a reality there. Due to their attractiveness and proximity to Los Angeles, the state beaches in Ventura County experienced heavy visitation. Of course, not all visitors left their problems at home, and the local lifeguards, rangers, and maintenance workers were kept very busy.

The Parks Department went through an exercise with the 20 ranger trainees in Greg's academy class as the time approached for being moved to their first permanent park assignments. While Greg had received a lot of valuable experience at Channel Coast, he was hoping that he would be re-assigned to a park that better fit his personality and personal goals. He really enjoyed the interpretive and resource management training he had received, and he wanted to focus on those parts of the job. And, although he was from Southern California, he was determined to relocate to Northern California – Greg had learned from his fellow trainees that there were many state parks in the north that sounded stimulating to him.

One ranger he had befriended in the academy was Matt Atkinson, who was working in the Santa Cruz Mountains District during his training period. When the "permanent" assignments were announced, Matt had been transferred to Jack London State Historic Park. Greg, meanwhile, was relocated to the Pajaro

Coast District, which was composed of the state beaches of Santa Cruz and northern Monterey Counties.

Greg was flabbergasted, disappointed, and a tad envious. He was a writer and a literature major – he felt that an assignment to Jack London State Historic Park would have been a perfect fit for his talents and skills. In typical fashion, though, Greg went about being the best ranger possible at Pajaro Coast.

Although Santa Cruz is quite a ways north of Ventura, the beaches there suffered from many of the same problems as did state beaches at Channel Coast. Santa Cruz was an easy drive for the millions of people who lived in the region around San Jose – the beaches and campgrounds at Pajaro were heavy law enforcement parks as well. It is telling that, once Greg ultimately transferred out of the beaches of Santa Cruz, he never once went back there to visit.

In the meantime, Greg had kept in touch with Matt Atkinson at Jack London SHP. The Department's policy at the time was that a ranger should stay at their district for two years before requesting a transfer to another park. Serendipitously, Jack London SHP was about to expand dramatically. When the park was opened to the public in 1960, it was only about 40 acres in size – it then included only the House of Happy Walls, the Wolf House ruins, and the gravesite of Jack London.

A major expansion of the park was slated to occur between 1977 and 1979 – it was to grow from 40 acres to about 800 acres, a 20-fold increase in size. This addition included the Jack London Cottage, a number of stone buildings, and several cabins from the Jack London Guest Ranch era.

The Parks Department recognized that extra staff would be needed, and an additional ranger position was authorized for the park. Greg had put in his two years at Pajaro Coast, and was successful in his request to transfer to Jack London State Historic Park. He never really left that park, even after he retired as a park ranger.

Greg was reunited with Matt, who worked at the state park the rest of his career, as well. They became best friends, and they were both totally devoted to the protection and interpretation of Jack London SHP. This dedication to the park was to be severely tested some 30 years later.

Matt, along with a ranger from nearby Annadel State Park, Bill Krumbein, had founded the Valley of the Moon Natural History Association. Matt and Bill borrowed some seed money and created the VMNHA to support interpretive programs, not only at Jack London SHP, but also at Annadel and Sugarloaf Ridge State Parks. The NHA would be allowed to sell books, brochures, and maps in the parks, and in return, they would funnel these funds back to help fill needs in the park's interpretive programs – equipment, research, and even brochure publication. One of the most attractive features of a natural history association – this concept was used at many of California's state parks – was that all income would stay at the local parks to help in interpretation, rather than go back into state coffers, never to be seen again.

The state, with the assistance of the VMNHA, was also able to recruit docents to help deliver interpretive programs and nature walks. Matt even started a Mountain Assistance Unit – volunteers who were trained to help patrol the park on horseback. The park's 28 miles of trails connected with trails in the adjacent regional parks, and they were becoming very popular.

Greg – writer and literature buff – immediately fell in love with the state park and with his job there. It is hard to imagine a better fit between job and ranger – working there was the dream of a lifetime for him. Upon his arrival at the park, he decided that he was going to learn everything there was to learn about Jack London and Beauty Ranch – the ranch that had formed the foundation of the state park.

He started reading and conducting research during every spare moment. Greg read all of London's books, as well as virtually every book that had been written about the author. He would not just read a biography or article about Jack London – it was almost as though he had memorized it. In addition, there were movies about Jack London, movie versions of London's books, and over 10,000 artifacts at the state park. His colleagues still joke – well, sort of joke – that Greg, quite possibly, knew everything there was to know about each of those 10,000 antiquities.

Jack London – author, sailor, adventurer, farmer. *Courtesy of California State Parks. (Jack London SHP collection. Image 241-76-23-30)*

In the '50s, two old buildings on the property had been pushed together to create a home for the ranch manager. When the state took over the ranch in 1960, the cabin was already in questionable shape. Although park employees had lived in the cabin in a couple of instances, it had seriously deteriorated in condition by the time Greg moved to Jack London SHP in the late '70s.

Every park employee with a family refused to live there, but it still made sense to the state to have a ranger residing in the cabin. Greg, who was single when he arrived at the park, agreed to move in. There were rattlesnakes living under the cabin, holes in the walls big enough to let light from the outside shine in, exposed bare electrical wires, pack rat nests in the walls, and piles of rat droppings large enough that shovels – not brooms – were needed to remove them. Greg set out to fix it up.

He patched the inside walls with old barn wood and found a wood stove that he installed for indoor heating. After Greg had finished, there were still holes in the wall, but they were a lot smaller. The rattlers and rats were "encouraged" to find new residences. This now "cozy" cabin was to be Greg's home during his early years at the park.

Another fateful early event in Greg's 25-year tenure as a ranger at Jack London SHP was the arrival of one Robin Fautley – a beautiful young blond woman who was assigned to work there. Robin did not work directly for the park – she was a crew leader for the YCC – the Youth Conservation Corps. The YCC is composed of youth who want to work and gain experience doing conservation work. Typical examples of their assignments include trail building, fire prevention activity, and habitat restoration.

Robin had supervised YCC crews locally for three years, and the park staff had come to know and respect her. Robin's crew was building a trail up to a local lake when brand new ranger Greg Hayes came walking up to check out the project.

She now recalls, "Greg was very handsome and very impressive. He was so pleasant to talk to, and extremely erudite. Even though I shortly moved away to work in Oregon for several years, I never was quite able to get the image of this man out of my head."

In the summer of 1983, Robin moved back to Sonoma County and quickly got hired at the park as a seasonal aide. At that time, she was putting herself through graduate school so that she could earn a teaching credential.

Robin remembers an incident that really revealed Greg as a man she might be able to fall in love with. One winter day, Greg and she both arrived at the office at 8 a.m. to begin work, and it looked as though it might rain. One of her daily tasks was to raise the American flag. Robin asked Greg whether he thought she should raise the flag, since the flag would just have be lowered immediately if it began to rain.

Greg reflected for a few moments, and then told her that she actually wielded a lot of power in this situation. He told Robin, "You know that if you put up the flag, it will rain. But if you do not raise the flag, it most certainly will NOT rain. So actually, you get to decide whether it rains today. You choose."

Apparently, Robin's decision about that flag pleased Greg greatly, because they began to date – and date seriously. Robin recalls thinking at the time that, perhaps, she and Greg did not have much in common, so she was cautious about entering into a relationship with him. Robin says, "Greg came from the big city and drove a Camaro, and I was a small town girl with an ecological ethic. When he showed me the cabin, though, I realized he had a sense of style and taste that matched mine."

They married the next year, and eventually they had a daughter – Nicolette. Of course, Greg had trepidation about asking Robin to move into the cabin – he thought that, while it might work well for a bachelor, it might not be as suitable for a family that would include an infant girl. To his delight, Robin loved the cabin. Robin laughs that she was never sure if she was more attracted to Greg or the cabin. Nicolette now says, "My mother liked to kid Dad that the only reason she dated him was that she really wanted to live in that house. Mom remembers the cabin as a truly delightful place to live, even though I would pick up splinters when I was crawling on the floor as a baby."

Robin recalls, "Fixing up the cabin kind of became a Catch-22. It was in a terrific location and was just so beautiful. And even though it was in horrible condition, the state would not let us repair it too much. I think the catch was that to bring it up to code would be very expensive and would require a monumental effort. But by allowing us to continue to live there, the state was taking on quite a liability – there were a lot of things that could go wrong and cause injuries. When Greg was the only one living there, I guess they could tolerate the risk. But with a wife and infant daughter – well, that was too much. The state just let it continue to deteriorate.

"Every time it would rain, Greg would have to climb up on the roof and patch holes. Inside, we would place buckets around to catch the rain, while we had to move the bed around constantly to keep the raindrops off our heads.

"The worst issue health-wise, though, was the septic system. It could handle – barely – two adults and a child. But if we had a friend or two over to the house, the system would back up and raw sewage would start flowing down towards the Jack London Cottage – park visitors must have loved that! Again, though, the state would not repair the septic tank or the leach fields. They clearly wanted it to appear that the decision to move was our decision – they did not want to be the bad guys by overtly forcing us out against our will.

"Finally, one day Nicolette touched an electrical plug in the kitchen and started a fire in the wall. That incident convinced me to give up the fight to stay in that house. It is too bad the state would not fund the necessary repairs there. It was helpful to have a ranger living there, but we just could not stay there with a child with such a dangerous electrical system in place."

Around that time, Ranger Matt Atkinson had moved out of the other park residence, so Greg, Robin, and their daughter moved into that house. Greg and Robin agreed to move out of the cabin, on the condition that the state would install a wood stove in the new house. Robin recalls that this new home was a standard state residence, but it was in a beautiful setting, and the living room windows looked out on the forest.

The state did install the wood stove – but only after several years of requests from Greg and Robin. She recalls, though, "Once that stove went in, it really made it pleasant to sit in the living room with a fire going – I got very fond of that house eventually."

Although Nicolette was too young to remember much about living in the first cabin, with all its charms, she remembers that she "absolutely loved" the second house. She became really frustrated when her parents decided to move out of the park in 2002 as they prepared for Greg's retirement. "I recall really being mad at Dad for a while after we left the park – I thought I should be able to live in that state park house forever."

Greg and Matt Atkinson, Nicolette's godfather, continued to work on expanding the volunteer program that Matt had launched – it grew from 45 individuals to several hundred during their tenure. Greg, along with many other instructors, really put a lot of effort into training them. By this time, Greg had become a recognized expert on Jack London and the ranch, and he was able to transfer a lot of his knowledge to these volunteers.

He was also quick to remind the staff and the volunteers, "Remember, we are not just spitting out facts. We are interpreters – we are trying to find ways to 'interpret' the facts and the theories and the historical accounts – and we are attempting to relate information to the park visitors in a way that gives them something to 'take away' from the park – something that they will remember."

Although Greg did not like to raise money – actually, like a lot of people, he did not like to make the "ask" for donations – he was very adept at laying out the case for his pet projects. For example, Jack's second wife, Charmian, who lived at the ranch and traveled far and wide with Jack for years, was an accomplished pianist. When she died, her 1901 Steinway piano was stowed away in a back room at the ranch. Greg had the notion that having the piano restored to operating condition and convincing volunteers to play piano music of the historic period would add to the experience of park visitors.

Greg mentioned this idea to the park volunteers, and, very quickly, sufficient funds had been raised to restore the Steinway. Greg knew that he would also have to find piano players who would volunteer, but this additional workload for him was obviated when one of the park docents "volunteered" her husband, Judd Goodrich, to play. Judd and his wife liked the idea of providing period piano music so much that they took over the job of recruiting, organizing, and scheduling volunteer pianists. That tradition continues during busy visitation times, and many visitors comment on the nice atmosphere that period music provides during their visits. It is also a joy for the volunteer pianists.

Greg also had the notion that the park volunteers could become more specialized. He knew that, while most volunteers were passionate, intelligent, and articulate, he did not expect them all to become experts on all aspects of Jack's life. So he set up teams of docents for different attractions, such as the Wolf House, the Cottage, Beauty Ranch, and the park museum. That way, the volunteers could become experts on that slice of the park and Jack's role at that facility.

According to Lou Leal, a volunteer at the park who serves as its historian, "Greg could see the big picture for the park's future, and he knew that the docents would have a large role in the success of the interpretation program. Not only did he have a great appreciation for the docents and their commitment, he was able to convey that sentiment to them in a sincere and meaningful way. There was nothing phony about the man."

Greg may not have had the "big picture" and the "long-range vision" for the park when he first arrived to work there. But as he gained more and more knowledge and experience, his vision for the park came into focus. Personally, he was committed to learning everything there was to learn about Jack London. Towards this end, he decided to go back to graduate school. Nearby Sonoma State University offered a master's degree in literature, so he enrolled in that program while continuing to work and raise a family. The focus of his advanced studies was, naturally, Jack London. Greg's master's thesis was entitled, "Jack London's Agrarian Superheroes."

Jack London admitted that his prolific book writing was really a vehicle for funding his real passions – farming and ranching. He had great regard for innovators in agriculture – farmers who were trying to find methods of working the land that were efficient, effective, humane, and sustainable. The reminders of Jack's commitment to trying to improve agricultural practices remain evident in the park to this day.

Jack himself was quoted, "I am rebuilding worn-out hillside lands that were worked out and destroyed by our wasteful California pioneer farmers. I believe the soil is our one indestructible asset, and by green animal manures, nitrogen-gathering cover crops, rotation of crops, proper tillage and draining, I am getting results which the Chinese have demonstrated for forty centuries."

An example of his innovation in agriculture was the construction of the "Pig Palace" on his ranch. When Jack was running Beauty Ranch, there was a real problem with pigs getting cholera and dying. So he built this stone piggery, whose design was based primarily on the principle of efficiency. There was a ring of homes for the pigs on the outside, while in the middle there was a two-story building where their food was mixed. The food was on the top floor and it was fed down to the sinks with hot water so the pigs had hot food. This was in the middle, so the fewest possible number of steps was needed to get to each of the pig stalls. Each of these stalls had a front yard where pigs could get food, and an indoor place where the pigs could go to rest.

There was also a "run" into the adjacent oak woodland where they could roam about. These were hard economic times, and Jack's neighbors thought that he was crazy – his pigs were living better than a lot of humans – "in hog heaven," they would say.

Jack was a fanatic about the health of his pigs. He made visitors stop at a place below the piggery and disinfect their shoes – Jack was sure that cholera was being spread by the stuff on peoples' shoes. His fanaticism seemed to work – his pigs always remained healthy.

In his quest to learn everything possible about Jack London, Greg had some strong allies. In addition to his best friend, Matt, he also connected with a seasonal state park ranger at Jack London SHP named Milo Shepard. Now, Milo was not just your run-of-the-mill park ranger – he also had a very strong historical connection to the park and to Beauty Ranch. Milo's grandmother was Eliza Shepard – Jack London's stepsister. Eliza ran the ranch after Jack's death until 1939, when her son Irving took over the ranch operations. Irving had several children, including Milo, who was still directing ranch operations when it became a state park in 1960.

Milo was born and raised on Beauty Ranch, so he had this deep knowledge of many topics, in addition to his famous relative. He knew where the chanterelle mushrooms (that Greg loved) grew, and where to find beautiful wild lilies. The location of Wildwater Creek and the waterfall – Milo would share this knowledge with Greg. These hidden treasures eventually became part of fundraising events – as a park volunteer, Greg would lead hikes to these special places, while members of the public would pay to go on these unique walks.

This friendship was invaluable for Greg. Knowing and learning from Milo was the closest he could possibly come to actually "rubbing elbows" personally with Jack London. Milo was famous for going into great depth when teaching Greg the secrets of Jack London and the ranch environs. Greg used to joke that when he was scheduled to meet with Milo for an "information download," he would have to clear half a day off his calendar. It was information, however, that was truly priceless, and it helped Greg to fill in gaps in the personal database he was creating in his head about Jack London.

Milo also helped to debunk some of the local myths that had arisen vis-à-vis the life of the park's eponym. Rumors that seemed to survive decades after Jack's death were that he was always drunk and could often be seen riding through the countryside on a white horse. Milo would laugh and point out that Jack had never owned a white horse or boarded one at the ranch, and, seriously, it was nearly impossible for someone to be inebriated ALL the time.

Oddly enough, as Greg's research on Jack London progressed and his knowledge of the author increased, his respect for Jack's writing talent diminished. Greg, who was himself a writer and a recipient of a B.A. and an M.A. in literature, was a serious student and critic. While it appealed to Greg to work in a park that focused on a literary giant, he eventually came to the opinion that Jack wrote too many books in too short a period of time. He thought London was sacrificing quantity for quality and income in his writing – he had published about 50 books over a period of 17 years.

It was rare for writers of that era to make a good living, but Jack London was the exception – his books sold very well, and the author earned a small fortune from his craft. Again, Jack admitted that his writing was a means to an end – he really loved being an agricultural innovator. According to Robin, "Greg, with his higher sensibilities to writing style, would have preferred that Jack show more of a 'literary edge' in his work."

Robin chuckles, "It seems odd, looking back, but I never read Greg's graduate thesis. Admittedly, he had nearly completed it by the time we were married, but I really want to go back and read it now. On the other hand, he read my dissertation that I produced for my Ph.D. in biology many, many times. I valued his critique – he made so many improvements in my dissertation, and he greatly helped my overall writing skills."

Robin adds, "Often, we would take hikes in the park with Nicolette – heck, we lived there! Along the way, Greg would make some biological observation, or identify a bird by its call, or stop and identify a plant. He delighted in his knowledge of the local flora and fauna, and he was a talented field biologist."

Nicolette also recalls some fond memories. "My dad was a very quiet guy. The school I attended was a 30-minute drive from our home. On many days, Dad would drop me off and pick me up. There were days when, in those 60 minutes, not a word was exchanged between us. We were not mad or anything – we were both just comfortable with silence.

"One of my favorite memories growing up in the park was having adult friends over for dinner. We would cook them a wonderful meal at our house, and after dinner climb into the golf cart or take a walk into the park. Dad would give us a whirlwind midnight tour and we would walk down and go to places that most people do not know about. We would walk through the spooky old ruins, and Dad would tell such amazing stories.

"I grew up there, so I thought I knew the park pretty well. But when Dad would give one of his informal night tours, he was this amazing fount of fascinating knowledge. When he was 'interpreting' the park, I could just listen to him all night long. It was so fun and entertaining – it was a great way and a terrific place to grow up. I look back on those night tours, and it was hard to believe this was the same guy who would not say one word on the ride to and from school. Dad loved sharing his knowledge, and he almost became a different person when he had an audience. He definitely was not showing off, but he really liked to help others get more knowledgeable about Jack London and the park."

As Robin recalls, "Greg especially loved interpreting to kids. He could really talk to them at their level. However, no matter how much he loved the educational part of his job, he was still a peace officer and had to carry a firearm.

"I remember more than once he felt a little frustrated. He had lost a finger in a bicycle accident as a three-year-old child. He would come home and say, 'Gee, I was giving these kids all this amazing information, and thought I was totally captivating them. Then I would ask them if they had any questions, and the first two questions would always – ALWAYS! – be about my gun and why I was missing a finger.'

"Well, Greg had this terrific, dry sense of humor. So he would tell them one of a million stories about how he lost his finger. He really got creative about that – I think his favorite answer was that he was picking his nose one day and his finger got stuck, so they had to cut his finger off. You can imagine school kids going nuts over that answer!"

Nicolette adds, "Even though Dad wore a gun at work every day, I didn't know that until I was about 10 years old. Before he walked in the door of our home after work, he would take off his firearm and stow it in his briefcase. He was a gentle man, and he did not want me to know that he carried a gun and had a job that could be dangerous – it was just one of the many ways in which he protected me."

Robin recalls, "Nicolette is right – Greg was truly gentle, and I think he even carried that trait into his law enforcement contacts. Greg wanted to ensure that the people he was dealing with understood the reason for the contact, and the reason why they were getting a ticket or going to jail. It was just part of his DNA – he

Jack London cottage. © *Jay Beiler, Dreamstime.com.*

was a teacher and interpreter – he never wanted to be a tough cop ranger.

"One afternoon, Greg had a run–in with some kids drinking beer in the park – they had broken into the barn and had stolen some of Jack London's historic saddles. He caught them with the saddles and had to arrest them. Since he was so nice about the whole incident, they poured out all their beer and totally cooperated with him – they never argued with him about any part of it. These guys even wound up thanking Greg, after he arrested them, for being so kind and treating them well."

Docent Lou Leal recalls an example of Greg's dry humor. "One time Greg and I were at Jack London's cottage in the park, and we were inspecting the damage done by the acorn woodpeckers to this wooden building. In some places, the cottage looked like it had been under attack by a machine gun. There were holes in the sides of the walls where the woodpeckers had drilled holes to store their acorns. They just loved drilling holes in the cottage. Of course, we like the woodpeckers – they are a colorful native species – but they were ruining a historic building in a park that had been established to preserve and interpret a particular place and time in history.

"While Greg and I were talking about them, a woodpecker flew down and landed on top of the roof and sat there looking down at us. Greg went into a half-crouch, slapped his hand on the top of his leather holster, and ordered me to 'Stand Back' – as if he were going to shoot that woodpecker on the spot! I was startled at first, but then I saw that Greg was wearing this huge grin, so I was able to breathe a sigh of relief.

"Greg was always extremely supportive of ideas – no matter where they came from – that supported interpretation. At one point, I became determined to improve the exhibits at Jack London's cottage. I talked to Greg about it, and he told me to prepare a presentation for the board of the VMNHA – he would help get them to provide funding. The project eventually resulted in an 11-panel photo display.

"I made sure to have the photos, display design, and suggested wording reviewed by Greg, Milo Shepard, and Glenn Burch – the district's park historian. I wanted to be sure everything was historically accurate and that it met the state's design standards. We finally got it approved, funded, and installed. To Greg's credit, he was happy to let me run with the project. He even submitted me for a statewide award for volunteers, and we had a grand opening for the exhibits, complete with a ribbon cutting. I truly think that Greg's happiness came from allowing me to manage the project – he was so supportive, and he was genuinely eager to let me take the credit for the successful end product."

The Hayes family also really enjoyed traveling. As Robin recalls, "Greg loved to take Nicolette and me to beautiful natural areas all over the world. We went to some pretty exotic areas, such as Kenya, China, the Tibetan Highlands, the Galapagos, Ecuador, Europe, Canada, and Tasmania. Greg was always mindful of

Nicolette, Robin, and Greg visit China. *Courtesy of Robin Fautley.*

Greg in Kenya. *Courtesy of Robin Fautley.*

the fact that we were visiting the home and culture of other people, and that we needed to be very respectful."

Nicolette adds, "I have to admit, my dad would 'let down his hair' a little bit sometimes. Admittedly it was rare – he was, by nature, quiet and low-key. I think that also, maybe as a ranger at a quiet park with a small staff, he felt the need to maintain decorum. After all, he was a park ranger living in the park, and he believed he should set a good example.

"One weekend, though, Dad officiated the wedding of my cousin Teresa. At the reception, apparently, the music hit my dad in the right spot at the right moment, and he just started to do this wild dance. Mom and I just started cracking up – wait – this is my dad?"

Robin adds, "Every year, Nicolette's school would have this 'Father and Daughter' dance, and they would just

Courtesy of Robin Fautley.

have the best time dancing. She would always come home from those evenings feeling like she had the best dad there – what a great gift Greg gave to, and was to, his daughter."

He continued to pursue his interest in writing. Greg published a book of poetry – *Earthsweats*. With fellow ranger Matt Atkinson, he also wrote a book on a crucial part of the history of Jack London State Historic Park – *Jack London's Wolf House*. The two rangers believed that the story of the Wolf House – Jack London's dream residence that burned down before the Londons ever moved in – had never been made available to the public in written form. In typical fashion, neither Greg nor Matt received any income from the sales of this excellent book – they wanted all proceeds to go directly to the association.

Greg loved to write – he wrote dozens of novels and short stories, many of which were not published. As Robin remembers, "One of my favorites was the short story Greg wrote as a gift to our daughter and me, called 'Nicolette and the Wolf.' It is a beautiful tale about Jack London's history and adventures, the legend

Courtesy of Robin Fautley.

of the Wolf House and the Valley of the Moon, and places within the park – Greg then tied all that into Nicolette's own story. It takes place on a windy night, when Nicolette's house (our old cabin) is blown away, and all that is left are magical creatures that help her find her house again."

In his off time, Greg also volunteered as a mentor at the local Santa Rosa Junior College's writing center. There, he worked with hundreds of writers and helped them improve their writing craft. Young men and women would bring their writing projects in, and Greg would help tutor them. In tribute, his photograph and a couple of his poems are still posted at the writing center. As Robin recalls, "He made a huge impact at the writing center in a short period of time, just as he did wherever he went or whatever he was doing."

Jack London's Wolf House

He also taught Nicolette and her classmates to write at her school – not only prose, but poetry and haiku as well. As Nicolette recalls, "Everyone I ever talked to about my dad's writing would describe his talent as 'phenomenal.' I think it took a very talented writer like my dad to dare to critique a famous author like Jack London."

Greg and Matt, similar in many ways, watched the job of ranger change dramatically during the course of their careers. As Matt recalls, "The Department, more and more, wanted our focus to be on law enforcement. After several years on the job, I no longer felt that I was being given the opportunity to be an interpreter or resource manager. I spent my shift driving between the three parks in our sector – many times I was the only ranger on duty in the sector. My job became one of writing citations. I really missed being a 'generalist' ranger – the job I was hired to do initially." Matt now says, "When a local winery made me an offer I – or anyone – could not refuse, I pulled the plug and retired."

Becoming a supervisor was never Greg's goal as a ranger. In the year 2000, however, a vacancy arose, and it was clear that Greg was the best person for the job. He reluctantly agreed to accept a promotion to become the supervisor for that sector, which included Jack London, Annadel, and Sugarloaf Ridge State Parks. He still lived and had his office at Jack London SHP, but his job duties really changed. He now would have to deal with more administrative issues, as well as personnel matters – often the bane of many supervisors.

Three years later, after he retired, Greg could focus on being a volunteer at the park, training other docents, and assisting the board of the Valley of the Moon Natural History Association. Susan St. Marie, who was then the volunteer coordinator for the state park – a role she now fills for the local nonprofit corporation – recalls Greg's time as a park volunteer, "He was the consummate interpreter. He loved the local history and natural history, and he was a writer and poet. All these aspects combined to make his role as a docent so spectacular – he did not have to do the law enforcement work any longer, and he could concentrate on the parts of the job he loved best.

"He spoke to the rest of us – paid staff and volunteers – in plain language, even though he was so much more knowledgeable than any of the rest of us in the story of Jack London. We never felt that he was talking down to us. Greg could relate the stories at the park to YOUR story – and that is the real gift of the best interpreters. When Greg was a ranger, we felt that he really showed sincere appreciation for the role and efforts of the park volunteers. Looking back now, though, I believe his favorite task here at Jack London State Historic Park was interpreting the park to our visitors – especially young people."

Retired ranger Robyn Ishimatsu recalls Greg's first days as a park volunteer. "One day, he was scheduled to lead a walk in the park. I thought it would be a great opportunity to watch 'the master' in action. Unfortunately, no one showed up except me. To my delight, Greg led the walk anyway for the only attendee – me – the park ranger! He gave the walk as if he had 20 VIPs in tow – he was just so full of information and enthusiasm. I was so fortunate to have known him. I went on many more walks with Greg, and I learned something new every time."

Greg became chairman of the board of the VMNHA, beginning in 2004 – one year after he retired from state service. Ominously, both of the two prior board chairs of the association had recently died of cancer. Greg did not seek out or welcome the role of chairman, but since he was the vice-chair of the board at the time, it was a natural progression in leadership. This ascension was also heartily endorsed by the board. What nobody knew at the time – either at the association or at the State Parks Department – was that the next few years would become one of the most important, frustrating, and groundbreaking periods in the history of the state park.

In the role of board chair, Greg's knowledge, experience, diplomacy, respect, and wisdom were soon put to the ultimate test. In May of 2011, State Parks announced that it must implement a $22 million-dollar, department wide, budget cut. In a small department like State Parks, that is a massive reduction. In order to deal with this large of a cut, the Department proposed to close 70 parks – fully one quarter of the state's parks. Not only was Jack London SHP on this list of park closures, Annadel and Sugarloaf were slated to have their gates and doors locked as well.

Local park supporters and volunteers were outraged – not only was every state park in the immediate area being threatened with closure, it was not clear if the state intended to close these units temporarily or permanently. Park closures have huge impacts on local economies, the morale of staff and volunteers, and the ability of local residents to have excellent places to recreate, camp, picnic, and be personally restored through contact with nature. This was a big deal.

Now, unlike a library, police station, or office building, it is really difficult to "close" a state park. With a park the size of Jack London SHP – now up to about 1,400 acres – you really just secure the doors and windows of the buildings and padlock the gate at the entrance station. The public, in theory, may not enter and use the park.

In reality, however, you are merely de-staffing the park. You are removing paid staff and volunteers from their role in conserving the park and its resources. Also, the visiting public plays a key role in protecting parks – they are often the "eyes and ears" that are out there hiking the trails and enjoying the park's beauty. In many cases, it is the park visitors who report wrongdoing to the park's rangers.

However, if the paid staff, volunteers, and the public are removed from the park, then there is no one present to stop the vandals, thieves, partiers, and others from damaging the park's facilities and resources. Redwood burl marketers, marijuana growers, firewood harvesters, illegal hunters and fishermen, snake and lizard poachers, and thieves who would love to break into park buildings and steal irreplaceable historic and prehistoric artifacts – these are a few of the people who benefit from park closures. The good people cannot enjoy the park, but the bad people sure can.

There are health and safety issues to consider as well – water and sewage treatment systems must be maintained regularly. If they are allowed to fail, it becomes very expensive to construct new facilities and systems. If people start to believe that the park may never be re-opened, vandals could begin destroying park buildings, thereby delaying any attempt to ultimately allow visitors back into the park. In order to prevent all these problems, it still requires capital to close a park and keep it closed. There is really no upside to closure, other than the shortsighted benefit of saving the expenditure of a minuscule amount of state funds. When lost revenue is figured in, along with the financial impact to local communities, damage to natural and cultural resources, and the immeasurable loss of good will, it seldom makes sense to close a park.

At Jack London SHP, the reaction to this proposed park closure was immediate and forceful – the staff, volunteers, and the board of the VMNHA vowed that they would take any and all steps necessary to keep the park open. As Lou Leal recalls, "The sense at the time was, if we fail to find a way to keep the park open, so be it. But we cannot stand by and not even try to keep this magnificent historic monument, the beautiful natural areas of the park, and facilities like trails and picnic areas available for the public to enjoy."

This threat of closure made Greg and Matt question whether their loyalty was really to the Department or to the state park – an extremely difficult predicament given their attachment to and respect for both entities. Matt now says, "The thing that mattered most to Greg and me was that the park was open and protected, and that its resources were available to help our visitors understand and appreciate this magnificent place. We both got to the point where we did not care whether it was the state or a nonprofit that could best accomplish that goal."

So here was Greg, in this position of leadership at the VMNHA. He was authorized by his board to contact the State Parks Department and open up a dialogue of the association's realistic possibility of operating the state park. It was not a role that was in his comfort zone, but his passion for the well-being of the park motivated him to lead this effort. As his wife Robin recalls, "Greg was the perfect 'go-between' at that time. He knew what State Parks would demand, and he knew what the volunteers could bring to the table. He was just so well-respected by all."

Although there were many instances of individual state park units being operated, under contract, by a local governmental agency, it was unheard of for a nonprofit organization to take on the full operation of a park unit. Even at Crystal Cove State Park, where the nonprofit Crystal Cove Alliance has an operating agreement to manage the cottage rental enterprise, the state still collects entrance fees, and it provides and funds the ranger, lifeguard, and maintenance staff there. Special legislation was passed by the state to permit nonprofits to take on this new, proposed role.

It did not help matters that, in July of 2012, when many groups like the VMNHA were struggling with the issue of how to keep "their" local park open, the state dropped the bombshell that the Parks Department actually had an extra $54 million stashed away. Presumably, in the opinion of many park partners, some of this hidden capital could have been used to stave off park closures. With good reason, groups like the VMNHA, and many individuals who were striving to prevent these closures, felt betrayed.

Although the legislature was able to authorize the expenditure of some of those funds to help avoid the need to close parks, the supporters of Jack London SHP continued to pursue their effort to operate the park. In the meantime, Sonoma County's Regional Parks Department took over the operation of Annadel State Park, under contract. Simultaneously, the county's Ecology Center began to run Sugarloaf Ridge State Park. Greg helped to get both of these contracts approved.

But it was at Jack London SHP where negotiating the contract between the VMNHA and the state proved to be trickiest. However, just about everyone agrees that, had Greg not been at the helm of getting this agreement under way, the process would have been much more difficult and much less trustful.

Because Greg was so respected by all – his former colleagues at State Parks, the volunteers, the community, donors, and members of the board of the association – they put a lot of faith in his ability to come up with a model that would be successful. He not only was able to create a "bridge of trust" – he WAS that bridge of trust.

As his wife Robin recalls, "There were just so many people locally that wanted to keep the park open – horseback riders, docents, and hikers, among many – but they had no idea how to operate a park. Greg had the knowledge of park operations, and he knew how to navigate the intricacies of the State Parks Department.

"From my standpoint, Greg was taking on an extremely difficult task, and this work was hard on both of us. He really was the only person who had the knowledge and expertise necessary, but that meant he was going into the park every day. He was still putting in 40 hours per week – he just wasn't getting paid for it anymore. The compensation never was important to him, but he was upset at the notion that the park still might be closed. This caused him a lot of stress, and that stress was not healthy."

Susan St. Marie adds, "Greg was just so calm and reasonable, at least on the outside. He would segue from being the true blue (okay, true green) park ranger, defending the position of State Parks, to encouraging the association board and the park volunteers about the future of the park. He had to be creative while remaining realistic. In other words, Greg had to help create a formal, contractual relationship – the likes of which had not existed before – while ensuring that it would be agreeable to both parties. Wow – that was not an easy task!"

Board member Chuck Levine weighs in, "I think it was particularly hard on Greg for many reasons. Here is a man who, really, spent his professional life making this park as special as possible. He went to great lengths, often on his own time, to become an expert on Jack London, went back to school to study the author, cultivated and grew the park volunteer program, met his wife and raised his daughter in the park, wrote a book on the park, chose as his best friends rangers and docents – he just held the park so dear.

"In the meantime, while budgets were declining, the list of deferred maintenance projects was growing. Rangers were being required to do more and more law enforcement at the same time that their authority to make decisions was being taken away. That is hardly a recipe for making your staff happy. And then there was the final straw, the final insult – they were going to close 'his' park and let it decline even further – possibly to the point of no return as far as maintaining the original structures.

"One of Greg's great attributes was his ability to recognize what his strengths were and what they were not. When we at the VMNHA went into negotiations with the state, Greg was our president, but he knew that he was not a skilled negotiator. I think it also concerned him that he was negotiating with 'the mother ship' – the Department where he had worked loyally for 30 years. So, he asked for help, and two of us came in to help conduct and execute the negotiations. Greg was always there, listening, and not getting involved in the things he did not understand, while participating fully in the discussions where he could contribute.

"We tried to minimize the appearance that we had any disagreements on our side of the table, but, of course, our team would huddle before and after each meeting to figure out a strategy for each issue. Sometimes I did not understand why something was so important, either to the state or to Greg – he was just so skilled at explaining the nuances and how we could finesse it. That was a great help to us, and he provided a terrific benefit to the state as well, although I am not sure they realized that at the time."

Just as the state and the association were rolling up their sleeves on the contract negotiations, Greg became ill – he was diagnosed with cancer – in early 2013. As Elisa Stancil remembers, "I was vice-chair of the association when Greg got sick. It is difficult for people who were not there to understand the impact his illness had on everyone.

"Of course, there was the pain on a personal level – the obvious shock and concern when a beloved friend or relative of yours gets cancer. Then there was the fear of what the future might hold – not only for Greg, but also for the park and the association. Greg was graceful, dignified, diplomatic, and intelligent. We all believed that as long as Greg was involved in the negotiations, everything would turn out all right. We knew that his former colleagues at State Parks respected him very highly, and somehow, we were convinced they would treat the association better because of that. So when Greg got sick and took a step back, we were not quite as convinced of a successful outcome."

It is fair to say that negotiations were not as smooth after Greg had to step down as board president. The bridge of trust had been built, in large part, on Greg's back. Creating a new model was a first for both parties, and some hard lines were drawn. When it is the first time that an operating agreement of this nature is crafted, both parties realize that they are setting a lot of precedents. All subsequent negotiators likely will reference positions that are accepted in that first contract.

This was not a "cooperating association" contract, and it was most certainly not a "concessions" contract. It was an operating agreement – a new concept that would permit a nonprofit corporation to run the park. The Valley of the Moon Natural History Association was dissolved, and the "Jack London Park Partners" was incorporated for the purpose of operating the park.

The details of those negotiations could fill another book. The take-away from the events that were occurring towards the end of Greg's life is that he fought to the end to ensure that the park would remain open, vibrant, historically accurate, and sustainable. He was successful in that legacy fight.

Robyn Ishimatsu reflected on Greg's impact: "Even when Greg retired and joined the board of the association, he remained very loyal to the goals of the park. He saw the association as a means of supporting the park's interpretive mission. From the first day I met him at Jack London SHP in 1995 until his death, 19 years later, he maintained this infectious enthusiasm about the park.

"It nearly crushed him when he learned that the park was on the closure list. Then he saw an opportunity for the association to play a bigger role. And in the era of budget cuts, deferred maintenance backlogs, and staffing reductions, he wondered if perhaps the park could even improve under a new operations model.

"The year that Greg died – 2014 – was an incredibly difficult year for all of us involved with the park. Not only did Greg pass, but local rangers Wardell Noel and Martin Stoye also died of cancer within a few weeks. Add to that the specter of park closure or, at a minimum, a whole new way of doing business, and things were really in an upheaval.

"There was not really a downside to him. Greg was dignified, strong, kind, intuitive, purposeful, gentle, soft-spoken, intelligent, kind, quiet, helpful, determined, curious, inquisitive, knowledgeable, articulate, and he was a true gentleman. It was like losing a big brother.

"Through his whole cancer treatment process, he never complained, at least not publicly. At times, of course, it was hard for him to even walk around the block. We all – rangers, other staff, volunteers, and friends – never took Greg for granted – he was not a man for whom that was an option. But we took for granted the belief that he would always be there for us. As a quiet and humble leader, he was just the most amazing man. People, even today, when considering how to approach an issue at the park or the association ask themselves, 'What would Greg have done in this situation?'"

Is there any greater legacy than that?

Ark

By Greg Hayes – 2000

The mountain sleeps

awaiting the arrival

of the next storm

unmoved as only a mountain

    can be

unlike the rest of us

anxiously eyeing

the hidden pearl of the sun

tucked away in the

dank oyster flesh

of the clouds

Or others of us

heads down grazing into a

    wind

heavy with water and

    information

we do not want

Or still others

gathering kindling

that might float away from us

and save someone else

All of us occupied

with our useless preparations

like Noah, who meant well

but should have left well

    enough alone

and slept and dreamed

he was a mountain

Greg passed away right about the time I began work on this book. Although our careers overlapped for several decades, I did not know him well personally. Therefore, unlike the other rangers and lifeguards featured in this book, I did not have the opportunity to interview Greg and get to know him better.

In addition to reading the books and poems Greg published, I relied on his family, friends, and colleagues to help me understand the depth and nature of his passion and dedication to Jack London State Historic Park. Thank you to Robin Fautley, Nicolette Hayes, Susan St. Marie, Lou Leal, Elisa Stancil, Chuck Levine, Robyn Ishimatsu, and Matt Atkinson for sharing their memories of, and reflections on, the remarkable Gregory W. Hayes.

Robin adds wryly, "My dad used to say that he never loved a man as much as he loved Greg, and my mom told me that if I ever left Greg, she would keep him instead of me. I miss him every day. He was so deeply loved by everyone he touched."

Greg is truly one of those people whom you wish you had known better. After hearing such touching and moving accounts from his family, friends, and colleagues, I am convinced my life would have been much richer and more beautiful had Greg and I been friends.

— *Dave Van Cleve*

For more information –

Here is a link to a talk that Greg presented as a part of volunteer training in April, 2012, shortly before he knew that he was ill. It is about 72 minutes long, and the most striking part of the video is the knowledge he demonstrates while answering questions from the audience. This segment starts at about the 60-minute mark. These 12 minutes are enough to convince any observer that, indeed, Greg was truly an expert on the topic of Jack London.

https://www.youtube.com/watch?v=DhAMHC6wsZQ

Hayes, Gregory W., and Matt Atkinson. *Jack London's Wolf House.*
Valley of the Moon Natural History Association, 2010.

Huell Howser. Huell speaks to Greg about Jack London and the State Historic Park named for him.
https://blogs.chapman.edu/huell-howser-archives/1994/12/10/jack-london-californias-gold-502/

AFTERWARD

When choosing the subjects for a book of this type, the inherent risk is that I had to choose to omit the stories of some terrific people. However, I did have to limit the book to a reasonable length.

To those who probably should have been included in the book, I offer my sincere apologies.

More importantly, I believe that the conditions that created the environment that allowed – no, mandated – these success stories can be recreated. It is not a magic formula – that blueprint is still available.

The Seventh Generation Principle. This ancient principle is thought to have originated with the Great Law of the Iroquois Confederacy – perhaps in the 12th century. The idea is that every decision that may have long-term impacts – particularly those that involve natural and cultural resource conservation – should take into account the effects of those decisions on the next seven generations. It is a reflection of the concept that we have a huge responsibility to leave our planet in a healthy and sustainable condition, well into the future.

Consider that President Abraham Lincoln established the first state park in the nation in 1864. An average generation is considered to be somewhere between 20 and 25 years long. Seven generations since 1864 would put us right about in the first quarter of the 21st century – that would be, well, today! We cannot continue to ignore the responsibility that our generation has to ensure that the "park movement," and parks themselves, are nurtured and supported in such a manner to provide for these parks' health for the next 150 years, and longer. Amazing people have created, nurtured, protected, and interpreted the very best places in California since 1864. Are we willing to let this legacy slip away on our watch?

BIBLIOGRAPHY

Engbeck, Joseph H., Jr.
State Parks of California, from 1984 to the Present.
Charles H. Belding, Publisher. 1980.

Department of Parks and Recreation. State of California Resources Agency.
From Little Acorns...

Hayes, Gregory.
Earthsweats. 2014.

Lynch, Michael G.
California State Park Rangers – Images of America.
Arcadia Publishing. 2009.

Steen, Karen E., Laura Davick, and Meriam Braselle.
Crystal Cove Cottages – Islands in Time on the California Coast.
Chronicle Books. 2005.

Williams, Terry Tempest.
The Hour of Land.
Sarah Crichton Books. 2016.

ACKNOWLEDGEMENTS

I would like to thank the following people for their incredible dedication and help in getting this book published:

Mary – my beautiful and talented wife. She encourages, supports, and assists me in so many ways. Mary is a true gift.

The rangers and lifeguards who graciously agreed to be featured in this book. These men and women gave of themselves in extraordinary ways in order to make their "slice of California" a much better place. The stories of these "persons of place" are for the ages.

Rose Marie Scott-Blair and Beth Edwards. In addition to their amazing grasp of technical skills, such as proofreading and graphic design, they know how to nudge an author towards a better product. They are also patient and kind.

Chuck LeMenager. Several years ago, I mentioned off-handedly to Chuck that I was interested in writing a book or two. He has provided strong and faithful encouragement and advice ever since.

The rangers and lifeguards of California's Department of Parks and Recreation, past and present. They have provided, and continue to provide, incredible public service and resource protection for the state's remarkable tapestry of parks.

The subjects of this book wanted me to mention, by name, the colleagues, teachers, mentors, managers, supervisors, park aides, and volunteers who helped to shape them and who assisted them in changing their world. This list would have been many pages long. To those of you who did fill these roles, please accept our thanks for your remarkable efforts. The world is a better place because of you.

Wil Jorae, at the California Department of Parks and Recreation. Wil provided excellent guidance on the procedures for utilizing the Department's images.

The **California State Park Rangers Association** and the **California State Parks Anniversary Committee** provided grant funds to assist in the preparation of this book.

The **California State Park Rangers Association (CSPRA)** is an organization of State Park professionals who are dedicated to the advancement of the highest principles of public service. The organization was established to support and preserve California State Parks for present and future generations. For over 50 years, CSPRA has been the professional organization that truly cares first about protecting and preserving the values of California's State Park System. CSPRA is the organization for every State Park professional. For more information: www.cspra.com.

The **California State Parks Anniversary Committee (CSPAC)** is a private, nonprofit that started as the 125th Ranger Anniversary Committee in 1990. This original committee was formed to organize, promote, and celebrate the 125th anniversary of the appointment, in 1866, of the first state park ranger – Galen Clark. After the 125th Ranger Anniversary, CSPAC sponsored and promoted the 150th State Anniversary in 2000. CSPAC was also instrumental in recognizing the state park anniversaries of Lifeguards, the Off-Highway Vehicle Recreation program, the K-9 program, and the Firearms program. CSPAC was one of the primary sponsors and promoters of the California State Parks 150th Anniversary in 2014. For more information: www.cspra.com and then find the link to Park Anniversary.

ABOUT THE AUTHOR

David Van Cleve spent nearly 32 years in the California State Park System as a park ranger, park ecologist, and park superintendent. He subsequently worked nine years as a senior project director and ecoregional director for The Nature Conservancy. In addition to *A Greatness of Spirit*, he has also written a humorous book on his career, entitled *Have a Nice Day Job*, also available on Amazon.

Visit his Facebook page – Rangers in the Night Books – or contact him at davidvancleve@yahoo.com.

Made in the USA
San Bernardino, CA
24 October 2018